THE PASTOR IN A CHANGING SOCIETY

THE PASTOR IN A CHANGING SOCIETY

Effects of Social Change on
the Role of the Pastor in Africa

ZAWADI JOB
KINYAMAGOHA

Foreword By
ELIA SHABANI MLIGO

RESOURCE *Publications* • Eugene, Oregon

THE PASTOR IN A CHANGING SOCIETY
Effects of Social Change on the Role of the Pastor in Africa

Copyright © 2014 Zawadi Job Kinyamagoha. All rights reserved. Except for brief quotations in critical publications or reviews, no part of this book may be reproduced in any manner without prior written permission from the publisher. Write: Permissions. Wipf and Stock Publishers, 199 W. 8th Ave., Suite 3, Eugene, OR 97401.

Resource Publications
An Imprint of Wipf and Stock Publishers
199 W. 8th Ave., Suite 3
Eugene, OR 97401

www.wipfandstock.com

ISBN 13: 978-1-4982-0052-3

Manufactured in the U.S.A.   09/25/2014

To my wife Tulizo with whom I shared the flavor of my pastoral ministry from the first day of my call, the day of my ordination, and my first encounters of social changes in the parish. Not only that, she also had words and actions of encouragement, tolerance, and endurance during the busy times of preparing this book

To our children: Loveness, Agape, and Awardiel. They may become neither pastors nor Church ministers because they plan for different professions. However, this is to remind them that social change faces all professions in human life

and

To pastors and other Church ministers in Africa who face the challenge of social change in their ministry

CONTENTS

Foreword by Elia Shabani Mligo | ix
Acknowledgments | xiii
List of Acronyms | xvi

1 Introduction | 1
2 Tanzania | 28
3 Pastoral Ministry in the Perspective of the ELCT/SD | 65
4 The Social and Cultural Context in which Pastors Work | 86
5 The Pastor in a Cognitively Changing Society | 143
6 In the Name of Social Change | 163
7 Responses Toward Social Change | 206

Bibliography | 231

FOREWORD

Doing Pastoral Work in a Changing African Society

"... being a slave of Christ is far better than being a slave of culture."
—Peterson, "Titus: Starting Out in Crete," 184.

Doing pastoral work in a changing African society is challenging not only because the work is difficult, but also because the pastor faces the reality of society in the context of globalization. The Ghanaian theologian Emmanuel Lartey in his book *Pastoral Theology in an Intercultural World* defines globalization as the changes that appear when, "in whole or in part, the lifestyle, worldview, values, theology, anthropology, paradigms and forms of practice developed in North America and Western Europe are imported into different cultures and contexts."[1] The work of the pastor in this context where African cultures and contexts are changing because of the imposition of Western cultures and values can mainly be to defend the truth as revealed in scripture; however, the reality presented by the changing working contexts dictates the pastor toward the existing situation. The main question behind the role of the pastor remains: "What should the African pastor do in order to exercise God's ministry in the midst of the various dilemmas of this time?" Should the African pastor adhere strictly to the revealed scriptures and forget the changing reality? Or, should the African pastor adhere to the existing reality and its

---

1. Lartey, *Pastoral Theology*, 43. Robert J. Schreiter defines globalization by drawing from two sociologists Robert Roland and Peter Beyer. For him, globalization is "the extension of the effects of modernity to the entire world [Roland] and the compression of time and space [Beyer], all occurring at the same time." (see Schreiter, *The New Catholicity*, 8).

changes and leave behind the revealed truth from the Holy Scriptures? These questions are fundamental concerning the ministry of the African pastor that need clear and articulate responses.

Zawadi Job Kinyamagoha's book is a timely contribution toward responding to these questions. Through his research in one of the churches in Africa (the Evangelical Lutheran Church in Tanzania) Kinyamagoha has managed to show that the role of the pastor in a changing society within Africa faces challenges economically, socially, spiritually, and religiously. In his very first chapter, Kinyamagoha states the major concern for his book: to study "the characteristics of the contemporary society, expectations, its strengths, pressures, and weaknesses or problems that pastors encounter when they perform their pastoral tasks." In order to reach this concern, Kinyamagoha studies the context that forms the working life of the pastor, the documents accepted by the church which the pastor uses as tools for his or her ministry, the ways in which the pastor interacts with other people in the process of implementing his or her role and the effects that interaction brings; and more important, Kinyamagoha conducted fieldwork among pastors to ascertain the real lived experiences in their pastoral ministry in the changing African situation. He finally suggests some possibilities on how the church should respond to the situation facing pastors in their ministry. By doing so Kinyamagoha demonstrates that the pastor is not only a theologian, but also a leader of the community in which he or she is in.

This book is a monumental tool for any African pastor working in this changing postmodern society because it addresses the question of great concern to pastors and their pastoral ministry: *How can a pastor live and work as a reliable minister whom society counts as credible person amid rapid social change in Africa?* Here, life and work are the major aspects that the pastor has to combine. These two aspects have to correlate because the pastor lives life as any other Christian within the changing society. Yet, the pastor has to perform a special ministry to the people he or she lives with. Kinyamagoha's book has shown clearly the need for this balance in order for the pastor's role and dignity to remain intact.

Basing on the Tanzanian political, economic, social, cultural, socio-religious context, Kinyamagoha carefully and convincingly presents his argument drawing on the dilemma of the pastor's role in the midst of the changing society. The book purports that social change is both good and bad at the same time. It is possible to minimize the dilemma facing African pastors on their work by capitalizing on the good effects of social change to make the role of the pastor more adorable in the midst of many bad effects existing around him or her. In this case, Kinyamagoha's book plays a major contribution toward pastors' and African churches' self-awareness about the potentials of social change to the role of ministers within it. The book also unveils the need for updating church ministers (both pastors and non-pastors) through education for them to suite in the contexts they minister.

Though Kinyamagoha's focus is on the role of the African pastor, one can still note that the powerful argument of his book touches every pastor in this world. This is mainly because social change is not only limited to African churches. The Christian church is One but the context of this church is not one. The One church of Christ is located in various contexts of people who confess allegiance to Christ in their own ways. The American Theologian and Pastor Eugene Peterson illustrates this point more clearly. In his article: "Titus: Starting Out in Crete," he begins with an overwhelming, but true statement about the reality of American Pastors: "Pastors have an extremely difficult job to do, and it is no surprise that so many are discouraged and ready to quit."[2] He further notes: "Our culture doesn't lock us up; it simply and nicely castrates us, neuters us, and replaces our vital parts with a nice smiling face."[3] The words of Peterson above indicate that pastors as workers of the One church of Christ experience different situations according to their cultural orientations. Their cultures have made them slaves of their calls. They are no longer slaves of Christ who called them to ministry. The pastor of the church faces challenges not because of the changes of the church, but because of the changes of the cultural contexts in which the ministry of the church has to be carried out. In this case, Kinyamagoha's focus on the African pastor does not entail that the effect of social change is only an African issue; rather, Kinyamagoha most likely chooses to focus on an African context in order to tell us that other contexts (as Peterson has just illustrated above) also have challenges of their own kinds.

In brief, Kinyamagoha has used a variegated amount of materials to present the argument of his book. His use of Taylor's spheres of society as a framework to analyze the lived experiences of African pastors is commendable. I acknowledge that this book is potential in study classes for practical and pastoral theology students, conference discussions, and to individual ministers in congregations. The book can also be a useful resource to scholars of practical and pastoral theology to further discussions on the role of the pastor amidst social changes worldwide.

Elia Shabani Mligo (PhD)
University of Iringa
Amani Centre
July 2014

---

2. Peterson, "Titus: Starting Out in Crete," 183.
3. Ibid.

ACKNOWLEDGMENTS

"Very few people work alone [if any]. Indeed, solitary confinement is often thought of as a major source of torture. Not only do most people work with others, but they do so quite specifically in groups, sections, teams or departments. [A worker is] part *dependent*, part *independent* and part *interdependent* on others. . . . Humans are social animals. They seek out the company of others and even the most primitive sort of work in hunter–gatherer societies is essentially cooperative and collaborative."[1] Another one concludes: "I OFTEN REMIND my . . . class that social research is a cooperative endeavor, built on relationship of trust. This book is no exception, and I have relied on the help of many."[2]

Reflecting on the above quotations, I admit that without a help from many people perhaps this book could hardly reach its present status. Therefore, in the first place I thank the pastors and other lay Christians of the parishes where I conducted my research. They showed good cooperation such that I was able to discuss with them the questions I posed; and hence, I got the data needed for this work. They tirelessly devoted much of their time in all sessions as we planned to meet. The focus group discussion deserves a mention for being ready to meet even in weekends to provide me with information relevant during data analysis, interpretation and discussion of the findings. I disturbed their timetables several times. Their help made this work fulfilled. I thank all who participated in this process toward the end of this publication.

My fellow staff members at the University of Iringa, Amani Centre, particularly in the Department of Counseling Psychology deserve to be mentioned as well. They sometimes allowed me to continue with this work

---

1. Furnham, *The Psychology of Behaviour at Work*, 477.
2. Ellingson, *The Mega Church and the Mainline*, vii.

and themselves carried out all matters that pertained my office responsibilities whenever was convenient to them.

Reverend Dr. Elia Shabani Mligo, Senior Lecturer at the University of Iringa Amani Centre also deserves my heartfelt thanks. In fact he is the one who came in the first place to encourage me to publish this research work. He assisted me on the processes regarding publications of books, and wrote the foreword of the book. I dare to speak that he was not selfish with all necessary information that I needed to undertake to the completion of publication at Wipf & Stock Publishers. If that was not enough, he was ready to read my manuscript from the very beginning. Despite his many official and family responsibilities, yet he tirelessly read and re – read my manuscripts. Sometimes he was even ready to postpone his manuscripts in favor of my work. He tirelessly read and critiqued, commented and corrected my work throughout the process. His home library is one of his contributions in my book. His help has enabled me manage to reach the work to this point. I admit that he was committed to help me, and had a close commitment to helping me in perseverance upon my weaknesses both in academic demands as well as in my human weaknesses.

Close to Reverend Dr. Mligo comes Ester Malekano, his wife. She hosted me almost all times that I had to meet with Rev. Dr. Mligo for assistance. I will not forget her good meals and other accommodation facilities she offered me. She helped me minimize all meal and hostel costs. Thank you *'mama* Mligo' for your kindness. It counts a lot in my work.

I also extent my appreciations to the librarians and their assistants for assisting me get some books and other materials relevant for my reviews. The libraries of the University of Iringa, at Iringa Campus as well as at Amani Centre—Njombe, and at Ilembula—Department of Counseling Psychology where I was allocated to teach. Their cooperation was of great contribution toward the publication of this book. Students, especially from the Department of Counseling psychology also contributed some ideas included in this book. Their critical questions in some of the issues arising in this book made me rework several times to minimize extremisms and fashion my thinking. They widened my horizons.

Moreover, I will ever remember Egidio Chaula, Assistant Lecturer at the University of Iringa – Amani Centre in this book. He corrected my English language expressions and other necessary grammatical reviews to make this book readable. I am very much thankful for his work. I can imagine how it may have been difficult to read and correct my language problems.

Thanks also go to the publisher who accepted my application and provided me with all necessary information and contracts for the publication of this book. I am grateful for their patience in handling my queries regarding the errors in the manuscript. I highly appreciate for their patience and openness in whatever needed improvement.

Finally, I am grateful to my family. My wife Tulizo and our three children Loveness, Agape, and Awardiel who provided me with love, encouragement and other support that enabled me accomplish the plan to publish the manuscript. Sometimes they missed my conjugal and parental love as father because of this work. May the Lord God bless them forever and ever more! I dedicate this book to them and to fellow pastors in Africa.

LIST OF ACRONYMS

AIDS	Acquired Immune Deficiency Syndrome
ATR	African Traditional Religion
CCM	Chama Cha Mapinduzi
Cf.	Compare with
ELCA	Evangelical Lutheran Church in America
ELCT	Evangelical Lutheran Church in Tanzania
ELCT/SD	Evangelical Lutheran Church in Tanzania, Southern Diocese
HIV	Human Immunodeficiency Virus
KKKT-DKu	Kanisa la Kiinjili la Kilutheri Tanzania – Dayosisi ya Kusini
KKKT	Kanisa la Kiinjili la Kilutheri Tanzania
MUCo	Makumira University College
NLC	New Life Crusade
SD	Southern Diocese
TANU	Tanganyika African National Union
TU-MUCo	Tumaini University Makumira University College
UWATA	Uamsho wa Wakristo Tanzania (Tanzanian Christians' Revival)

1
INTRODUCTION

AIM AND OBJECTIVES

THE PURPOSE OF THIS book is to bring alive some 'lived-experiences'[1] regarding social change in relation to the role of the pastor. The book studies and puts forward the characteristics of the contemporary society pertaining to its demands, its expectations, its strengths, pressures, and weaknesses or problems those pastors encounter as they perform their pastoral ministry. It is my belief that social change has some intense effects and challenges on the Church and on pastoral ministry in this postmodern era. To reach that purpose I have developed the following objectives:

I. To examine the context in which the pastor lives and performs his or her roles. I examine the contemporary social setting and its social changing trends.

II. To survey some church documents that regulate the roles of the pastor.

III. To explore how pastors implement the prescribed roles and some practical consequences they encounter due to social changes.

IV. To assess the present context of the Church that emanate from the people that I interviewed. This assessment of social change would help bring out two pictures: first, of the changing face of the Church from one stage or phase to another and, second its implication on the role of the pastor.

---

1. By 'lived experience' I mean somebody's practical life under a particular circumstance in a particular time.

v. To identify the challenges and suggest some possibilities to respond to the changes and challenges that pastors are facing in both, their individual life, and in their ministry.

BACKGROUND AND STATEMENT OF THE PROBLEM

Tanzanian theologians and pastors Peter A.S. Kijanga, George M. D. Fihavango and Solomon Y. Swalo, acknowledge that like in any other society in the African continent, the Tanzanian society has been undergoing fast social changes. For example, Kijanga states that changes that happen nowadays affect and far more will continue to affect both, the secular part of society and also the Christian Church. He declares:

> Priests and *pastors serve in Ujamaa villages*. . . . And as *many Tanzanians move* . . . many things will probably change. The *changes may* in turn *affect the ecclesiastical structures*. The fact that priests and pastors serve congregations . . . indicates the extent of that *change in the Tanzanian society*. . . . *What will be the role of priests or pastors* . . . ? . . . priests or pastors . . . do . . . *ministries* . . . *in a changing society*. In the eyes of many missionaries, Christianity brought to a Tanzanian Christian 'good' life. The argument is that *social change* . . . *made possible the development of* . . . *societies*.[2]

Kijanga is pointing out to the introduction of '*Ujamaa villages*' that implies the change of many things that in turn affects the ecclesiastical structures of the Church. The exercise of *Ujamaa* greatly includes the movement of people from one area to another. *Ujamaa* brought people close to each other. As a result, congregations also had taken a new face. Pastors had to serve in new contexts that hold on the *Ujamaa* ideology. This had become a collective and open social change to the Tanzanian society. That change brought some effects on pastoral roles. The roles of 'priests or pastors,' to use his words, were in questions. Kijanga notes that now there was a need to rethink the role of the pastor in the changed and changing society. Kijanga's ideas imply that the development emerging due to social change pushes, both the pastors and Churches to change certain things in order to go well with the active context. He envisions that "priests or pastors . . . do . . . *ministries* . . . *in a changing society*." My questions to the statements of Kijanga are these: What are those "many things [that] will probably change"? What are those effects that pastors and the Church should expect to encounter?

---

2. Kijanga, *Ujamaa and the Role of the Church*, 66–67, 85 (Italics mine).

How will they affect the ecclesiastical structures? How should the pastors and the Church respond to them in order to cope with the changing society?

Similarly, Fihavango argues that the changes that are taking place in Tanzania are also in the African continent as a whole. He states that, to the years of 2000, the whirl of change in all spheres of life was already in rapid rhythms and beats in the African continent. That is why he is confident to declare that throughout the continent, all people and social institutions are "in the changing Africa."[3] For Fihavango, all people living in Africa are entirely controlled by change. If his argument is true, pastors are no exception. As he confirms the dominance and rapid social change in Africa today, Fihavango goes further to describe:

> The dominant *feature of life in Africa today is change*. Whilst it is true that everywhere modern *man is living in changing times*, yet the essential difference between life in the west and life in Africa is the *faster tempo of change in our continent*. This whirl of *change in all spheres of life: social, economic, religious and political,* has created tremendous problems for the church which are, at the same time, both a challenge and an opportunity for it to life and growth of the new nations . . . concerning *Christian responsibility toward areas of rapid social change.* . . . There are great waves or storms of change going through Africa in all spheres of life . . . *People seem to take different steps in reaction to these waves*. Some attempt to resist, and they are swept or carried away. Others are carried away with these changes unknowingly. The *right way of reaction is to learn the behavior and patterns of these changes and follow their rhythms and beats without being carried away*. May be there are people who hope that the waves of change will stop and the situation will return and be like in the past. This is a dream. *Today and tomorrow will never be like yesterday*. From now on, "*nothing will be as earlier anymore*."[4]

In the quotation above, Fihavango notices that as Africans and shepherds, pastors have to realize and become aware of the challenges and opportunities that social and other factors bring onto life and ministry in Africa. He suggests that the best reaction toward social change and all other change factors "is to learn the behavior and patterns of these changes and follow their rhythms and beats without being carried away." For him, life in Africa is in daily change. There is no turning back. Each day remains unique from the other. This is the contemporary context in which African pastors

---

3. Fihavango, "Leadership and Family," 183.
4. Ibid., 183–184 (Italics mine).

live and serve. However, what and how should African pastors learn from those behaviors and patterns of changes so that it becomes easy for them not to be away?

Furthermore, supplementing to his statements above, in the same article, Fihavango illustrates that the contemporary society is causing some dilemma to the Church and its leaders even in the learning institutions. Once in one of his e-mails to his friends and colleagues world-widely, Fihavango shares the dilemma occurring at Tumaini University Makumira University College (TU-MUCo) in Tanzania. This university is the most prominent religious institution in training pastors. It trains both, Tanzanians and non-Tanzanians from different Churches within and outside Tanzania. Fihavango describes how trainers, theology students and other new trainees are in dilemma due to the complex mixture of students who study theology and those studying secular courses in that institution. At that time, MUCo had just established other secular programs that include students who are not for church ministry as pastors. There were new programs being introduced at bachelor's level in the fields of law, languages, music, and education, to mention but a few.

As a lecturer, a pastor, and Dean of Faculty of Theology in that university at the time he was writing that e-mail, Fihavango wanted his fellow Tanzanians, friends, and other colleagues in the African context become informed on how life at that university had and was rapidly changing into complex and challenging situation. In that e-mail, he calls an attention to all contemporary church ministers and leaders, especially theologians to be aware of and take hold of constructively coping with the challenges and influences made by the secular disciplines. He insists pastors in Africa to have enough, both theological and secular education for meeting numerous questions and challenges that the contemporary society was posing.[5] But, what evident long-term training strategies are both, the teachers and the university as an institution doing for Church ministers toward curbing and coping to the situation they encounter as it is being revealed while in the process of training?

As we have seen above, the above quotations show that African pastors have been undertaking their roles being trained within various circle of rapid changes, amongst them is this of social change. Both quotations and descriptions regarding the arguments of Kijanga and Fihavango highlight that social change has been bringing some effects or problems and challenges in and outside the Church. Together with the challenges and problems, however, social change provides some opportunities for people to stay stable

---

5. Fihavango, "Mambo Mbalimbali," E-mail Communication, 8 November, 2006.

amid the transforming spheres of life. Moreover, it seems that social change might even continue in future. Nevertheless, there are immediate questions that flow out of my mind as I read the quotations above: what are those effects that contemporary social change brings upon the roles of the present pastors? What are those challenges? Furthermore, which opportunities or alternatives can social change and the church provide to pastors for them to respond to those effects and challenges?

Following Kijanga and Fihavango's testimonies above, I want to follow up their information about the effects, opportunities, and challenges that social change brings on the role of the African pastor and hence, on the mission and life of the Church at large. Again, to me, there is a big gap between the times when Kijanga made his research to that of Fihavango and Swalo. Nevertheless, as Fihavango recounts and asks: "It was acknowledged in 1962 that Africa was already in a process of rapid change. How far then is it true today in 2003, in the twenty-first century, a century of science and technology, a century of communication? At a time when . . . as far as communication is concerned there are no longer boundaries."[6] Although they tried to highlight some issues according to their own experiences, I found it important to make an in—depth research from the lived experiences of the contemporary African pastors, evangelists and some groups of lay Christians themselves about this phenomenon of social change.

Again, Solomon Y. Swalo[7], in his speech during a retreat for Church ministers, among the striking ideas were the questions of awareness in pastors about social change and the strategies for coping with those changes. Swalo seems to feel strongly touched by the fast social changes in the African context. He urges pastors to be awake of the great changes in society. I find two important contributions that touch my feelings and add to other questions that I have presented above. First, Swalo maintains that in the twenty first century everything is changing, while others have already changed. Both the pastors and the Churches as institutions are in the same revolving world. Second, he asks, "What should the church do? How should this church accept and cope with new emphases, demands, needs, interests, and lifestyles of its contemporary Christians? Are all pastors and other ministers aware of this? And how are they prepared to face them?"[8]

The questions that Swalo raises to Church ministers call for the church to perform three essential tasks: first, to understand that there are severe changes in the contemporary society; second, the changes are bringing

6. Fihavango, "Leadership and Family," 184.
7. Swalo, "Mtumishi wa Bwana," 25–26 May, 2006.
8. Ibid.

some new emphases, demands, and expectations upon the ministers and to the church; third, that pastors seem to be unaware of the changing realities, and therefore the church has to inform and prepare those pastors in order that those twenty – first ministers can face and deal constructively and adequately with the social change. The main problem that I see from the descriptions of theologians above is the tension that faces the current African pastor in the pastoral role. The pastor is caught between two tensions: the rigid demands of church authority (guiding principles and superior leaders) and the changing society that brings the role of the pastor in a difficult situation. On the one hand the church authority obliges the pastor to work according to its needs and interests according to the norms set and provided. On the other hand and at the same time, the changing society wants this same pastor to respond to realities of its life. I will illustrate it more in the concluding chapters.

After disclosing the problem that requires to be studied, I now recall my personal experience to the existing tension between the prescribed church principles and the changing society in my own role as a pastor. My personal experience serves to illustrate the problem underlying this tension. During my pastoral ministry, both my parishioners as well as the surrounding community asked me several questions whether I was aware of the changes that had already taken place and those that were in progress in the area where I was working. They told me of the changes in terms of multiculturalism, mobility of people, complexities in social values or morality, and many other changes in relation to lifestyles of people. To help me understand well the society in which I was living and serving, most people whom I conversed with told me that people struggle to improve their standards of living. Due to this struggle, people are also changing to improve their life styles. Parallel to their struggles, people expect even their religious affairs will match this process. They demand that whatever is done in the church has to reflect and respond to the realities at hand. There are also some comments on the messages to be preached. They comment that it would be good if the gospel preaching responds to people's problems. There are so many issues that people have been sharing to me so that I perform my pastoral responsibilities according to changes in society. Currently, parishioners ask several questions pertaining to pastoral roles in this century. For example, several times we hear them asking the following questions: does the church know that things have changed? Can church leaders not adapt mostly to the attractions from contemporary Christians?

Anthony Giddens once studied this problem. He writes:

> The problems of the world are no longer just 'out there' at a remote distance, but tend to be brought into the centre of every – one's lives. Global problems confront us personally, no matter how much we would like to switch off from them. . . . It is fraught with meanings and potential meanings. . . . But all realize, and in some sense react to, the wider world significance of their style of dress. There are difficult issues of how societies that have become fundamentally secular confront religiosity and a reaffirmation of the sacred. Battles that seemed to lie in the past now reassert themselves in the present. One could argue that the very principle of an open society is the acceptance that 'nothing is sacred' – all beliefs, of no matter what kind, are open to critical scrutiny. Inherent tensions exist when sacred symbols are invoked in relation to social attitudes and practices in everyday life – and where these conflicts with those of the majority, or even the foundational principles of a democratic society. The issue of freedom of speech, which once seemed more or less wholly resolved in contemporary societies, comes to the fore again in a dramatic fashion. There are two reasons: one is the return of the sacred, and the other is the threat or actual use of violence where beliefs or symbols are in some sense said to be defiled.[9]

In short, Giddens indicates that to date pastors live and work in an open society, critical questioning society, free society, corrupt (morally decaying) and confused society, developing society, and all that we can list down. Pastors are in the very centre of all social, economic, cultural, political, and technological crises. This is the pastor's ground. He or she has to be aware and keep examining the status and development of our society.

I can try to remember some of the questions they ever shared to me a few days after my arrival in one of my parish appointments. Some of them are these: how will you perform your work in this century in which, currently, the society is rapidly changing most of its features of life? What will be your program for our Church? What strategies can you suggest in order to deal with such challenges and problems? They deliberately told me that such questions call for awareness of the contemporary context in which pastors and other leaders live and work. The questions above reflect the ideas of Giddens and also of Carroll who said that, in such situation, society's life affects the clergy's ministry and life. Carroll states:

> There is a growing crisis in church life, which robs . . . churches . . . [and] good pastoral leadership, and brings pain and hurt upon pastors' and pastors' families. [C]onflicts in congregations

9. Giddens, *Europe in the Global Age*, 130–131, cf., 133–152.

> between parishioners and clergy are increasing because of the changing nature of the church and . . . the . . . cultural values. . . . Pastoring has become . . . nearly inhumane to expect the person to consistently manage all multiple and conflicting expectations.[10]

Carroll notices that the contemporary task of pastoring is in the midst of strong and pressing ambivalences and tensions. The church as well as the ministers are highly confronting entire problems of "multiple and conflicting expectations" of society. To manage this situation, Carroll remarks: "we must . . . consider relevant characteristics of the broader social world in which the congregation is located."[11]

In addition, during my parish ministry, I myself noticed that some parishioners and other surrounding communities were highly educated. Those parishioners were very inquisitive to know whether pastors are being trained about the status, needs and other challenges facing and being posed by the contemporary society. Among other problems, there were many challenges regarding marriages and mobility of parishioners. In those times, I encountered numerous problems due to interfaith marriages and movement of Christians from my denomination to others. People had so many demands that they wanted me to fulfill. Their questions, requests, demands and comments put me into fear about my pastoral ministry.

The issues that I conversed with those members of my Church community were very challenging. That was because I was completely new in pastoral ministry itself and because I was just coming from my pastoral training. I had never worked before as a pastor in any parish. Many problems that I encountered created tensions to me as a parish pastor. Even when I went to seek some advice from my nearby pastors and other church superiors, they told me that they were also in the same situation. Most times, they claimed to encounter the same problem of social change. The changes that constantly happen in society bring several pressures on their process of fulfilling their responsibilities, and hence even on the whole mission and life of Church. As a result, I had to remain alone with my problems as my fellow pastors and superiors were. Hence, I realized that pastoral ministry in the church is facing severe tensions and challenges.

Eventually, I came to remember a testimony from a certain pastor. That pastor shared to me his experience a few days before we were ordained as pastors. The pastor told me that society in which he had served brought to him several questions that he never finished to respond to. Transformations

---

10. Carroll, *God's Potters*, 160, 196.
11. Ibid.

always happened to people. So, he noted to me that social change was one of the forces that sometimes made him feel to be in a desperate situation. He finished his testimony by wishing me a good life and ministry at a time and society of varied changes and attitudes.

As we have seen from the quotations above that there are some effects caused by social change on pastoral ministry. Social change is also said to possess a continuous feature of rhythm change. Even if my fellow pastors and I had undertaken some pastoral training, yet social change seemed to be a strange issue when we reached the reality. This surprise of social change was an outcome of less training on socio-cultural life setting. We (pastors) undertake our pastoral roles basing on the prescribed principles of the church only. I became profoundly surprised when even the church constitution and other church documents were silent about the existence of changes in society. Several times when I felt stuck in a ministerial problem, I tried to consult the constitution in order to find a solution, but there appeared no exit, nor were there a clear description for other immediate resolutions. The constitution was certainly very confined that its referral was too far from immediate solutions to the problems at hand. Most of the time people did not show to worry with the constitutions that usually pastors use as a focal reference for pastoral responsibilities and other matters that people appeared to face. The behavior of not worrying about the constitution still exists even to date.

Then I asked myself, why do some people come and tell me that society is changing? How are they sure that I have less information about it? Why are almost all pastors complaining about society and its changes? Why does social change seem to be a strange issue to most of the pastors? What is wrong with the pastoral training for meeting the social change? What is wrong with the constitution from which the church and pastors rely on for their pastoral roles in society? Does it not provide a clear alternative when problems emerge? Why then does the church itself and pastors remain reluctant to respond or depend on the strict rules in the face of many pressures from society? What challenges are the pastors and the church encountering as they perform their roles? Consequently, many of these questions remained unresolved throughout the three years of my pastoral ministry in the parish before I left for my further studies.

As if the above experience is not enough; during my master's program in Inter-contextual Theology at the University of Oslo, social change appeared to be among serious issues of discussion and emphases. We studied it in the subject '*Models of Contextual Theology: Faith and Cultures,*' the book written by Stephen Bevans. One of the most important issues that Bevans pinpoints is social change. As well, in this book, Robert J. Schreiter put some comments regarding the statements of Bevans on social change. In his foreword, Schreiter observes that all people, especially theologians (pastors inclusive), there is "the need to find theological expressions more attuned to changing realities."[12] Due to this urge, "Stephen Bevans has done us a great service in proposing a way to think more clearly about the interaction of the gospel message and culture, and about honoring tradition while responding to social change."[13] For Bevans, effective honor to tradition goes hand in hand with faithful response to social change. Thus, once social change is forgotten or ignored, pastors fail to constructively and appropriately control society then work effectively.

Seeing that, Bevans himself puts more emphasis that, together with other theologians, we pastors ought to live and work 'in a situation that calls for creative pastoral action.'[14] He adds that the issue of social change ought to be studied and constructively dealt with in order to help pastors work with a comfortable spirit. The main reason for his arguments is that social change touches the whole life and ministry of a pastor. It is in the full daily interaction of the gospel and lived experiences of the people. Creative pastoral actions are important if we want the pastor be constructive in his or her personal life and to the ministry he or she has been set for.

In reflecting on the above observations, I ask myself, if it was acknowledged that in 1978, 2004 and 2006 the Tanzanian society was so far in a process of rapid social change. How far then was it not true in 2000s to the present in the twenty – first century where society, Church and the pastor were and are in a growing global and technological village?[15] Thus, it is from such situations and experiences above that I chose to explore the relationship between social change and the prescribed church authority on the role of the pastor. The questions about social change and its repercussions on the role of the pastor ran into my mind and made me think of them hence, I had to delve into this practical issue in social interaction and pastoral ministry. It is my conviction that, the tension that exists between the church authority and the changing society causes the role of the pastor to be in dilemma.

RESEARCH QUESTION AND BOOK OUTLINE

From the above experiences and questions, therefore, I draw some important issues that this book will address: first, the church and its ministers seem

12. Bevans, *Models of Contextual Theology*, ix.
13. Ibid., ix–xi .
14. Ibid., 15–16, 37, 42–43, 54–55, 59, 70, 76, 139.
15. Fihavango, "Leadership and Family," See quotation above.

to be uninformed or reluctant to respond to the realities of the changing society in which pastoral roles are performed. Second, the changing society seems to hinder pastors from performing their given roles. Pastors and their co-workers are in a tense plight because they are not yet fully prepared to respond to social changes. Third, yet, despite the dilemmas and ambivalences; pastors ought to remain firm to the call to reach an ever-changing society with the changeless purposes of the Church.[16] Fourth, the constitution that pastors relied on was either for the administrative structures only or it was so static and individualistic that it provided minimal or no room to address the changes in society. With such a situation, pastors would likely encounter very difficult problems. The church and society were matching along different lines. The church had not yet up-to-dated itself with its ministerial guidelines into the realities of the daily lives of society. Thus, the main question to be answered is: *How can a pastor live and work as a reliable minister whom society counts as a credible person amid rapid social change in Africa?*

The six parts of this book deal with some aspects of social change and its consequences on the role of the pastor on the one hand, and on the mission and life of the whole Church on the other hand. After the general introduction in chapter one, in chapter two I present an overview of the life situation of society in the Tanzanian context. By using literature, my discussion in chapter two focuses on the political, economic, social, cultural, socio-religious, and the educational or cognitive life of the people and how there has been some development or changes in those aspects. The main aim for this chapter is to give a general picture of the context in which Christian pastors live and perform their tasks. In chapter three, I present a discussion of perspectives on the pastor and the roles that the pastor has to perform. I make my analysis and discussion basing on the church documents, mainly from the Constitution of the ELCT/SD and from some parts of the ELCT Constitution.

In chapters four and five, I analyze and discuss the field work findings. These chapters serve as the main concern of this book. That is, to investigate the relationship between social change and the role of the pastor. In these chapters, the main aim is to see how a pastor implements the given tasks and the difficulties he or she encounters due to social change. In most cases, the analyses and discussions in these chapters illustrate that pastors encounter severe tensions and pressures from both the church and from the changes in society. The pastor is in tensions between two equal strong poles, the church authorities (leaders and the prescribed principles and policies) on the one hand, and the changing society in which he or she lives and serves

16. Cf., Carroll, *God's Potters*, 56.

on the other hand. Both bring great demands, needs, and interests upon the pastor. The church authorities demand him or her to work according to the prescribed rules and principles, while society pressurizes him or her to observe the realities of life.

In chapter six, I try to summarize the analysis by discussing how social transformations also change the expression and phase of the Church and consequently, the changes bring up some other implications for the roles of a pastor. Chapter 6 shows how the roles of the pastor appear to widen or multiply due to the changing phase of the Church. This chapter also describes the reflections of some Lutheran Bishops from the American context on pastoral ministry in relation to the changing society. Again, the discussion in this chapter portrays the reflection to be a model for the ELCT authorities. Furthermore, the discussion in this chapter highlights also how the changes put many demands upon a pastor to play significant and huge tasks that require some other skills and essential qualities for the work. It is seen vividly that most of the pastors seem to lack certain knowledge and skills for them to respond to the social changes through their roles. At last, in the same chapter six there is an additional role apart from the prescribed roles so that a pastor can also advise society about its economy.

Chapter 7 draws out the results from chapter two to chapter six, and sets out the framework for a new outlook toward the contemporary society and an urge for awareness on the changes in society. Therefore, it is in this later chapter that I discuss some needs requiring attention and proactive decisions and actions amid the effects of social change. The chapter calls for the church and the pastor to become fully aware of how social change is part of the life of society, and of the mission and life of the Church. It is also an essential issue in their pastoral ministry as a whole just as it is in their ordinary social, cultural, political or economic life. I conclude my discussions in this book by proposing some areas that need further exploration regarding the existing effects of social change.

SIGNIFICANCE OF THIS BOOK

Social change seems to be an obvious issue almost in the African continent and in the Tanzanian society in particular. Like any other institutions or leaders of society in the African continent as well as in the Tanzanian context, the church as well as pastors and their co-workers live within that changing society. However, it seems that most pastors are very suspicious of the changing trends of society. Despite some positive consequences that some informants highlight in this book, social change depicts to bring several severe effects as pastors perform their roles both in the Church premises and outside it. Most of the informants describe social change as more of a threat than an opportunity to the church, to pastors, and to other leaders for them to learn from the changes in society and use any new potential aspect they encounter from it.

By using the drawn sample of interviewees used during the collection and analysis of data, this book defines the context of the contemporary society, the context of rapid change in every state of human life. The analysis points out that pastors as well as the entire church should positively perceive and accept social change as a reality that has always existed, but with some additional transformations depending on time, space and type of people. Again, the book also discusses and exposes "that rapid change has become a characteristic of our society" and therefore it argues that it is essential for all pastors to have a solid understanding of their leadership role given the fact of the contemporary era of society.[17]

Furthermore, the book also describes how both the church and pastors of the ELCT themselves ought to understand the realities of society and respond to the assumptions of people regarding the developments that society undergoes. It calls for all church ministers to understand the phases of society and of the Church. As well, the book reveals how people deal with their economic strengths and weaknesses, how people share information globally, and the way this society practices its self-governance.[18] Hence, it calls for the Church to rethink and reformulate some long-held guidelines, doctrinal theories and treasured traditions to respond to the challenging issues, such as those of multiculturalism, freedom, mobility of people, religious pluralism, morality, old and long liturgy, and long worship services.

The results of the research presented in this book attempt to contribute to the need for further training so that pastors are updated with education from time to time according to the changing reality of society. Besides, we may suppose that constant training to both, new and long-service pastors might help a pastor to respond to the changing face of the Church and hence be able to carry out the many aspects of the roles according to time and needs of society. The survey's results also anticipate to help enlighten even other church ministers of what is happening and how to meet up the changes. Moreover, this book attempts to suggest some pastoral leadership approaches particularly in the Evangelical Lutheran Church in Tanzania with open consideration of multicultural, changing society and its challenges to pastors and the Church at large.

17. Ibid., Carroll, 128.
18. Taylor, *Modern Social Imaginaries,* 71–141, 76, and 101 – 115.

As a whole, the book strongly calls for awareness in all pastors and all Church authorities that the transformations that constantly take place in society's lifestyles in turn change the face and phase of the Church. Hence, there may be a need for adjustments of systems and modes of daily operations of the church. In my opinion and according to the testimonies of most witnesses in this book; we can hardly avoid or stop changes from happening, but we may be able to try to live them or discover and travel some pathways beyond our negative attitude toward social change, beyond hate and fear of it.[19] Besides, this book suggests that by listening and learning from the community, the church itself, pastors as well as other church ministers can get some tools for their real role-play in pastoral ministry.

METHODOLOGICAL APPROACHES

The research results obtained dispose both the nature of exploration as well as the book to belong to both practical and pastoral fields of theology. We see this link clearly in their characteristic interrelationships in theory and practice. According to Lartey the praxis and maintenance of interaction between theory and practice are among the interrelated characteristics of practical theology and pastoral theology. To confirm this argument, Lartey argues that practical theology "Is committed to facing up to the importance and relevance of religious experience in the contemporary world. Practical theologians avoid merely abstract considerations of real life experiences of pain and suffering – . . . and rather seek to find better ways of thinking about and responding to such situations."[20] Whereas for the maintenance between theory and practice:

> Pastoral theologians practice the art of maintaining dialectical and creative tensions between theory and practise, tradition and experience, the real and the ideal, literary and the non-literary, different disciplines, the sacred and the secular. . . . Pastoral theology entails the art and craft of maintaining the mutual interaction between the critical, interpretive, constructive and expressive abilities of persons in communities of faith, practice and culture.[21]

To fulfill the above perspectives for this book; I undertook both a fieldwork and library reviews. I also consulted both, oral and written sources. In

---

19. Browning and Reed, *Forgiveness, Reconciliation, and Moral Courage*, 222.
20. Lartey, *Pastoral Theology*, 19.
21. Ibid., 20, 21.

conducting this research, I used both sociological and theological approaches. This is because the exploration has both disciplines' characteristics. Besides, this kind of research is in line with contextual studies. It is in the category of a qualitative (contextual) research or approach. According to Bryman, a "qualitative research is a research strategy that usually emphasizes words rather than quantification in the collection and analysis of data. [Qualitative research] is too subjective."[22] Again, it is contextual in the sense that it applies those methods: "To a specific locality, . . . case or social setting; it sacrifices breadth of coverage and statistical generalizability in order to explore issues in depth. Contextual methods attempt to understand . . . the dimensions within the social, cultural, economic and political environment of a geographical or social locality."[23] The quotation above reflects and points out that in contextual research, in most cases, the reality is the first reference before other factors are given a chance to respond or testify. It means that the lived experience is studied in the first place, and then other references are consulted or made in order to respond or support the existing reality.

Theologians Paul Ballard & John Pritchard contribute on the efficacy of the above two approaches. They state that the pastoral, practical, and systematic theological researches never escape from using social research methodologies and approaches. It shares the descriptive, normative, critical and apologetic tasks. For example, some questions asked in such a research concern the way in which the small community and society share and accept the gospel. "[is it done] adequately or should it be challenged? Are we learning from this context? What should be formulated, said or done or urged in the name of the gospel in and for the world?" 'What about the ways through which faith expresses itself in languages' because of "its focal concern for pastoral, practical and systematic Christian faith practice;" a theological research "draws on the [critical] methodologies of the social sciences as its critical partners . . . [they become] its basic tools for understanding the social reality in which we are set and which has to be served in the name of Christ. All theological disciplines employ critical tools from other disciplines."[24]

Ballard and Pritchard go further to describe that the Church has to be discussed both sociologically and theologically. For them the whole Church itself is a sociological entity (group or institution). They state that sociologically, the church also has some problems that require a sociological and theological contextual consideration, especially, when pastors carry out

---

22. Bryman, *Social Research Methods,* 266, 284.
23. Holland and Campbell, *Methods in Development Research,* 2, 3.
24. Ballard and Pritchard, *Practical Theology in Action,* 18–20.

their roles in the community. To Ballard and Pritchard, although there is an ethical dimension to the church's understanding of itself that suggests how this church is ought to behave in its contemporary mission to society: "Sociologically, the church is fragmented, loosely identified scattered reality, caught up in nationalistic, class and cultural conflicts. It is hard to know what counts: is it the institutional structures, the devotions and liturgies, or the professed belief? Theology provides a description of reality as understood in relation to God, whereas sociology tries to make empirical, historical sense of a pattern of human behavior."[25] Therefore, Bryman, Holland and Campbell, and Ballard and Pritchard convince that it is necessary to combine sociological and theological approaches in learning people's experiences, interactions, feelings and thoughts in the contemporary realities of fragmentations, devotions and beliefs resulting from patterns of human behaviors.

I agree that the Church ought to combine those two disciplines as it searches the efficacy of its efficiencies and constructive ministry in the contemporary times. If my understanding above is somehow accurate, then it might certainly be accurate also to understand that the Church belongs, affiliates and exists in society that is constantly changing. A pastor is both a theological leader of a religious institution as well as a leader of society like other leaders. Following this perception then, Ballard and Pritchard urge that the pastor works and should continuously try to examine the society in which the Church belongs and lives.

Additionally, together with other scholars, Ballard and Pritchard, Slee, and Lartey suggest that every pastor should learn the characteristic realities of society. For them, a pastor studies and serves the community by using varied theological and sociological methods and approaches that put the reality in the first place. Such approaches are linear, correlational, praxis, narrative, artistic, cyclical and the habitus.[26] Lartey expands the explanations of *habitus* as an approach. He uses a sociologist Pierre Bourdieu to content that:

> *habitus* (habit) refers to an orientation or way of being disposed toward things . . . so that the implied practice is seen in terms of structures, strategies and cultural products. Christian theology, in this renewed thinking that seeks to reconnect it with . . . the concept of theology as *habitus*, is seen as related to the life of the Church and to the life of and faith of Christian people. Christian theology in this sense is the articulation of the nature

---

25. Ibid., 118.
26. Ballard and Pritchard, 128-143; Slee, *Women's Faith Development*, 7.

and understanding of the Christian faith as it undergirds and is expressed through practical living.[27]

For Lartey, the correctly articulated and connected Christian theology with practical living of Christians usually portrays the real structure, strategies and cultural products. At this time, the Christian faith becomes real because it manifests itself in real habits.

THEORETICAL FRAMEWORK: CHARLES TAYLOR AND THE SPHERES OF SOCIETY

In my analysis of the lived experience of society and the context in which pastors perform their roles, I used the perspectives of Charles Taylor as expressed in his book *Modern Social Imaginaries*. As a philosopher of social and political theories, Taylor presents his reflections about the development of Western history that is Western societies in *"Multiple Modernities."* Thus, Taylor continues his contributions by using the term *Social Imaginary* in the book *Modern Social Imaginaries*.[28] Very early in the introduction, he suggests that it is essential to use both the past and contemporary issues in order to have a clear understanding of modernity and the place we are throughout history. Such senses are the ones that comprise the phenomenon of *social imaginary*.

Taylor says that "the social imaginary is not a set of ideas; rather, it is what enables, through making sense of, the practices of a society."[29] The forms that social imaginary provides gives some new outlook on the common paths or forms of contemporary Western modernization within the moral order of society. Taylor defines the term *Social Imaginary* as "the people imagine their social existence, how they fit together with others, how things go on between them and their fellows, the expectations that are normally met, and the deeper normative notions and images that underlie these expectations."[30]

Taylor differentiates *Social Imaginary* from 'Social theory'. He provides three reasons as to why the term *imaginary* is important in his reflections. First, it reflects "the way *ordinary people* 'imagine' their social surroundings." They express their imaginations in images, stories, and legends, but not in theoretical terms. This was his focus on describing the social forms

27. Lartey, *Pastoral Theology*, 23 (Emphasis original).
28. Taylor, *Modern Social Imaginaries*, 1, 2, 3.
29. Ibid., 2.
30. Ibid., 23.

or spheres of the contemporary society. Second, a small minority possesses social theory, but all or a large group of people share social imaginary. Third, Social imaginary reflects the common understanding that makes the common practices possible and provides a widely shared sense of legitimacy.[31] Thus, according to Taylor, social imaginary means the way ordinary people collectively imagine their social life in the contemporary world. The concept "ordinary people" is one of the reasons for opting to use this perspective.

Why do all these things happen in this contemporary society? Taylor states that it is because of two reasons: first, we are all in a different space; and second, we are all in a different time. In social space, "we function through the grasp we have on the common repertory, without benefit of theoretical overview. Humans operated with a social imaginary well before they ever got into the business of theorizing about themselves."[32] In this example, Taylor seems to maintain that social imaginary is as old as society itself. The social theory came later because of education. Thus far, Taylor gives an example that people for example, can organize a demonstration, they can make violence or act collectively without a certain social theory.

The contemporary space and time is full of transformations. This started to happen with speed in the Western world in the eighteenth century.[33] Society is in transitions from traditional way of thinking and actions into the contemporary outlook. Society of the contemporary world can easily make revolutions. This was not so much an experience in the past. Almost the same, the people I conversed with testified that in the contemporary society; revolutions, strikes, conflicts and wars even in religious organizations are very common. People are against top-down modes of leadership. They want democratic governments in both the church and in secular institutions. People seem to be self-conscious if leaders do not emphasize to help people on their economic development.[34] In this general information about the history of social imaginary, Taylor accounts that people, or as he call it, population, has a long march in the process of developing or modifying old practices into new ones. Finally, Taylor describes the spheres or social forms of the contemporary society.

According to Taylor, the social imaginary defines three key social forms or spheres that seem to characterize features also of the contemporary Tanzanian society. First, is the market economy sphere.[35] In this

31. Ibid., 23 (Italics mine).
32. Ibid., 26, 27, 30, 31.
33. Ibid., 30.
34. Ibid., 28–29, 33–46.
35. Ibid., 47, 69–82.

economic sphere, society appears to be a commercial society. Economy can link people with others around the world through travels and communication means. Economy is becoming dominant and determinant factor of the life of society.

For example, Taylor notices and reports the power of economy in the Western culture. He writes: "But the economy could become more than a metaphor: it came to be seen more and more as the dominant end of society."[36] For Taylor economy can even affirm a person's ordinary life, family life or relationships. Economy underlies the fundamental importance of equality in our social and political lives. That is why social, political, material and spiritual factors help explain the gradual promotion of the economic power of people to its central place of decisions and practices. Commercial and economic activities are currently appearing to become the path to peace and orderly existence. Taylor illustrates that: "The more a society turns to commerce, the more polished and civilized it becomes, the more it excels in the arts of peace. The impetus to moneymaking is seen as a 'calm passion.' When it takes hold in a society, it can help to control and inhibit the violent passions. . . . moneymaking serves our interest, and interest can check and control passion."[37] Consequently, it implies that in all people, poor economy can lead them lack peace, become violent, and voiceless. Most African pastors are without exceptions. They are vulnerable to the problem of poverty. This problem of poverty has plain evidence in the analysis of data. It portrays the existence of a low economy level among most pastors. They complain daily about low salaries and low standards of life.

Ada Newaho Simkoko Mwendamseke when writing about *Mass Media and Female Images* confirms that it is becoming obvious that in Tanzania as well as in other parts of the world, people with good economy become the dominant class. It reads:

> Structural relationship in a society is determined by class relations. Those who dominate economically, politically and socially in a society, tend to control not only the economic production in the society but even the social relations of the people. These relations in turn tend to influence the views expressed in the mass media. Thus, the social relations which emerge in a Tanzanian society are a reflection of the relations of the dominant class. . . . the dominant class becomes the reference group. . . . in most cases the dominant class controls . . . .[38]

---

36. Ibid., 72.
37. Ibid., 74.
38. Mwedamseke, *Mass Media and Female Images*, 44; cf. 26, 84.

As the discussions ahead will illustrate, Mwendamseke verifies the theory of Taylor which reflects the Western World. Economy dominates and determines one's living and socialization. Economy controls the social relations of people. Economy is a powerful weapon.

Since the informants in this book are aware that they belong to a poor country and context, then, most of them point out that economy has been an important agenda for the development of the church and of individual members of society. All people are always engaging in their struggle to eradicate poverty. Therefore, society dares even to urge worship services be shortened in order for them to go for their economic businesses. The same is among the reasons for their movements into urban centers and the tendency of being mobile in search of employment.

Second, the public sphere. This is a "common space"[39] where there are multiple media for communication. It is a public space. In this sphere society communicates through mobile phones, has face-to-face encounters, use written (newspapers) and electronic (emails) devices to make the work and communication simple and attractive. It means that, in this public space "we are already in some kind of conversation with each other."[40] For Taylor, it is an intimate space. People can use those electronic devices to communicate regionally and globally until they reach a public opinion through several discussions. Media is the most useful tool for connecting societies. It reaches fast and many people at once. This was one of the developments of the modern society. Sometimes, the leader receives information after other members of society have been informed and reacted toward it. They discuss the issue first and reach consensus. The leader becomes the last to get that information.

Taylor continues to state that it is a common space because people discuss sensitive issues and reach certain common opinions for actions by using different media, such as, through books, pamphlets, newspapers, even through drawings – that is artistic works, during coffee hours, in salons, and in other formal public places, like the parliament.[41] The messages they convey to each other make society reach a public opinion. People use their freedom to discuss their issues pertaining to their life. The people may or may not pronounce in words what they would like to be changed. Therefore, Taylor suggests that leaders take seriously those expressions because they are essential opinions of society. He urges that the "government ought to

---

39. Taylor, *Modern Social Imaginaries*, 83–141; cf. Dobbelaere & Jagodzinski, "Religious Cognitions,"
197–200.
40. Ibid.
41. Ibid.

listen to it. . . . . Government is then not only wise to follow opinion; it is morally bound to do so. Government ought to legislate and rule in the midst of a reasoning public."[42] This is how the contemporary society utilizes the modern knowledge and development in order to survive in this modern (contemporary) era.

The third is the self-governing sphere.[43] It is a democratic space. Taylor states that in this sphere, people practice self-rule or self-governance through democratic elections. Taylor calls this sphere "inventing the people' as a new collective agency." He adds: "the society in which we live is not just the politically structured order; we also belong to civil society."[44] In social imaginary, the contemporary society demands full freedom from undemocratic rules and regulations from parents, social administrative structures (the church is included here), freedom from traditional patriarchal powers and top – down approaches of leadership. In this social imaginary, Taylor maintains that in the pre-modern society before the early eighteenth century society followed hierarchical principles. Nevertheless, in the late eighteenth, the situation started to change drastically. People started to criticize the ruling class due to their old forms of authority and principles. That spirit of criticizing the existing old styles of leadership continues to grow with people to date. Taylor testifies: "Similarly today, we feel the need to criticize and even transform many of our nonpolitical relations, those that are insufficiently "democratic" or egalitarian. We find ourselves speaking of the democratic against authoritarian family, for instance. . . . our lives are organized around a contrary principle."[45]

It is to be noted that, Taylor was aware of what it meant to be free. Freedom did not mean keeping oneself separate from the society that you belong. He argues that if individual persons and some organizations want freedom or a self-governing, yet, they should not detach themselves from the whole society because they are part of humankind who have to live a horizontal life with each other. This is because, "in the direct – access society, . . . each member is 'immediate to the whole.'"[46]

Why then did I choose to use this framework of "Social imaginary" in my analysis of data? First, the perspective is not biased to minorities; that is, for example, the educated alone or the rich; rather, the phenomenon is inclusive of all people. It does not make distinctions in society; that is,

42. Ibid., 88.
43. Ibid., 143–154.
44. Ibid., 143.
45. Ibid., 146.
46. Ibid., 157.

between the literate and the illiterate, the rich and the poor, and so on. It attempts to unite leaders and the followers so that they come together and make consensus on matters pertaining to society's life, whether spiritual or material or secular life. Second, throughout my research and in the analysis, I discovered that most of the time both ordinary and the educated members of the Tanzanian society could come together and share information about their economic development, their needs, interests and experiences of life for their common decisions and practices. Almost all people seemed very influential and strong to pressurize pastors to undertake their roles by observing their contemporary needs and interests.

I agree with Taylor that sometimes Christians can even organize a strike against their government or leaders if they become tired of the ways practices are.[47] The approach of organizing a strike against the government or leaders also applied to a pastor in the area of my research if the community felt unsatisfied with the services or interaction with their spiritual ministers. The theory describes the reality that this research presents. People are very mobile due to freedom of movement, faith, of speech and freedom of expression. Whenever they feel unsatisfied, people can speak up so that their pastors and other church ministers can make some adjustments in order to respond to the contemporary problems of society. However, most church ministers seemed reluctant to the rapid changes that had put the contemporary society into those three key spheres.

Thus, one will notice that although I do not arrange the themes into those three spheres, however, the whole analysis reflects them. Taylor's theory demonstrates a great part of the experiences of the Tanzanian society drawn as an example of all African pastors, especially, those in the context in which the investigation was undertaken. Christians wanted democracy, and were critical. As I have stated above, in the concluding chapter of this book, I try to make another deeper discussion about the economic sphere. I reflect from data on how economy role is to be an essential mission of the African pastor. This obligation stands on the fact that economy seems to be dominant in the twenty-first century. In this century, the power of economy dominates and controls almost every factor in life-decisions. Fihavango describes that the world has passed through four challenging civilization (phases) – powers of development phases. He lists *the four powers of civilization* as follows: first, the military power which operated during the times of establishing and expanding chiefdoms. Second, the power of religion that operated during the times when religious organizations controlled the world. The third is the power of politics that operated during the times

---

47. Ibid., 25.

when political ideologies emerged and ruled the world. The fourth is the economic power that operated during the times when economy with the political powers dominated and ruled the world. This is the contemporary century. For Fihavango, those with better economic status are the ones deciding for others. He views the economic power to be a great challenge to postmodernists. Therefore, he urges Church leaders to be aware of these changed and changing phases and they ought to struggle with them.[48]

SOURCES AND SELECTION OF DATA

Choosing the question of social change as my subject matter for this book was just the beginning. I needed to find out how to do the research. Therefore, in this section I describe the location in which I undertook the investigation, samples for data collection and discussion. These represent the rest of locations and samples of the African context. First, I decided to carry it out through a fieldwork within my home Church and country, the Evangelical Lutheran Church in Tanzania, specifically, in the Southern Diocese (ELCT/SD) area. Second, in the research process, I had two categories of informants: the first category had four individual pastors and two group interviewees that comprised of lay Christians from two parishes, one group from each parish. Moreover, one was from a rural parish, and the other one was from an urban parish. I considered this first category as my major focus group.

Then I had a secondary category that was also a group interview with separate group of other pastors and of evangelists within the ELCT/SD. Under the second category there was also a group of informants from one of the training institutions (within Tanzania) where some pastors of the ELCT/SD got their theological orientation before they were ordained and appointed for workplaces.

Each of the individual pastors from my focus group had at least an experience of two years in parish ministry, and had both rural and urban parish experiences. Among them, one was a female and others were male pastors. Gender sensitivity helped me obtain data that comprised varied experience patterns. Accordingly, the second category of my informants thus served to supplement and substantiate with their lived experiences the information from my focus group. Therefore, I devoted much of the time in interviews with the focus group. Most important also is that I limited myself to interview with the members of society who were also members of the Christian Church within the ELCT/SD.

48. Fihavango, *Tupate Wapi Mtu Kama Huyu?* 19–20.

I did the task of transcription, interpretation, discussion and presentation of the findings in my last year 2008 of studies at the University of Oslo. For my library exploration, I used the published literature from the libraries of the University of Oslo, from other Universities within Norwegian context, from internet, from the then Iringa University College, and other materials in my own possession. Different approaches and resources as mentioned in this book were of great use in the whole process of research and presentation of the findings and responses for this exploration.

Moreover, in this book, unless stated otherwise, the term "Church" with a capital letter 'C' will denote the universal church; while, the "church" with a small letter 'c' will denote the trained theologians and pastors who are decision makers on issues of pastoral ministry in their respective parishes and dioceses. Additionally, the small 'c' will not denote the ELCT- superior power of the Church in Tanzania.

INTERVIEW AS A METHOD OF RESEARCH

In the whole process of collecting data, I used interview as my method. To reach that goal, I opted to utilize both the semi-structured and unstructured form. To use the semi-structured interview I prepared some guiding questions that helped me converse with people to get some relevant information that I wanted and have analyzed and used in this book. This method also left the informants with a freedom to express their experiences in terms of their feelings and thoughts about social change and the role of the pastor. Furthermore, this method also provided me with flexibility to ask some follow-up questions from the informants to clarify their descriptions. In addition, this method helped the informants to feel free to ask me if they did not understand well the guiding questions.

Stephen B. Bevans points out that the "contemporary postmodern thinking is moving away from correspondence understanding of truth and understanding truth more in terms of relation, conversation, and dialogue. The methodological attitude of openness and dialogue is the most useful approach in this postmodern world which is greatly filled with radical pluralism, ambiguities, and multicultural consciousness that emerges almost everywhere." He emphasizes this especially when one undertakes a study in issues such as of social change. For Bevans, reality emerges in true conversation between authentic women and men when they "allow questioning to take over."[49] David Tracy further insists in this point of conversation:

---

49. Bevans, *Models of Contextual Theology*, 93.

> Conversation is a game with some hard rules: say only what you mean; say it as accurately as you can; listen to and respect what the other says, however different or other; be willing to correct or defend your opinions if challenged by the conversation partner; be willing to argue if necessary, to confront if demanded, to endure necessary conflicts, to change your mind if the evidence suggests it.[50]

Bevans and Tracy above emphasize on the usefulness of this method because it interacts with real contexts and allows dialogue. Bevans comments thus, "Because contexts constantly change, theology has constantly to change as well."[51] It implies that the task of transforming theology should be done by using this methodological approach.

Additionally, regarding the significance of interview in a form of conversation as a method of research in issues pertaining to obtaining the lived experiences, Howard Clinebell states that when one deals with people's problems, the methodological approaches have to be therapeutic. For Clinebell, therapeutic approaches use much conversation. He argues that, for example, if the pastoral psychotherapist wants to reach the purpose of obtaining important information that will be useful to control certain situations in life and bring a complete healing and growth in a person; the discussions ought to be in a conversation form. The process of conversations allows both the psychotherapist and the client, in this case the interviewee, to discuss the problem extensively. Conversation method is within "insight-oriented approaches to pastoral psychotherapy [which] employ methods that enable persons gradually to become aware of and change those out-of-awareness (repressed) feelings, images, impulses, desires, memories, and conflicts, which limit their effectiveness in living."[52] Furthermore, the reflections from Clinebell indicate that, interview in a form of conversation can easily open the long-sealed doors and the hidden rooms gradually become open. "By "working through" deeper and deeper levels of life-constricting inner forces, persons gradually diminish inner blocks to aliveness and self-acceptance. They deal with obsolete, inappropriate feelings and resolve growth-blocking inner conflicts from the past."[53] Through interview in a form of conversation, a person airs out some views about life. He or she has enough room to express the views regarding the question at hand. It implies that, for Clinebell, a conversation that reflects the above arguments is part

50. Tracy, *Plurality and Ambiguity*, 19.
51. Bevans, *Models of Contextual Theology*, 94.
52. Clinebell, *Basic Types of Pastoral Care & Counseling*, 380.
53. Ibid. 380–381.

of healing and growth in a person. Interview provides detailed information as he envisions:

> It allows persons another chance to experience, [express], and learn more self-affirming attitudes toward [and about] themselves and others. The [interviewer] goes down with people [in this case, informant] into their "little private hells," allowing them to face their inner "devils" and find liberation from them.[54]

In addition, as I highlighted above, interview allows the interviewer to intervene where there are no clear descriptions or seek further clarifications on the subject in discussion.

As I pointed out above, methodologically, this book reflects a contextual research while using interview in a form of conversation as its technique in obtaining required data. Therefore, it is important for me to emphasize that my primary data was from the lived experiences of both the pastors and the community. I conversed with four individual pastors and two groups—one from a rural parish and the other from an urban parish. I considered both those pastors and the two groups as my focus groups.[55]

Either, I would also notify earlier that unless otherwise stated or done unintentionally, I use *italics* in two forms: first, in quotations from fieldwork voices; and second, if the direct quotation from the written source contains that italicized word, phrase, or sentence. Otherwise, throughout this book I expect not to italicize the quotations from any written materials. Still, this is exception with the quotation principles.

CONSIDERING RESEARCH ETHICS

The *Guidelines for Research Ethics in the Social Sciences, Law and Humanities* (NESH) maintains: "'Research Ethics' refers to a complex set of values, standards and institutional schemes that help constitute and regulate scientific activity. Ultimately, research ethics is a codification of ethics of science in practice."[56] I stated above that the research process conducted for this book is a 'contextual research' in which I used both sociological and theological approaches due to its nature, scope and the aim of this book. I was aware of the ethical considerations as I interacted and conversed with the informants. I interviewed the informants after their free and informed consent. Moreover, I used Swahili language that the informants themselves

---

54. Ibid., 381.
55. Bryman, *Social Research Methods*, 2004: 318–324, 345–351, 357, 359–361.
56. NESH, *Guidelines for Research Ethics*, 5.

were conversant. I also respected their freedom to participate – especially in group interviews, dignity, and integrity, especially, when they sometimes changed the appointment time due to their commitments.

Furthermore, I also observed the professional ethics of my informants and mine. In this book, I have anonymized the real names, places and dates to secure confidentiality and dignity of informants. I keep the data about the informants and their responses separate from this book. By following the ethical issues of research, I managed to obtain the data that I needed and in preserving the data after the analysis and submission of the manuscript for publication.

2

TANZANIA

HISTORICAL OVERVIEW ON PEOPLE AND THEIR SOCIO-CULTURAL LIFE

INTRODUCTION

TANZANIA IS AMONG THE East African countries. The Evangelical Lutheran Church with its Southern Diocese are in Tanzania, where I carried out my research. The pastors, other informants and society on research are therefore Tanzanians. Thus, I find it essential to start with some descriptions about Tanzania. The main issues that I discuss in this chapter mainly relate to some of the recent social changes that both, directly or indirectly affect the social and individual life of people; hence, the ministry and life of the church. Thereafter, the description of the Southern Diocese will follow in chapter three.

By presenting the historical overview of Tanzania as a whole with its people's socio-cultural life, the aim is to highlight and understand the social life of the people within which pastors and the Church are living and working. We ought to have at least a brief knowledge on the cultural, social, socio-religious, economic, political and educational life of society we live in. Why is this important? Sociologists Paul H. Chalfant and Emil Labeff in their book *Understanding People and Social Life: Introduction to Sociology* state that, it is necessary for all people, especially leaders, to understand people and the way they live. Leaders need to know people's interaction, social movements, religion and religious behavior, individual and collective behavior, demographical growth, social problems and other related issues.[1] Chalfant and Labeff emphasize that people have their ways of life, and if one will not study and understand them well, there will be more difficulties in life relations and leadership. People have varied backgrounds. Among ultimate backgrounds that Church ministers and other theologians ought to understand appropriately are environment and customs. In those two backgrounds, people set and practice their life styles. Chalfant and Labeff argue that societies change their life styles due to people's interactions between individuals, one group to another, and hence one community to another. Some other factors that cause society to change are change of needs, various problems, economic status, population growth or decrease, type of activities that people engage in their daily life and toward life philosophy in general. All these and many other factors that Chalfant and Labeff have depicted do influence and challenge each member within society and in the surrounding communities to alter some standards and styles of life.

The description above from Chalfant and Labeff help us learn some essential life aspects that characterize society. By using varied literatures in this chapter, I try to relate what Chalfant and Labeff are trying to explain with the context of my research, as well as my reflection on the current changes in African societies. From the outset, if we can reflect and compare the observations above with the contemporary life, it indicates that the society of Tanzania represents complex, varied, growing, and changing context and life styles. It is in such circumstances that the pastor performs and incorporates the ministerial and social roles. It seems there is no way for pastors to work without meeting such problems and challenges.

Every pastor ought to understand the people and their social life so that he or she can be able to practice the given roles within a multicultural and changing characteristic of society and contexts. Therefore, the following section presents an overview of some general important aspects of Tanzanian people's life; namely, the political, economic, social, cultural, socio-religious, and educational life. 'Most of the references used are those talking about Tanzanian perspectives. The main interest and focus in those facets are on the recent changes that have happened. The section is titles 'people and their life backgrounds.' As I undertake this overview, it is good to assert that, in most cases, the situations discussed in this chapter are similar in many African societies. I will not overlook this fact if I have to be sincere because I belong to an African background.

---

1. Chalfant and Labeff, *Understanding People*, 6–9.

PEOPLE AND THEIR LIFE BACKGROUNDS: SOCIO-CULTURAL LIFE

Political Life

Tanzania's political history is so long that we cannot exhaust in this small presentation. However, this is not the main intention of this book. I will touch some issues that relate to the work I am doing. The reason for this is that it may be difficult to account on the society's life setting without mentioning something about people's political awareness and involvement in its principles that govern them as both secular and religious citizens. Therefore, in this section my detailed discussion will not be on how political parties form or on how Tanzania obtained her independence. The purpose of this section is to show the background of the Tanzanian society's awareness and its relationship between the religious life and the political life of the same people. For example, Niwagila argues: "Political awareness was at work within religious circles, Christians, both Protestants and Catholics were asking themselves how long it would take the Africans to take leadership in the church. . . . if freedom meant to be free from the colonial yoke, it also meant to be free from the . . . yoke of making the church property, both in administration and in theological thinking."[2] Moreover, it is to show how Tanzania united as one nation, the start of strong integration and the introduction of the *Ujamaa* (socialism) concept, the effect on the Church and ministerial role of the church leaders and the challenges brought by the political proclamation on self-reliance. Different scholars discuss about political life and people's awareness of politics. However, in this part I mainly use literature that relates to Tanzania.

Katherine Snyder in her research about *The Iraqw of Tanzania* observes that, before the state was called Tanzania, it existed as two separate countries called Tanganyika for the Mainland and Zanzibar for the Islands. Even during the time of independence, there were two political parties: The Tanganyika African National Union (TANU) for the mainland and Afro-Shiraz Party (ASP) for the Islands.[3] The two political parties united on 5th February 1977 to form the present ruling party *Chama Cha Mapinduzi (CCM)* – which in English is commonly called the 'Revolutionary Party'. However, this was formed after the 'villagization', we will see this later within this section. Therefore, from 1977 to 1992 Tanzania was under one political party system.

---

2. Niwagila, *From the Catacomb*, 70.
3. Snyder, *The Iraqw of Tanzania*, 46–47.

Snyder continues to state that during postcolonial times, that is from 1960's to 1970's; at first the clans were somehow resistant to some of the political ideologies of the state. As the political leaders noticed that resistance, they found some strategies to win those clans. Among the strategies that political leaders used to influence people to accept these ideologies little by little were: first, to appoint or select some clan leaders into parliamentary representations. The second was to draw upon traditional and colonial boundaries and units so that people would not get shocked with the political powers that the government wanted to have upon the whole life of society. The two strategies proved to be effective in most parts of the country even though some clan traditional authorities were slow to adopt the imposed political structures. Later on, as they were slowly convinced and encouraged, they also started adapting to what government leaders were proclaiming. The adaptation was slow because people had been under colonial domination for a long time.[4] Accordingly, people wanted to differentiate between the new governments from the colonial ones.

For Snyder, from her research in the Tanzanian context; some significant changes need to be realized. Those changes have been growing very fast. First, from the time of colonialism, soon after independence to the time of villagization and the birth of CCM (1977) still most villages had no important social services. Consequently, after the birth of *Ujamaa* ideology and of CCM party some of the things started to move more rapidly. It implies that a change in political system and ideologies also led to a change of some policies relating to availability of social services and a more close community life. Progressively, to the year 2005:

> Within villages, the government had built schools, health dispensaries and government offices. Thus, the penetration of the state is quite thorough. . . . This political system is a highly effective means of communicating information particularly from the [district] headquarters to the grassroots. . . . The intended outcome of this structure . . . [is] to enable those at the grassroots level to communicate their wishes and affect policy at the district, regional, and national level. . . . The flow of information and power moves [at least as] . . . stated national ideology.[5]

However, Snyder argues that despite this national political ideology and the growing changes; there are some weaknesses. Some information and power move primarily in one direction from the core to the periphery.[6] I

4. Ibid.
5. Ibid., 47.
6. Ibid.

agree with the contention in the quotation and her awareness on the way the Tanzanian government is operating. Despite some weaknesses it has, no Tanzanian who can deny the current strong involvement and influence of politicians and government in social affairs. Political parties are strongly fighting for people's rights and, more freedom of speech, of movement, and other related interests. Anthony Giddens supports that the issue of speeding the process of free speech links with influences of globalization. For example, he states blatantly, "Immigration has changed its nature in a world of instantaneous communication. 'Internal globalization' – the internal make-up of societies – mirrors globalization on a world scale. . . . Migrants and cultural minorities can interpret their local experience in terms of events happening elsewhere in the world."[7] This problem connects itself to clothing styles.

Another change that has been in great move in Tanzania is the rapid growth of social movements and organizations that fight for their rights. Niwagila observes and states that among them are the strong women and youth's movements. He points out that, for example, from 1994 women and youth have been struggling for recognition, inclusion in various issues for equal monopoly in leadership and in other roles in society. There has been a struggle for land ownership and youth's interests in Tanzania. This struggle happens because only men and old people who own pieces of land according to African culture. Women owned it in virtue of their marriage to their husbands.[8]

Thus, through political system changes, women and other marginalized groups are awake and have room to fight for their rights of equality, recognition and in many other issues from which society has marginalized or silenced them. Therefore, the Tanzanian society now emphasizes strongly the interests and rights of both women and youth. No one group is dominant in all issues. Today these groups have their conferences and other functions that are recognized and incorporated into leadership structures from the village to the national levels. Consequently, for Snyder, "the incorporation of communities into state structures resulted in new structures of authority."[9] The state has been regulating and restructuring its leadership roles and structures so that most groups are inclusive and functional like any other secular groups in the country. The church is pushed to do the same.

The third recent change in Tanzania is on the multiplication of political parties. This is a change from a single party to a multi-party political system.

---

7. Giddens, *Europe in the Global Age*, 129, cf.130–131.
8. Ibid., Niwagila, *From the Catacomb*, 305–308.
9. Snyder, *The Iraqw of Tanzania*, 49.

This ideology started to grow strong in 1993 such that the government had to rethink the single party system. Before the announcement of a new political system of multi-party, there formed a Presidential Commission to make a research as to whether most Tanzanians were now in favor of a new system of multiparty type or not. Hence, during the general national election of the president, the members of the parliament, and other representatives in 1995, the system of political multiparty started in Tanzania. This was a great political change in society of Tanzania.

Again, Snyder acknowledges that the rapid political change very much affects all organizations and any other social groups. As a result, the political systems, movements and structures of authority influence social or religious, institutions. People communicate freely their wishes and affecting ideas or policies in society; similarly, they do even in their religious institutions. Their political strength applies even when they are in religious communities and programs. A good example is on the 'villagization' whereby as the state decided to move its people into *Ujamaa* villages so the religious institutions had to move and re-arrange their allocations, modes of practices and programs. This also affected their religious philosophy and membership.[10]

When one reflects such arguments and expositions above, there are indications that may also imply that Tanzania has been in great political influence and transformations. To some extent and especially on political issues in the Tanzanian society, there is an attempt to use political influences in almost all groups of people in society. There is no excessive imposition of authority and power into society compared to the previous years. Political ideologies have given society a power to communicate and strongly argue for their interests. Sometimes one can notice that the political life of the state influences and provides some strategies for people to fight for their rights in the religious circles in which they affiliate. Whenever some, both religious and none religious organizations, are found not making satisfactory agreements with their members; people from socio-political spheres encourage their people to use the social strategies to influence their religious leaders to listen to what the communities want. In general, it implies that just as they are influencing other secular aspects, Tanzania's contemporary political ideologies are highly affecting the religious ideologies and practices.

As I stated earlier in chapter one, *Ujamaa* is mentioned as an ideology which needs some special attention in relation to a political life of the Tanzanian society. However, I ask myself, what is *Ujamaa*? What implications can we draw from it? Before going further, it is better now turn to the discussion of such issues. Besides, in this discussion about *Ujamaa*, the

10. Ibid., 49–50.

reflection of a Tanzanian pastor Peter A.S. Kijanga is dominant. I centre to his work because he relates *Ujamaa* and the role of the Church.

Describing Ujamaa Concept

Kijanga reports that *Ujamaa* is a Swahili word with its literal meaning 'familyness or familyhood. Mwalimu (teacher) Nyerere is the first one to use this word and coined it to describe the African traditional way of life.' For Kijanga, Nyerere described a kind of socialism that Tanzania adopted. It seemed a better term because it brought in the mind of the people the idea of mutual involvement in the family. It is contented that Nyerere himself maintained that this concept could be helpful to ensure that people care for each other's welfare. It provided better notion and description of socialism.[11] This concept was emphasizing that "a socialist society can only be built by those who believe in, and who themselves practice, the principles of socialism." If people had this as their attitude of mind, they could become really socialists.[12]

Kijanga argues that according to Nyerere, it was very necessary to grow a Tanzanian society out of the roots of African traditional societies and that could contain no exploitation and individualistic attitudes. The second thing was to develop society "in a particular quality of life."[13] Kijanga states further that *Ujamaa* was not a completely new kind of life. Rather it was building on the traditional life of African families. "The traditional African family lived and still lives according to the basic principles of *Ujamaa* which relates first and foremost to persons and then to property. The former gives people the sense of social solidarity and respect and the latter thrusts to the individuals the obligation to work and the universal hospitality which is reflected in the sharing of the necessities of life."[14] Kijanga observes that the *Ujamaa* attitude aimed at helping people to have a sense of sharing and cooperating in matters that affect a wide community. For example, issues of basic needs and social services were and are ought to be put under the control of the community. Each member of the family is obliged to them. However, before the introduction of *Ujamaa* idea, the social solidarity, universal hospitality, and respect to persons already existed in African families. As stated above, *Ujamaa* was not introducing a new thing; rather, it was just adopting, officiating and pronouncing it as a national ideology. Additionally, at the birth

11. Kijanga, *Ujamaa and the Role of Church*, 2–3.
12. Ibid., 4.
13. Ibid.
14. Ibid., 14.

of *Ujamaa* ideology, people had less quality life. Now *Ujamaa* had to emphasize strongly the need to run toward quality life. All basic social affairs (services) were to have a quick establishment or improvement. How could Ujamaa introduce and emphasize this? The next subsection responds to this question.

Ujamaa: A Political ideology of Tanzania?

Historically, when you mention *Ujamaa* in Tanzania; you also mention TANU and Nyerere. As I stated earlier, this nationalist movement began in 1954 under the leadership of *Mwalimu* (teacher). At this time, the country was under the leadership of the same Julius K. Nyerere. However, TANU dissolved in 1977 forming the present ruling party *CCM*.[15] At first, *Ujamaa* appeared as an approach and not as a doctrine of the Tanzanian society. However, the ideology seemed to develop into a kind of philosophy that political leaders (Nyerere being their champion) wanted to influence into society. Preliminarily, it is asserted that 'Ujamaa was only an attitude of mind not a dogma. It just based on assumptions and beliefs about African view of man and society. It is opposed to exploitation of one person by another.'[16]

However, TANU developed *Ujamaa* as its ideology and a political system during the times of struggle for independence. Reflecting and focusing on *Ujamaa* for the Tanzanian society, TANU's primary aim was to achieve *Uhuru* - that is independence. Other tasks after independence in 1961 were "Africanizing, reforming and remodelling society. Now, colonialists had to start using African indigenous leaders in local administration." Therefore, TANU had to attempt to make *Ujamaa* as its ideology. This ideology had to reflect the policies that will deal with education that strengthens the feeling of responsibility to the African society in which the individual and communities were poor or rich depending on whether the whole tribe was rich or poor.[17]

TANU challenged all British colonialists and even the old African establishment that were not sensing toward community centred life being part of its emphasis on *Ujamaa*. *Ujamaa* emphasized on social life that considers equality and hospitality. TANU also promoted *Ujamaa* by using 'Kiswahili' language. This language was one of the instruments that helped the *Ujamaa* philosophy to create national integration. Together with other

15. Westerlund, *Ujamaa na Dini*, 25.
16. Kijanga, *Ujamaa and the Role of Church*, 113–114.
17. Westerlund, *Ujamaa na Dini*, 30; Nyerere, *Ujamaa: Essays on Socialism*, 9; Kijanga, *Ujamaa and the Role of the Church*, 1, 4.

aims, *Ujamaa* also aimed at integrating rural and city people. Through *Ujamaa* society became a mixture of external and internal influences. In 1967, *Ujamaa* became more explicitly a socialist ideology. From that time on it started other struggle on establishing concrete policies of change that would lead to a fight against enemies of capitalism, poverty, ignorance and many other social problems. It had to fight for self-reliance, education for and to all people, to improve agricultural (and other economic) activities, rural development, good leadership and democracy.[18]

At this instant, we can ask ourselves this question: was it ultimately inevitable time for Tanzania to adopt the idea of *Ujamaa*? Niwagila responds to this question by describing that:

> The birth of the *Ujamaa* ideology in modern Tanzania was inevitable because of the socio-political situation in the country. Firstly, the country had suffered from the colonial imperialism and exploitation that robbed man of his [sic] dignity. Secondly, the country was divided into more than 126 tribes with non-common identity as one nation. Thirdly, the country is inhabited by people who have three major problems—poverty, diseases and ignorance. All these three circumstances led and his party TANU to launch a political struggle . . . to unite the 126 tribes into one nation and to mobilize this big family to fight for its freedom . . . The philosophy of *Ujamaa* made the Tanzanians aware of the social, cultural and psychological consequence of colonialism. After achieving political independence, the *Ujamaa* policy which was outlined in the Arusha Declaration . . . on 5th February, 1967 marked a turning point in Tanzanian politics. War was declared on poverty, diseases, ignorance and exploitation . . . The whole nation was called to support the policy of *Ujamaa*, of self-reliance which is the backbone of the whole process of development and modernization in the local communities, changing the economic structures . . . into a Tanzanian context – under the leadership of the people.[19]

Niwagila shows the long life of the concept *Ujamaa* and the way in which all communities were involved in this political ideology. Moreover, he points out that this attitude of mind developed policies that were to fight against the big three enemies. At last, it had become a full political ideology of Tanzania, and as well, it became a philosophy of the nation.

18. Kijanga, *Ujamaa and the Role of Church*, 2; Westerlund, *Ujamaa na Dini*, 25–28; Nyerere, *Ujamaa: Essays on Socialism*, 13–74.

19. Niwagila, *From the Catacomb*, 391–392.

Since its establishment, it was and has been proclaimed and practiced for many years in Tanzania. The Church and ministers are among significant members who faced challenge, influence and hence participated much in proclaiming and implementing this ideology.[20] However, in one way or another, although this political ideology still exits to date in terms of actions, its explicit proclamation and emphasis seems diminishing due to social, cultural, economic, and technological changes. People are rethinking about it (*Ujamaa*).

Ujamaa and Villagization: A Struggle for Rural Development and Socialist Country

In discussing *Ujamaa* to have influence and thus become a political ideology in Tanzania; I also touch that this ideology or assumption also aimed to struggle for rural development. So, one of the most important aspects and goals of *Ujamaa*, in a broader sense, is its attempt to transform life in the rural areas through the formation of *Ujamaa* villages. Westerlund describes that, due to the apparent state of a very poor status of rural life of Tanzanians, similar to many other Africans, this was also among the most radical rural development policies in Africa. Parallel to the above ideas, Nyerere outlined by emphasizing that socialism in Tanzania should primarily focus on rural development. For Nyerere, the land and people had to be the basis of Tanzanian socialism. He had in mind that Tanzanians can change their poor life into better one by being co-operative through community life. In order to make community life possible and effective, people were politely encouraged, motivated and persuaded to shift from their residences into new villages. The movement was possible first because "traditionally most people had lived scattered, and therefore it was considered necessary to have them settled in proper villages, where they could be provided with modern facilities like schools, dispensaries or hospitals and tap water."[21] This formation of *Ujamaa* villages seemed to be vital for Tanzanian's development into a socialist country. Therefore, apart from the need for communal co-operation and better services, the less economically developed areas established the vast majority of the new villages. Hence, other villages were just encouraged to continue improving more and more of their standard of life.[22]

Given the poor response to the first attempt, by using a polite approach to transform the pattern of living in the rural areas, TANU eventually

20. Ibid., 393–405.
21. Westerlund, *Ujamaa na Dini*, 28.
22. Ibid.

decided to apply a new approach. Thus, in 1973 the government announced that to live in villages was no longer optional, but compulsory for all Tanzanians. "This policy of creating villages was called *Ujamaa Vijijini* which in English is . . . referred to as the policy of 'Villagization.'"²³ Westerlund continues to account that this step was the first and then the second was that of socialist units. People first gathered in villages so that they could start a life of socialism. Socialist life would be impossible if people are scattered. Consequently, the government moved all people by force using soldiers and political leaders so that by 1976 all could settle in new villages. It is elaborated that the basic principles of customary *Ujamaa* living are mutual respect, equality, human dignity, sharing of joint production and other necessities of life, and a universal obligation to work. To meet these principles, two things are reality and things to fight against them: the inferior position of women and other groups of people, and awareness about the persistence of domination, poverty, ignorance, diseases inflictions in society. Since it was a nation's struggle, even religious organizations joined *Ujamaa* policies; otherwise, they could be in controversy with the government. Therefore, there were great interaction and interrelationship of *Ujamaa* and religion that bare its significance.²⁴

Hence from Nyerere on *Ujamaa: Essays on Socialism*, Kijanga on *Ujamaa and the Role of Church in Tanzania*, Westerlund on *Ujamaa na Dini* [literary translated as 'Socialism and Religion'], and Niwagila's book *From the Catacomb to A Self-Governing Church* we can realize, draw, and predict the following implications and implementations of *Ujamaa* principles for society of Tanzania:

Ujamaa: A Vehicle and Tool for Change toward Development

At this stage, *Ujamaa* emphasized on human dignity and equality. However, Tanzania was to accept change but remain stable to defend the national freedom. In defending the national freedom, Nyerere emphasized: "we are also determined to change the condition of our lives. . . . we must have both change and stability."²⁵ Nyerere perceived change as part of human development. Whatever done in the nation was to be for the purpose of increasing people's freedom and developing their self-awareness. Schools buildings, good roads, and an increase of crop output were to be among the

---

23. Ibid., 29.

24. Westerlund, *Ujamaa na Dini*, 29–32; Kijanga, *Ujamaa and the Role of Church*, 2, 4, 6, 79, 85–86.

25. Kijanga, *Ujamaa and the Role of Church*, 5.

signs of development if those things were to change and improve the health, comfort and the understanding of the people. Self-awareness was a key to other aspects of life—the corporate responsibility, economic transformation and self-reliance.

As a vehicle and tool for change toward development, *Ujamaa* had to relate to persons and to economic prosperity. Political freedom without economic development was no longer enough for Tanzanians. A change in society's conditions of life could bring human dignity, and put the country into full freedom. The socio-economic struggles and goals are one of the issues that *Ujamaa* focused to improve by changing economic systems. How can the people attain economic prosperity under dependent economy?

There is no true and free economic development under external dependent economic influences. That is why *Ujamaa* had to emphasize on self-reliance to all Tanzanians so that they can enjoy a healthy life and access basic education. The concept 'self-reliance' is "here understood as regeneration through people's efforts." From the day of its inauguration, the emphasis was that self-reliance is an essential ingredient to human development. Self-reliance is said to consist principally in the people, and the people alone could be the motivating force in the making of their history, and hence their own contribution to world history. The Church and her ministers had to play an important role to assist the process of self-reliance and self-sufficiency of society.[26] It implies that among other people, pastors have been great agents of proclamation on self-reliance and self-sufficiency.

We have noticed that after the struggle for political independence, Tanzanian people had now to look toward a future of their better life. They had to look for ways to transform their economy. They also had to avoid any kind of life stagnation by working hard and have a corporate responsibility. It was a dream of *Ujamaa* that active participation is a key to a genuine life that reflected its (*Ujamaa*) ideological assumptions. In this struggle, the *Ujamaa* ideologies held in mind that all people have to know and be ready to meet even some other challenges and problems that they do not anticipate.

Ujamaa: A Tool for Democratic Decision Making

Ujamaa villages emerged basing on democratic principles. In most cases, from then and in all their life, people were to plan and decide for themselves what they will do. Therefore, one of the characteristics of a particular *Ujamaa* village life was to have power and authority to make decisions for their particular village. It is possible to argue that freedom from interferences is

---

26. Ibid., x–xi, 9–10.

part of a self-reliant society. Kijanga quotes Nyerere when he emphasizes on real freedom: "a nation's real freedom depends on its capacity to do things, not on the legal rights conferred by its internationally recognized sovereignty."[27] Too much dependence upon others puts all aspects of life in humankind into imprisonment. The same imprisonment can face the nation regarding inability to make democratic decisions. In this sense, *Ujamaa* played a role of being a tool for society to make its own democratic decisions. *Ujamaa* emphasized this spirit to all people.

Ujamaa: A Vehicle for Educational Change

Education is one of the most important instruments of liberation and since a few are receiving it, it is 'an investment by the poor in their own future.' *Ujamaa* policies emphasize on changing the poor conditions of education in which massive people in the Tanzanian society are living. Education needed was that one which could reinforce the values of society and prepare children to live and work in it. Besides integrating social values of *Ujamaa*, the education aimed at developing self-reliant Tanzanian citizens. Schools were regarded as real part of society. Education for all people is one of the changes that *Ujamaa* leaders anticipated and practiced. Primary school education (that is, each one had at least have to reach standard seven) was regarded as a basic education level that each Tanzanian ought to have attained. Hence, education was to help people use their knowledge to exploit available opportunities and resources, improve their living conditions. Education should serve as a lamp for people to see and realize their problems and look for ways to solve them.

Ujamaa: A Mechanism for Good Leadership

Leaders and technicians were supposed to play their roles as faithful and active participants and as resources for people to learn. Moreover, leaders were to become and have an inspirational leadership. They had to remember their social responsibility; otherwise, they would find themselves becoming obstacles of change and development. *Ujamaa* was against abuse of power for it (abuse of power) deterred the initiatives of people and blocked their participatory democracy in all levels of social life and leadership. *Ujamaa* was searching to inspire people to harmonize word and action. Both, leaders and society were to follow this ideology.

27. Ibid., 9.

Ujamaa: A Tool for Solidarity, Self-Determination, Human Dignity and Equality

Ujamaa anticipated and urged to produce genuine solidarity among the people. It emphasized on people's solidarity, self-determination and equality where the superior and inferior were to have good relationships. In addition, individuals were to be responsible to society and an attitude of human dignity and equality of all human beings. Thus, the introduction of *Ujamaa* and *villagization* seem to be among strong starting evidences for a social integration life of the Tanzanian society.

Economic Life

As I highlighted above, one of the most important aspects of people's life is economy. The current economic life situation in Tanzania has been improving as compared to the time before and soon after independence. We have seen in the political life history that, *Ujamaa* noticed that people's economic development needed transformation. As a result, to improve the economic life, hence economic development of society was one of the aims and goals that leaders were to deal with. Then, how is the economic life of the Tanzanian society?

In general, historically, considering the economy and population in Tanzania; we are told that,

> As an African country, Tanzania is economically a part of the third world where the average life-span is 42 years. The annual income per capita is approximately § 120. While the population increases at a rate of 2.7 percent a year, the mortality rate for children is still very high as many of them die from the ages of six months to five years. Parents are always unsure of how many of their children will survive during that period of life. . . . Consequently, the parents in the Tanzanian society are still scared and concerned about sickness . . . and death.[28]

However, the above demography has extremely changed to date. Therefore, before I proceed with the discussion on the economic changes and their impact on society and the church at large; let us have a brief picture on demography of Tanzania. This will give us a picture of the changes that relate to the forthcoming discussion on the economic life of the people.

---

28. Lutahoire, *The Human Life Cycle*, 13.

Lutahoire presents an idea that the people's economic status was not all that much good, though there were strong and progressive efforts to improve it. There are more explanations about the life setting with emphasis on the economic life of society in Tanzania. We are enlightened that:

> about five percent of the population lives in cities and urban areas, whereas ninety-five percent live in rural areas. Therefore, most of the people are dependent upon cash crops such as raw cotton, banana, coffee, maize [beans] and other forms of consumables that they raise for their own subsistence each year. The government's goal for Tanzania is socialism, rooted in communitarianism. To reach this objective they encourage the people of Tanzania to settle in villages. Community life is important because it represents the common welfare of a people. Men and women are not a means but the central focus for all development. They must be free from ignorance, disease, poverty, hunger, injustice, prejudice, fear, racialism and tribalism. Therefore, those who live in villages must be willing to work on a cooperative basis. Tanzania is agricultural; however, the indigenous people are still untrained and unskilled peasant farmers. As the soil is one of Tanzania's greatest assets, it is important that new methods of farming be learned. In addition, the agricultural people are now being introduced to mixed farming and are being taught to be self-reliant. . . . Tanzania is struggling toward economic development.[29]

In the book *Ecology and Change*, Knight agrees that Tanzania is a nation that has been depending much on traditional agriculture than from other sources of economy. "Human societies require energy and material from their environments for survival." . . . For most societies, agricultural systems provide the means by which environmental energy and matter are channelled for human use. . . . Agricultural systems follow the rhythm of the seasons, and although they may change through time, . . . for survival . . . [of the] society."[30] The author continues to explain that through agriculture Tanzanians get produces for home consumption and for cash. Just as others mentioned maize, millet, wheat, cassava, beans, fruits and many more, all serve as one of the crops grown in Tanzania.[31] Yet, Knight discusses the changes that both the indigenous and the government have been emphasizing and practicing in order to improve this kind of economy as well as avoiding land dreadful conditions. One of the measures taken was to have

29. Ibid., 13–14.
30. Knight, *Ecology and Change*, 82.
31. Ibid., 83–97.

agricultural extension officer whose role was to be an agent of change. People were to start farming by using modern tools such as plough, tractors, and by using ridges. The new ways of economic production activities has made society to improve in many living standards.[32]

Despite of the social problems, such as HIV/AIDS, that the Tanzanian society is facing, the economic situation above has been changing to a better one from time to time. Niwagila is one of the witnesses of the changes. He states that Tanzania has a blessing of good climate. Of course, there are places where both food and cash crops cannot grow stronger compared to other areas. Bukoba and Iringa regions are among productive regions in Tanzania. Together with them, there are other regions with valleys and plateaus, flat land, fertile soil, favorable rainfall, and weather that Tanzania as a nation gets food and other goods for home and industrial activities. Niwagila observes that the physical features of Tanzania and their climatic conditions do shape and influence the socio-religious life of the people. Moreover, such situations or conditions help to determine the economic situation of the people. This means that most of the Tanzanians are agriculturists and engage themselves in animal husbandry. Coffee, cotton and tobacco are among cash crops in Tanzania. But there are beans; bananas, maize, millet and sorghum are among domestic items that Tanzanians depend on them.[33] We can site one example from him. Niwagila indicates that: "[T]hese food crops have been grown not as commercial crops but as the major food crops for family use only. It is in recent years that the banana crop has proved to be of commercial value, . . . in the whole of Tanzania . . . Another crop which ... has proven successful in the economy of the country is coffee. Today the [country of Tanzania] grows two kinds of coffee: Robusta . . . and . . . Arabica . . . ."[34] What have these changes to do with the life of society, the pastor's ministry and of the Church in Tanzania? How does the Church and pastors benefit from those economic produce?

Crop production, cattle, and other business activities with all their improvements have played a big and important role in the religious life of the people. The practice of economic activities is for both social and religious reasons. Both farmers and business people as they increase their economy they build modern houses, extend their small farms and other businesses, buy more cattle, send their children to schools, and so forth. As Christians earn something so are their good offerings and donations in the church or in religions and denominations. Therefore, as most Tanzanians improve their

---

32. Ibid., 197–198, cf., 158.
33. Niwagila, *From the Catacomb*, 48–53.
34. Ibid., 49.

business careers for the economy of the individuals, of their personal life, of families, and so they do for the Church and for the country as a whole.

In addition, improved economic status and information technology has also brought rapid changes in the mode of communication. Previously, there were landline telephones. However, that landline type of communication was mainly in government offices or other big organizations. It was very rare that individuals owned a private telephone. May be it was due to less technology or economic problems that African countries have been facing. Today, people possess and use cell phones. The number seems enormously growing. People seem to live in a global village. Due to business activities, many people have become very mobile. Niwagila substantiates that an improving economy has made and is still exposing people to new ideas, education (knowledge), beliefs, and new ways of life.[35] That is, new expositions envision new practices.

Peter Gibbon, as an editor, in the book *Social Change and Economic Reform in Africa* states that the problem of raising up and falling down of economy in Tanzania was also vivid in the 1990's. From those years, the government has been aware and daily struggling of it. Economic fluctuation destabilizes the nation. Gibbon shows that, consequently, instability of the nation affects even other social living. It rises up people's life and it falls down. The efforts for adjustments that the government and all other private organizations employ are parallel to social change. Yet, Gibbon shows that there are some improvements compared to some years back.[36] The process of economic change in Africa has been influencing people to change their lifestyles and standards. Going against that may lead them into failure.

The next studies confirm that there have been some developments. Snyder, and Lwehabura and Ndyetabura are among the witnesses of the fall and development. They point out that despite the prevalence of social problems that attack society each time; there are some growth indicators in people's economy. Snyder points out that, currently, society is within:

> the process of globalization that began in the colonial era and continues at an accelerating pace today. Development entails bringing individuals and communities into a national and global political economic system. Therefore, the story of development in rural Tanzania and elsewhere entails the chronicle of change and specifically how once "local" cultural forms and practices

---

35. Ibid., 50, 67–68.
36. Gibbon, *Social Change*, 161–243.

have been transformed or sustained by the ever-changing global political economy.[37]

Snyder notices that from year to year, Tanzania has been undergoing the processes of rapid socio-economic and political change. Those changes are parallel to the process of globalization. Furthermore, as the global political economy ever-changes, the local cultural forms and practices transform or sustain. Once those changes have occurred, the transformation of society occurs. Accordingly, economy becomes the major factor for social change.

However, Lwehabura and Ndyetabura in their article *Implementation of the Tanzanian National Policy* . . . provide us with a highlight on the product growth or drop rate and the recent population in Tanzania. Two elucidations are important from their report. The first is about the population growth, while the second is on the death rate. They report that "according to the 2002 census, Tanzania then had a population of some 34.4 million. . . . With an annual population growth rate of approximately 1.83%, Tanzania had an estimated population of 36.8 million in 2005."[38] The second thing is the mortality rate. While drawing references from the World Bank; they report that economy and life expectancy rates have been changing. There are dramatic signs in the economic projection (1985-2010) of the nation.

> The average real gross domestic product growth rate for the 1985-2010 period could drop from 3.9% without AIDS to 2.8%-3.3% with AIDS. These are serious economic implications for Tanzania. . . . an increased mortality rate was estimated to have reduced the life expectancy of Tanzanians from the previous 56 years to 47 years by the year 2004. . . . mortality . . . increase [and] orphans. [In] the 2005 estimates takes into account the higher death rate due to AIDS. This has resulted in a lower life expectancy . . . and a lower population growth rate. . . . There is also a change in the distribution of population by age and sex than would otherwise have been expected.[39]

The quotations above bring the implications on the fact that even if there may be an increase of birth rate, but also there is an increase of death rate. Both the growth and decrease in population may affect positively or negatively the policies and practical roles of the government and other institutions in society.

---

37. Snyder, *The Iraqw of Tanzania*, 2, 163–166.

38. Lwehabura and Ndyetabura, *Implementation of the Tanzanian National Policy*, 126.

39. Ibid., 125–126, 127.

Therefore, as Church leaders come across population growth, they also ought to be aware of the problems that associate the same society. Diseases and mortality rates are among the examples. They need the type of leadership that can be able to address the present population and its problems. It is in this Tanzanian context in which church life and ministry are taking place. Lwehabura and Ndyetabura advise that there is a need to have leadership with committed service spirit and strong efforts from the government and other social organs. Taking Tanzania as a model, they point out that the economy of society contributes much on the growth and decrease of the life expectancy of people. The Church and her pastors cannot exclude themselves from being touched by the two dimensional characteristics of society – that is, its growth and its decrease, if at all they are human beings who live and serve within society.[40]

The Social Life: 'I am because We are and We are because I am'

I have adopted the notion *I am because we are and we are because I am* from Wilson B. Niwagila. He uses it to mean that Tanzanians with other Africans as a whole live a communalistic type of life. They have a sense of togetherness in thought and actions. The emphasis is that in whatever you think or do should reflect others' survival, that is, a sense of sharing.[41] One's thinking and actions affect the life of the other. Only positive effects are welcome. For Niwagila, the *I* survives because the *We* is alive, and vice versa.

To enter the discussion on the people of Tanzania and their social life, it is better to start by some descriptions and evidences from Sebastian K. Lutahoire. This serves as our opening statements here and as the general highlight on how African societies lived and continue to emphasize the type of life for its people. Lutahoire writes:

> Sociologically, the African people live in communities. The community is the integrating factor in the lives of our people, and it may also be seen in terms of a natural phenomenon. The individual is expected to participate in the social group. Everything must be done in harmony, agreement and for mutual fulfilment almost to the point of symbiosis – that is, as the clan and extended family lives under a common ancestor. There is no question of individualism; the primary emphasis is on communalism and not on communism.[42]

40. Ibid., 126, 128, 149.
41. Niwagila, *From the Catacomb*, 35; cf., 34, 36.
42. Lutahoire, *The Human Life Cycle*, 16.

Lutahoire reveals a social style of life which African people live whereby the community is central. What does this imply? Why is it so necessary? What effects does it bring to the individual and to the community itself? What happens if one of the members decides to separate from his or her community? Can this be an everlasting form and composition of life in future generations? Such questions need addressing. I will discuss them in detail when I analyze and discuss my fieldwork data in chapters four and five. At this stage, I just bring forward some aspects that we ought to understand prior to the preceding topics. Let us reflect some of the most important issues that Lutahoire raises.

First, most Africans (Tanzanian people inclusive) live a community life. The community reinforces an integrated life style. It means that through community life and its influences people find themselves integrated. At this point, we learn that Tanzanian's life system is first characterized by a shared life. Second, the shared life creates the notion 'I am because we are and we are because I am' as Niwagila points out. For example, while mentioning the *Haya/Nyambo* communities who live in the Northern part of Tanzania; Niwagila who is from the same ethnic group extends the arguments of Lutahoire by describing the composition and formation of a shared life of Tanzanians. He supports that Tanzanians:

> Live in a society which is composed of clans, families and homes. They hold the view that every individual has a place in society, clan, family and home. His/her identity is credited to his [sic] clan and family. 'I am because we are and we are because I am' plays an important role. There is always a tendency to discourage the "I" idea of individualism. From childhood the individual is taught to think about himself [sic] in terms of others, with a "WE" emphasis.[43]

There is some truth in the above statements of Lutahoire and Niwagila. Although the situation is changing, in the quotation above each member of the community has to feel a sense of participation in the social group. Every member has to have a sense of a harmonious life toward and in the group. A member should realize that the community to which he or she is belonging lives in an extended family life, and that it keeps itself conscious of the ancestors. In this kind of life, society does not like ignore the previous context that the past generations experienced. The emphasis is on trying to preserve the clan's full history as well as, " . . . like other 'tribes' in Africa, [societies] regard the 'dead' as belonging to the family; . . . 'the living dead'

---

43. Niwagila, *From the Catacomb,* 35–36, cf., 34.

group."⁴⁴ The structure of society is formed from the family unit, to the clan and hence to a big society. There is a chain of relationship.

However, as I stated above in the political and economic life, even if some ideologies have discouraged the "I" idea of individualism, society seems to alter some identity accreditation of individuals. None has a permission to teach the opposite in society. As we shall see in the next chapters, the contemporary society seems to influence people to think about others in terms of himself or herself, with "I" emphasis. It implies that, for the contemporary society, the success of society depends on the success of its individuals, but not vice versa.

Snyder has some more ideas about the community life of Tanzanians, like other Africans. She adds to Lutahoire and Niwagila that, in community life no one has an opportunity to break it. We can read from her work: "for those, . . . , particularly male and female elders, who see their idea of moral community eroding in the face of development, this change is perceived as bringing a great "selfishness" or individualism, which has its cost at the level of community."⁴⁵ In this respect, old people view the contemporary society to be in a new and different outlook. It is changing so fast while altering most of the old traditions. New styles of life are in a daily change process. Thus, Snyder is on the opinion that:

> In Tanzania, *maendeleo* . . . [progress or development which also is referred to as 'modernity'] provides a set of categories and premises that continue to shape people's experiences and interpretations of their lives. . . . *maendeleo* is a bit of a moving goalposts, for both the government and Tanzanian citizens, as once one milestone is achieved, another appears on the horizon. . . . Development . . . and modernity . . . are frequently contrasted with the past.⁴⁶

Snyder's observations and evaluations validate the existing situation in Tanzania. Due to economic variation, Tanzanians are placing themselves into sets of categories. On the other hand, one should not perceive completely that *maendeleo* (development) in Tanzanian is just a bit and that it starts during the years of 2000 as Snyder describes. Rather, *maendeleo* has been greatly taking place even in some years before. Moreover, in any other country around the world, it is true that usually development may put people into contrasts, some on the front and some on the back yard. Appearing on the horizon does not necessarily mean that *maendeleo* is in a bit of moving

44. Ibid., 36.
45. Snyder, *The Iraqw of Tanzania*, 2–3, cf., 10.
46. Ibid., 4.

goalpost. The availability and ability to access both, the possible opportunities and resources are one of the factors for fast or slow development in people. Again, as people change their ways of thinking and doing things, the new ideas, products, and practices may differ frequently from the past. The contemporary society may have some differences in terms of socio-economic, cultural life (as shown below), and also in terms of political and technological advancement. These factors determine the mode, variation and status of development in the nation.

Meshack Edward Njinga had his observation regarding the social life of the Tanzanians. He reports that until the year 2003 the Tanzanian society has been very mobile. People have been migrating into towns and cities because the life in villages is not good. Less attention has been paid to people who live in village than those who live in urban. This movement seems to deconstruct the social structures. For Njinga, urbanization is an impact of globalization. Urbanization and other features of globalization do bring challenges to Churches and ministers because society is constantly transforming. The community life that traditional societies used to live undergoes reconstruction daily. Societies in Tanzania are currently reconstructing almost all aspects of life depending on the present life situation, time, and place in which that particular society is living. Due to this migration, even the economic, political and religious statuses keep changing into new forms.[47] As I will refer him persistently Anthony Giddens in his book *Europe in the Global Age,* argues that migration due to several compelling factors will continue to affect both, positively and negatively the clerical pattern of ministry. Others move and will obviously continue moving in search of economic prosperity, or for job vacancies. This is analogous to a strategy to solve the problem of unemployment. Giddens gives at least one example on this: "There can be no going back on pluralism, and immigrants will keep coming, legally or illegally. . . . Not just cultural acceptance, but economic integration is crucial. [For example, at one] point immigration was actively encouraged in Western Europe because of high levels of job vacancies."[48] What should we do on this kind of social life that contains the ever-changing forms? How should pastors and other Church ministers perform their prescribed roles in this kind of transformations? I will address these questions and more others in the next chapters.

In this section, I have briefly discussed the social life of people. It shows that first; still, the Tanzanian society lives in a community life. Second, each member ought to have a sense of participation in the social activities. These

---

47. Njinga, *The Shift from Ujamaa,* 20, 61–68, 85–90, cf., 92–96.
48. Giddens, *Europe in the Global Age,* 126, cf., 126–129.

two qualify a person to be a member of that community. However, the third observation is migration. The discussion shows that now people have become mobile. They move into towns. They are in search of better life in other places. This behavior seems to be new especially to old people. Fourth, the movement deconstructs the social structures. This is an effect of movement. As a consequence, those who will have moved may not have again the previous sense of participation in their original social groups because they are in another social group. Therefore, according to the above arguments, it seems that the community life of the present society is different from the previous one. Movements deconstruct the social structures.

Cultural life

Tanzania, as far as Africa is concerned, is a country with many tribes. Before and after independence, Tanzanian people lived in a mono-cultural life whereby each tribe owned its separate sites. Those geographical locations have names that indicate a type of tribe in that context. For example, there were *Ubena* – to denote the area covered by *Bena* people, *Uhehe* –for *Hehe*, *Ukinga* –for Kinga, *Unyakyusa* –for Nyakyusa, and so forth. On this, Leonard A. Mtaita states that, "Tanzania, like various other African countries, is populated by different groups of people with diverse ethnic origins. All these groups of people came to their present homelands through many centuries at different times in history."[49] The main idea that I want to draw from Mtaita is the fact that Tanzania comprises many ethnic groups.

Although they had some of their own, and may be today, they still have in slight elements, customs and traditions; yet, Tanzanians in most part had, and still now have common customs and traditions. For example, some customs like kneeling down when greeting each other had some variations from one context to another. For the *Bena* and *Hehe* cultures, they are only women who bend knees down. Such variation is found in other tribes in Africa; however, there are so many similarities in the African culture. In the following discussion, I will mainly highlight the cultural and moral changes.

Concerning the cultural changes, just as I have stated in the political life of the Tanzanian society; today there are no longer tribal distributions where you can find only one tribe. People interact and share common life. Even the type of communication is a new one. People used to communicate by interaction, where one meets the other and hence they share information. In those times, all communication modes were physical.

---

49. Mtaita, *The Wandering Shepherds*, 20–21.

As discussed above in the political life, Kijanga states that during the introduction of the "operation *Vijiji vya Ujamaa*" (Villagization for socialism) in the year 1974, people started a new system of life by forming one village that now had more tribal integration than before. People can stay separate from others. This form of society continued to communicate while now close to each other than before. Referring to this new cultural setting of the people and its way of teaching and sharing information and values through communication methods; Kijanga tells that one of the characteristics of culture is to be learned by members of the social unit or society. Tradition, ritual and beliefs are among the issues that society communicates and teaches members. He observes: "culture . . . consists of patterns of learned behavior that are shared by and transmitted among members of a society from generation to generation. Society's durability and self-sustaining is in a community of persons who share a culture and feel themselves to be a unit."[50] He argues that the cultural life of Tanzanian society is to share their behaviors. It shares traditions, rituals and beliefs.

Kijanga emphasizes that cultural life moulds the organization of society. He continues to state that the church and ministers in Tanzania have to be aware that they are in society that has the above characteristics. Since the church is an institution which meets generations in their varied and different times and contexts; it has to be kin and observe the existing and changing culture of people with its language of communication. He asserts, "culture provides the language of communication and the ways of social organization within which the church lives and works."[51] Kijanga goes further to state that the present society is in another different and multifaceted organization due to people's free interaction, new science and technology, and society's self-consciousness about the importance of individual, community development and the quality of life.[52] From the early year of the introduction of *Ujamaa*, Tanzania was moving ahead with cultural reconstruction, although in those first times the 'Christian church', as Kijanga calls it, appeared to accept the changes with great uncertainties. From the early time when the Tanzanian society's life entered into the present and solid integration, the church was slow to adapt to the new ways of life. "In spite of that, young people in the church are always bringing traditional songs into the church. The state of affairs may get out of hand if the Christian church will not be involved and promote inspiration and guidance."[53]

50. Kijanga, *Ujamaa and the Role of Church*, 80.
51. Ibid., 80.
52. Ibid., 4, 86.
53. Ibid., 86.

Katherine Snyder supports the above arguments in her research held from 2002 to 2005 in Tanzania. Snyder testifies that as time, needs, contexts and generations have been changing; people have also been changing so that whatever they do is in their present interest. My question is: if there are many generations that have past, now, why is this happening in this contemporary society? Snyder responds to this question by stating that Tanzanian communities have now entered into a modern world. It is now in a world that is strongly emphasizing on *maendeleo* (progress or development). This struggle has 'aimed at lifting people out of their traditions to a modern world which is more global than it was very local in many generations past.'[54] Yet, she adds that the societies in Tanzania are surrounded by other societies that are in a global perspective or are already moving fast toward that outlook. For her, the local cultural forms seem to disappear due to powerful of global influences. People adapt and accept some other new ways of interacting, entertaining, communicating, thinking and any other dimension of life that seems to be better for them at that particular context in time.

On the other hand, Snyder continues to argue that there are potential local cultural forms of Tanzanian communities that need to be preserved. For her, although the "local", as she puts this emphasis, cultural forms and practices undergo transformation or sustenance from the ever-changing global political economy, yet there is something to be born in mind. This is because the stories are characteristically competitive global forces that if society is not very stable, it will lose even good forms and practices. Snyder puts her standpoint in this way: "while this is a story with resonance for communities around the globe, it is important to keep the "local" in mind because, . . . local cultural forms (the rituals or narratives of a particular place) deserve to be given special weight, yet the framework of domination can never be understood within narrow boundaries."[55] Snyder shows that the notions of tradition and modernity are results of the struggle about identity and the meaning of community. People may want to find an identity that resembles to their time, context and situation.

Snyder also discusses the issue of moral change among African Tanzanians. She states that the modernization that is staking place in this globe seem not to comfort other people, especially to the elders. They argue that even if there is a fight for development, the modern Tanzanian communities have lost and are still losing their morality. Even if they feel to be in a modern society, elderly people complained about this modernity status

---

54. Snyder, *The Iraqw of Tanzania*, 2.
55. Ibid.

when they come across moral breakdowns. Magesa observes, "There is a decline in morals at all levels of society today. . . . We are living in a 'throw away' age."[56]

Concerning marriage and rites of passages, Snyder asserts that in the past, elders controlled such rituals. Nowadays these events are facing fraught with tension in many ways. Wedding ceremonies undergo transformation to suit the youth's interests. Moreover, there are numerable conflicts and contradictions brought out in wedding ceremonies. On the other hand, sometimes weddings are public and have a very interesting combination whereby there are elements of both traditional and modern ones. She reveals that even the way the bride and groom are clothing, preparation and types of food, dance, and song are features of all cultural styles, both cosmopolitan and localist (she borrows this term from Ferguson's terminology). In the past, parents and other relatives had a strong emphasis on betrothal, bride wealth, and time to get married and how to interact with in-laws.[57] Couples rarely married without consulting and seeking the consent of their parents. If it happened that they are living far away from their homeland, they would return home or send a message to their home parents and elders so that they could determine their prospective mates. Surprisingly enough, despite the marriage to be a critical issue in the cultural life of Tanzanian societies:

> Elders complain that young people today disobey many of the rules of betrothal, [bride wealth] and marriage. . . . Most young people ignored the advice of their elders. Today young people do not care. A father tells his son not to marry a girl because they are related, but the son goes ahead anyway and marries her. And now, you can see the problems that result. They discover they cannot have children. Maybe the children are born, but they do not live long, or they are very weak.[58]

In the quotation above there are much blames toward many young men who feel good to exercise a complete freedom, although, parents seem to want to help them not enter into such problems. Nevertheless, why do the young men ignore the advice from their elders? Among the reasons that young men give out is about the lengthy negotiations. To them such negotiations give them frustrations and humiliations. Young men argue that "It takes too long to get married in the traditional way, and the girl's father likes to stretch matters out as long as possible, trying to get more bride wealth, or

56. Magesa, *Anatomy of Inculturation*, 73.
57. Snyder, *The Iraqw of Tanzania*, 69, 71.
58. Ibid., 71.

just being difficult."⁵⁹ It shows that, most of the contemporary members of society in Tanzania dislike long procedures of marriage processes, especially the youth.

Snyder describes further that, like any other society in the world; the society in Tanzania is encountering the "Multiple Modernities" which is the play of all people in the world. Currently, around the world, there is cultural dualism between "localism" and "cosmopolitanism" styles of life whereby people change their "cultural styles" due to cultural integration, interests, urbanization, and international communication with a satellite, and other forms of communication.⁶⁰ Society is transforming its appearance as the world changes its outlook and practices.

Socio-Religious Life[61]

Even before the coming of Christianity, Africans already had their religious beliefs and practices. Westerlund provides that:

> It is obvious that the African religious system should be seen in the context of their integration in the various cultural and societal systems. Yet there were many religious ideas and practices which were widely shared, ... One religious idea which was shared by most or perhaps all ethnic groups in Africa was the belief in God, the Supreme Being. In general the Bantu-speaking peoples in mainland believed in the High God as Creator, the ultimate origin of life.[62]

Westerlund opens our discussion about the religiosity of the African people. He argues that Africans have their African religions. Those religions have some characteristic practices. He tells that African religions have a characteristic of sharing with many societies from all ethnic groups within the African context. Another characteristic is the belief on God as one who is the most high and powerful to make life of organisms. This shows that since then Africans have been worshipping God.

Westerlund goes further to arguing that Africans have been using names, symbols or objects to explain how God looks as the Supreme one. The name and symbol of 'sun' is one of the references that many Africans have been using when identifying and describing who and how God is the

---

59. Ibid., 72.
60. Ibid., 6.
61. This concept originates from Niwagila, 1991.
62. Ibid., Westerlund, *Ujamaa na Dini*, 36.

most high; and why should people worship this God. I agree with him that the name *Mungu* (God) is one of the Swahili names attributed to God. However, he argues that there has been a belief on spirits (*mizimu*) that they could bring disasters if one went wrong or removed an affliction or misfortune. Another word is *mtume* (prophet). They had their sacred places. Each African society had produced its own customs, rules, taboos and laws. In addition, African traditional societies had a direct link or connection between religion and morality. Morality ties, kinships and chiefdoms.[63]

Concerning Tanzania, the same characteristics existed. For Westerlund, the coming of Christianity and the Arusha Declaration (which emphasized integration through *Ujamaa* villages) started to change that traditional outlook of African religious life. He asserts: "Christian missionaries as well as ... the Arusha Declaration stressed the responsibility of individuals. This influence contributed to breaking up the traditional kin units, pointing to the much larger unit of the modern nation."[64] Therefore, when Christianity and Islam came into Africa met African religions through which the societies believed and worshipped God, whom, Christianity and Islam wanted them to worship through Jesus Christ or Prophet Muhammad. Moreover, politics was integrating with religious life of the Tanzania's societies.[65] There are several scholars giving descriptions in almost the same points of views.

Gomang Seratwa Ntloedibe-Kuswani in the article "The Religious Life of an African" while quoting Mbiti, argues that 'the believers of African religions have an inner attitude,' which paves the way for an understanding of the Christian message.' The reason for this is that, already indigenous religions were God-given or divine. God had put into them a sense and spirit of worship, though it may have differed from that of the Christian or any other foreign religious missionaries. For Ntloedibe-Kuswani, the coming of Christianity, for example in 1880s changed African societies into Christian philosophy. On the other hand, although in the first attempt conversion into Christianity was not in a rapid change. There were some resistances. Later on, many were converted. The process grew up that many joined and until the present time they continue converting into Christianity. This conversion has been extremely growing due to their pre-knowledge of God and the Christian influences through the use of "some African Concepts of Christology," the incarnation, healing messages of the Gospel and good witnesses of some missionaries.

---

63. Ibid., 36–38, cf., 39.
64. Ibid., 38.
65. Ibid., 41–47, 49–91.

On the other hand, as he explores Mbiti's standpoints on African Religions and Christianity, Ntloedibe-Kuswani argues that since Africans are not new religious converts, rather they complement each other; thus, Christianity and African traditional religion should not fight each other. They are not enemies; rather, they are complementary. Most African and Tanzanian theologians agree with Ntloedibe-Kuswani that, the sense of community life, elements of religion, religious experiences, practices, and places are among many symbols, objects, language, and many other cultural elements that Africans have had in their daily life. One can use those signs as the basic starting point when doing mission and evangelism and in pastoral ministry in the African context. This helps the minister to be flexible where necessary and address people's problems.⁶⁶

Again, it is easy to note that, when Christianity came into Africa, particularly the Tanzanian context, it met people with their religious life. The Christian influence is very affective than other religions that many people are eager to join it. People are changing their faith and ways of life. This is both a religious and a social change in terms of religious affiliation.

Furthermore, Niwagila, in his same book *From the Catacomb to a Self-governing Church* supports that the understanding of people and their religious life in their social and religious setting is an essential task. With strong emphases, he writes that:

> In order to understand an African and his [sic] ways of life, one has to take into consideration both his social life and religious life as one entity; to separate the two is to do injustice to the African. The socio-religious life of an African society is just like an egg. You cannot separate the egg from its shell unless you have the intention of destroying it. The African life is a socio-religious one which has for generations played a big role in politics, social, economic and religious life and but together the unity of the whole society. This socio-religious life has been influenced by tribal beliefs and philosophy.⁶⁷

Again, while quoting from John Mbiti; Niwagila describes that "religion permeates into all the departments of life so fully that it is not easy or possible always to isolate it . . . Philosophy of one kind or another is behind the thinking and acting of every people."⁶⁸ He makes an emphasis that Tanzanian society has been a religious one since then. No one should perceive

---

66. Ntloedibe-Kuswani, "The Religious Life of an African", 97–114, 117–118; Mtaita, *The Wandering Shepherds*, 32–68, 118–119; Niwagila, *From the Catacomb*, 406–425.

67. Niwagila, *From the Catacomb*, 34.

68. Ibid., 34, 44–48.

that the coming of Christianity in Africa in 1880's was the starting point for Tanzanians to have a socio-religious life. They worshipped, had the divine names of God, offered sacrifices and many other religious functions when Christianity arrived.

Again, Sebastian K. Lutahoire, states that apart from the new faith, that is Christianity, 'African people in Tanzania' have been religious since early on. The concept 'African people in Tanzania' reflects people, both being Tanzanians by birth as well as them being Africans by continent in nature. Either, one uses the same meaning interchangeably with the phrase 'Tanzanian Africans' or 'Africans in Tanzania' or 'African Peoples of Tanzania.'[69] Lutahoire argues that Africans accepted Christianity during the missionaries and colonialists' age. People have had their:

> Own historical background, culture, traditions, political, economic and religious organizations, both in ethnic and tribal groups. But the first thing the white men did was to discourage and destroy African religious and philosophical life. They came as if they were to command the Africans to start life from a bare beginning. They came to Christianize and civilize the savages of the African continent. . . . of course, they had their own goals and achievements in mind.[70]

From the quotation we can extract two issues: first, that 'Tanzanian Africans'[71] for several centuries have religious life. But, the second is that Christianity has been added to the number of religions in Africa. This is because; there is also African religions and Islam. The introduction of Christianity has been presented as if it was bringing a new religious life. Lutahoire continues to contend that the:

> Missionaries and colonialists called the people of Africa out of their culture and traditions as if they were to start life anew- from scratch. . . . Many Africans were reported to have found Christ because they accepted [Christian] baptism. . . . Gandhi's complaint was that the moment a person becomes a Christian, he [sic] . . . almost changes his [sic] nationality. . . . He adopts foreign dress and ways of life. He cuts himself [sic] off from his people.[72]

---

69. Lutahoire, *The Human Life Cycle*, 6, 7, 9.
70. Ibid., 5.
71. Ibid., 6, 7, 9.
72. Ibid., 6.

The contention above shows the missionaries' problem for they misinterpreted the Christian faith. They preached the Christian faith that people would deny when came to realize that missionaries had their own goals and achievements that do not mean what Jesus Christ meant. If to be a Christian would mean to belong to a new and different nation or continent; then it also implies that a person now belongs to a different culture and tribe. To me, it is difficult to think that this is a kind of religious life to accept from any type of belief. Again, the same quotation shows some Christians who adopt any foreign forms of religious, social, or personal ways of life. They adopt every new and foreign dressing styles even those that sometimes put them half naked even while in the Church. Others put on transparent clothes. Some pastors have been complaining over *mmomonyoko wa maadili* (moral decay). They sometimes consider such ways of behavior as identities of civilization.

Lutahoire continues to describe that, today, Africans in Tanzania are very much affected by Western culture and other new forms of life style. For example, there is a new style of Music in the Church, the *Hip pop*. I will discuss this kind of Church music in detail in my chapter of presentation and analysis of interviews.

> On the other hand, even though preachers presented the gospel in varied ways; as people continued to hear the Gospel, they continued to learn and accept Christianity in multitudes. What is the situation now? Subsequently, at present, "to some extent, Christianity is looked upon as a group or tribal religion because of its many diverse doctrines and theologies. Each tribal denomination of the Christian religion in Tanzania has been preaching the universality of Christianity that . . . is no salvation outside Christ Jesus . . . and teaching its promises (that Christ Jesus is the man in whom all people can have salvation and unity).[73]

Lutahoire continues to reveal that African Tanzanians have been religious even before Christianity came in. However, despite the challenges that it encounters with her ministers, Christianity has been growing in Tanzania through proclamation in the Church and public meetings, pedagogy, life practices of Christians, witness through evangelism and mission work, and other strategies. The second is that there are many and varied religious beliefs and denominations in Tanzania. Although all Christian faiths preach the same gospel, however, they differ in styles and areas of central weight; for example, emphasis on baptism or holiness or Eucharist or Sabbath.

---

73. Ibid., 9–10.

Most progressing explorations about Christianity in Africa, as well as around the world, (that is the Church), show that the Church is encountering a massive challenge and influences from eruption of denominations as well as religious pressures from non-Christian religions. As an example, apart from non-Christian religions, there is a daily birth of Christian sects and denominations. Generally, the Church with her Christian faith and ministers are living and working in the midst of religious pluralism. The author admits that pastors and other ministers in the Tanzanian society are leaders and servants of people who have many and varied ideological perspectives.

There is another observation supporting that Christian religious life and the mission and evangelism work in Tanzania as well as in many African countries is enormously growing. The speech by Pope John Paul II reveals the situation when he held an apostolic visit to Tanzania, Burundi, Rwanda, and the Ivory Coast. His address to priests and other religious leaders of Tanzania at Saint Peter's Church in Dar-es-Salaam on Sunday, 2 September 1990 portrays the expansion of the Church, increase of indigenous priests and devout church servants and Christians, African image of the church in Tanzania, and how ministers should work cooperatively, creatively and visionary at present. In his address the Pope said:

> I thank *Archbishop Pengo* for his words of welcome, and *Father Itatiro*, whose description of the expansion of the Church in this land invites us to praise God who is the Author of this growth (Cf. *1 Cor.* 3, 6–7).... Through God's grace, by increasing numbers of *indigenous priests and religious Sisters and Brothers*.... You show that ... the Church in Tanzania is both truly Catholic and truly African. Indeed, if you are to be genuine witnesses of Christ to the world, it must be apparent to all that "you stand firm in one spirit, with one mind striving side by side for the faith of the Gospel" (*Phil.* 1, 27).... The rapid growth of the Church in Tanzania is a pressing invitation to consider the most effective ways of building upon the foundation which you have inherited. The *continuing evangelization of Africa* is, as you know, a priority for the Church and has been chosen as the theme of the forthcoming Special Assembly for Africa of the Synod of Bishops. Evangelization belongs to the essence of the Church's life.... The great number of vocations to the priesthood and consecrated life in Tanzania bears eloquent witness to the *growing maturity of your young Churches*.[74]

---

74. Pop John II, "Address of this Holiness John Paul II," 1990.

The speech from the Pop highlights to us about the significant and challenging role of pastors and other church ministers regarding their mission work in the contemporary era. If the Church is putting her main efforts and concentration on evangelism, then pastors as daily servants in the respective mission areas will have more tough work to fulfill the witness.

Relative to religious, historic and practice; for Lutahoire the religions of Africa have functioned primarily as moral codes. Among important issues of religions are to deal with morality, loyalty, divorce, juvenile delinquency and other social problems. Lutahoire argues that, different from today, during the arrival of the early colonialists and missionaries in East and Southern Africa tribes were more just a socio-political unit. Today, religion is a part of life whereby people have beliefs based on socio-religious practices.[75] What Lutahoire argues has support from other Tanzanians as well. Niwagila in his same book *From the Catacomb to a Self-governing Church* calls this topic as "the socio-religious life." He affirms that today Christianity has become a big religion in many parts of Tanzania. Kagera region or the mostly used name is Bukoba is one of the examples where society has adapted Christianity. Many people have joined, and continue joining Christianity. He gives an example that "in the census of 1967 there were . . . the majority of the population in this region being Christians, who are about 62%, Moslems being 9%, traditionalists being 28% and others being 1%."[76] From this exposition, we come to understand that the Tanzanian society is characteristically having a religious pluralism. With these examples, Tumbo-Masabo and Liljestrom argue that, despite the newness of Christianity and some other religious sects in Africa and Tanzanian context in particular, it implies that Christianity has been daily multiplying the number of its members.[77]

However, Niwagila wants people to be aware of the fact that "traditional religion . . . in one way or another shaped and made a big impact on the life of the people of [Africa and Tanzania]."[78] In this case, when a Christian missionary talks about faith or beliefs; Tanzanian people do not get surprised. Thus, it has become easy even to share the Gospel of Jesus Christ. Their religious experience has paved the way for Christianity to penetrate and settle in people. Niwagila argues that, since Tanzanian people

---

75. Lutahoire, *The Human Life Cycle*, 16–17.
76. Niwagila, *From the Catacomb*, 34.
77. Tumbo-Masabo and Liljestrom, *Chelewa, Chelewa*, 5.
78. Niwagila, *From the Catacomb*, 34.

hold religious beliefs; this situation influences their social life within the community.[79] Faith shapes their lifestyles.

To conclude this subsection, I now highlight again about the religious pluralism. Further detailed discussion for this religiosity will follow in the analysis and presentation of data where I will show also how it affects the pastoral ministry. As I have stated above, another socio-religious life aspect that is very important to be well understood as we explore the effects of social change, is the mushrooming of Christian denominations. At present, the Tanzanian society is in a religious pluralism. There are so many Christian denominations. Christian denominations are being born almost every day. The same is in the Islam religion. Many lay and volunteer preachers establish denominations. Even Islam has been multiplying in terms of denominations. It has been building many mosques through various donors. As a result, many people, both Christians and others have been converting into Islam. This mushrooming of religious denominations has been confusing society. This is because, at one moment and religion, they are told that a particular religion or denomination is the true way for salvation, at the same moment another religion is proclaiming the same claims. People get confused as to which religion or denomination is the best for them to join.

EDUCATIONAL OR COGNITIVE CHANGE

When Tanganyika (after the union until now is Tanzania) attained its independence in 1961, there were very few schools. Most of the schools were under the control of religions—meaning that Christian religious institutions owned them. The Catholic Church was the leading institution in having involved in education. In general, in Tanzania for example, "In 1968 TEC (Tanzania Episcopal Conference) was linked with the following numbers of different educational institutions : 1378 primary schools, 44 secondary schools, 10 catechist schools, 8 teachers' training colleges, 2 commercial schools, 15 trade schools and 48 home craft & domestic science centres."[80] At first, churches aimed that their schools could be useful for strong Christian education. Nevertheless, later on it seemed bringing problems if other non-members of the church would want to get access to education.[81] Westerlund describes that since there were few schools and training centers; a few people got formal education. This is also witnessed by some Muslim's complains that they had been given less chances to join schools. As a result,

---

79. Ibid., 34.
80. Westerlund, *Ujamaa na Dini*, 118.
81. Mtaita, *The Wandering Shepherds*, 120–121, 124–125.

from 1962, non-Christians and non-Catholic pupils had a permission to join but not forced to attend religious instructions. Through government leaders, the discussions on how to make education accessible to all people were held constantly. The government had to nationalize all schools that were under private institutions so that every Tanzanian could have access to all schools. The exercise of nationalizing the schools came unexpectedly. Churches were not aware. Westerlund reports:

> The government in 1969 made known its intention to nationalize the school system. . . . the nationalization of the school came overnight, and that churches were not prepared for it. . . . In fact, it was argued that the change would not simply be a nationalization of schools but a nationalization of *education*, . . . it involved . . . the task of propagating political education . . . [all people] became more easily mobilized for the [educational] development process.[82]

In the observation of Westerlund, the main agenda is about the ways in which the government took over the schools for the sake of limiting some sanctions toward putting all Tanzanians equal in terms of accessibility to social services. Westerlund discloses some other hidden aims in the fact that, the process of nationalizing education was not mainly for people's benefit. Nationalization would also benefit the propagation of political education. In this sense, it means that schools as central places for intellectually awakening of people could also be for political issues. This is true because, some lesson such as civics were included as core subjects. On the one hand, this was useful for people to have their sense of home and self-awareness. On the other hand, the government had taken a huge burden that it could not manage appropriately. Moreover, religions were limited their education role for individual, for the national as well as for world development at large.

We have seen in the above descriptions that, after *Ujamaa* had taken place; the government controlled almost all educational institutions, except those that were specifically set for training religious ministers. This nationalization was then reverted in 1990's when Tanzania had now become strong in political stance. At this time, *Ujamaa* had strong roots. Some schools went back to religious institutions. Now it was a matter of close co-operation and limits of student recruitments that had no allowance. The discussion has given us with a historical picture of the educational life and practice in Tanzania. The available data shows that due to fewer schools, there were very few Tanzanians who were accessing formal education. Now I turn to the discussion on the present situation.

82. Westerlund, *Ujamaa na Dini*, 120, 122 cf., 119, 121.

Therefore, from 1977 primary education from standard one to seven started to be the right for everyone in Tanzanian. The same was and is for the remaining years, whereby, four years are for lower secondary education, two years for higher secondary education, and then, three to five years of university education depending on the course taken. It is in the same year 1977 when the "Universal Primary Education policy (UPE) was initiated.... Full equality of access to primary school was achieved."[83] Historically, from 1991 there has been rapid growth of schools and colleges. The government, private institutions, as well as individuals were free to establish educational centers where all people can be free to get education. This growth has led many people access education. Many parents send children to school, and also youth and other adults go for further education. Consequently, there are many youth and adults who have at least attained, or are now continuing with, their studies at a form four level secondary education.[84] Accordingly, if many people are getting educated, then one can dare to think that many Christians in Tanzania now have education; hence society and the church will largely become educated.

Consequently, Mtaita is on the opinion that if people become educated then the knowledge acquired helps "to enable them to cope with the changes which they are facing."[85] There are three questions to ask here: how and what does the church as an institution reflect from this situation? What is the educational status of the pastors? How is the minister prepared in relation to the availability of those schools and other educational opportunities? What advantages does the church get from the growth of educated society? I will discuss these and other questions in detail in the preceding chapters.

CONCLUSION

In this chapter, I have presented an historical overview on the socio-cultural life of the Tanzanian society basing on political, economic, social, cultural, religious and educational narratives. The main aim was to explore some changes that have happened or are taking place in the contemporary society. Furthermore, I also discussed the concept of *Ujamaa* as the main starting point for the integration life of the Tanzanian society. In this respect, the discussion has highlighted on how '*Ujamaa* Villagization' concept has been one of the tools for social change in Tanzanian society. The main sources of

---

83. Tumbo-Masabo and Liljestrom, *Chelewa, Chelewa,* 55.
84. Ibid., 57; cf., 54–55, 60–62, 68.
85. Mtaita, *The Wandering Shepherds,* 124.

information was from literature, mostly, those which gave us some important details about Tanzania or Africa as a whole.

This chapter also serves as a gateway to the discussion of the context in which the ELCT lives and performs its mission in order to reach its goals. Therefore, in the following chapter, by using church documents I shall present the analysis and discussion about the ELCT perspectives on pastoral ministry. The aim of chapter three will be to explore how the ELCT recruits, allocates and directs its church pastors into its intended mission and vision to facilitate the fulfillment of the set goals of the Church within Tanzanian context and in the globe.

3
PASTORAL MINISTRY IN THE PERSPECTIVE OF THE ELCT/SD

INTRODUCTION

IN CHAPTER TWO, I highlighted that the ELCT/SD is within Tanzania. Up to the time when the study for this book was undertaken, this diocese was among the twenty dioceses that composed the ELCT.[1] According to the government's regional divisions, the diocese is located in the Southern Highlands Zone. However, in relation to the divisions of the head office of the ELCT, the SD is in the Southern Zone of Tanzania. To the time of this research, in this Church's zone, there are nine dioceses: Southern, Konde, Southern Central, Southern-West, Iringa, Ulanga Kilombero, Eastern and Coastal, Dodoma and Central Diocese. The zones seem to have formations according to the closeness of the dioceses with the aim to enhance more and strong relationship in terms of communication and cooperation amongst dioceses' within the larger ELCT.

During the research and analysis of data for this book, the SD was divided into nine church districts, namely, Chimala, Ilembula, Kidugala, Lupembe, Makambako, Mtwara/Lindi, Mufindi, Njombe and Ruvuma. There were 80 parishes, 175 pastors and 180170 Christians.[2] Therefore, in this chapter I will mainly concentrate on the SD being a sample for African

---

1. KKKT, *Kalenda*, ii – front cover, cf., 20–62.
2. Ibid., 46.

Christian dioceses and or Churches, as well as SD being one of the constituents of the ELCT.

Apart from the brief descriptions I have presented in the above paragraphs; other areas to follow are the ELCT and SD perspectives on the pastor, the pastor's call into church ministry, training, oath and ordination, and work allocation or appointment. The second subsection is on the roles of a pastor and ministry in the Church. In the second subsection, I present five issues regarding the pastoral responsibilities. Again, as I stated in the previous chapter, the church literature and other relevant documents serve as my focal references. The main church documents for my analysis and discussion are the diocesan constitution (of SD), the ELCT constitution and any other documents or articles from SD and outside it. Nevertheless, some important information from other diocese of the ELCT or any other church constitution may be under my review in order to supplement wherever important information might be missing. All the same, other literature and articles will be useful in my discussion of these issues.

As I enter into the discussion of the pastor's roles and ministry in the church and in the midst of society, I hold the Constitutions of dioceses to be the primary and important documents to open up a room for the presentation of arguments. The reason for using church documents and constitutions is that, the ELCT documents, especially the constitution(s) specify that every pastor of the ELCT and SD be bound to perform all roles as they are specified in the respective constitution that was the basis for their ordination. The constitution is an essential and a primary church document that depicts the roles of a pastor. Therefore, this section will serve as a point of reference when I present and discuss the research findings in the forthcoming chapters.

THE ELCT AND SD PERSPECTIVES ON THE PASTOR

For one to become a pastor in the ELCT, there are significant steps to be followed and passed through. Before we look at the steps for one to become a pastor, let us have a look on some important procedures, for example, the meaning of being a pastor according to the constitution of the church, the call, training, ordination, and work allocations.

Who is a Pastor?

In the Constitution of the ELCT, article number seven is about 'pastorhood.'[3] The term pastorhood is usually used to mean both the church ministry which is performed by the ordained ministers – the pastors, and it refers to a pastor as a Christian minister and spiritual adviser. It reflects the official role of an ordained minister - a religious leader of the Christian church in the ELCT. Pastorhood is the central service for life and evangelism and mission of the ELCT in Tanzania, and in the world at large. As the leading document of this Church in Tanzania, the constitution defines a pastor, the procedures in calling a person for pastorate, the preparation (training), ordination, recognition after being ordained, articulates roles, and also the dismissal or withdrawal from pastorate. It specifies further the three hint-points that:

I. The Pastorate of this Church is to serve the Word of God and administration of (Holy) Sacraments through those who have the authority by the Lord of the Church to work in each Diocese.

II. This Church, through her dioceses, will call pastoral students, educate them, to ordain them become her pastors and to oversee their moral conduct.

III. After a pastor has been ordained by his or her diocese, he or she will have the recognition as a pastor of the ELCT. If this pastor becomes withdrawn by his or her diocese, he or she will not have this recognition as a pastor of the ELCT. Thus, any service that he or she performs will be worthless and unrecognized by the Church.[4]

The article above shows how the ELCT perceives a pastor and the roles that this minister is ought to perform. Part (a) depicts that the ELCT's pastoral ministerial role is primarily to proclaim the Word of God and administer the Holy Sacraments. Thus, in the ELCT, a pastor is one who has been bestowed with special authority to carry out those roles by the Lord of the Church, Jesus, to serve those functions in the diocese in which he or she has been called and sent to work. Part (b) the ELCT perceives a pastor to be the one who has undergone a set of preparatory steps in an individual diocese. This pastor should have undergone a formal call, pastoral training and ordination. I will discuss more in the 'pastor's call' sub-section. The third part (c) deals with recognition. The ELCT recognizes one as a pastor if he or she belongs to one of its (ELTC) constituents. This can mean that

---

3. In the *Katiba ya KKKT* (English: '*Constitution of the ELCT*') it is written *Uchungaji* (pastorhood).

4. KKKT, *Katiba*, 6. Translation into English is mine.

the ELCT's pastors are those who belong to individual dioceses within the ELCT. Once membership is lost from the diocese, automatically that pastor loses membership in the whole ELCT; rather, it remains to him or her, only the ordinary Lutheran Christian membership.

Before I move into discussion of the SD perspectives on the pastorate as specified in the Constitution; I will mention that the ELCT Constitution did not have any provision about so-called 'part-time pastors', neither did the SD constitution provide one. Once they are ordained, all pastors work as full-time ministers. However, the SD provides that a retired pastor may continue serving parishes or preaching points or in learning institutions (schools and colleges) by request if he or she is healthy, willing to do so, and has qualifications. This seems different from other churches, especially the American context. For example, Jackson W. Carrol in his book *God's Potters* states that some pastors can work either as full or part-time ministers.[5] For one to be a full or part time pastor it depends on the type of task, for example, "pastoral care responsibilities are also significantly higher for full-timers. . . . preaching . . . along with wedding and funerals . . . part-timers are primarily expected to perform in many small congregations." He adds that, however, this is somehow different in Protestant pastors of the mega churches if congregational size increases.[6] Conversely, usually the ELCT/SD pastors whether continuing or retired, all work as full-time ministers until he or she gets a complete rest after retirement.

In addition to the ELCT constitution, in the SD constitution rule number seven is about priesthood of all believers and the special ministry. The constitution stipulates as follows:

I. In the Priesthood of all believers, God calls every Christian to serve Him and become a Witness of Salvation in Jesus Christ.

II. This ministry is one; but, in order to preserve order, this Diocese will minister the Word of God, preserve the Sacraments and care people spiritually by those whom the Lord through this Diocese called and bestowed them with authority.[7]

Therefore, from the stipulation above, one can understand that in the ELCT/SD a pastor is any Christian within the ELCT/SD who has a call and a special authority to perform pastoral roles by the diocese itself. Consequently, on the one hand, the whole ELCT recognizes the authority conferred to a

---

5. Carroll, *God's Potters*, 2006. See chapters three and four, 57–126.
6. Ibid., 110, 111.
7. KKKT-DKu, *Katiba*, 3 Translation into English is mine.

pastor. On the other hand, if the diocese withdraws the authority, it affects the recognition in the whole ELCT.

Pastor's Call

The Tanzanian L. Festo Bahendwa was once invited in a retreat for ELCT bishops with their spouses to make a presentation about "to Administer the Word and Sacraments"[8] as one of the pastor's roles. He opened his presentation by stating how a person receives a call into the Church ministry as a pastor. His opening account states: "The Lutheran Church, ever since the time of Augsburg Confession (AC) teaches that: Churches among us teach that nobody should preach publicly, in the church, nor administer the sacraments, unless he or she has been called by order (AC, 14)."[9] In his presentation, Bahendwa starts by emphasizing that the pastor's call into the church ministry has to follow the prescribed and inherited Lutheran traditional orders. What are those prescribed and inherited Lutheran traditions? In this question, he himself is silent about its answers.

Bahendwa continues to describe the two types of call for a person to become a pastor:

> In order to get a pastor, normally, there are two kinds of call: internal or inside call and the external or outside call. Due to different reasons that a person by himself or herself can feel, pushes the inner most heart to love and to carry out God's ministry in the church. A person feels a call to join and become a minister of God. This is an internal call. The internal call has goes together with the external call. The one with an internal call discloses his or her inspirations to become a pastor. Once the parish or diocese gets satisfied with the applicant's status, it calls him or her and then sends into the colleges so that he or she has training to become a minister in the Church. This is an external call. Both, internal and external calls depend upon each other because the service of the Word and of the Sacraments is for all believers. The internal call can enhance the external call and vice versa, whereby, the external can establish the internal one (Exodus 3: 10-14; 4: 10-15; Isaiah 6: 1-8; Galatians 4: 4; John 10: 36; Luke 10:1).[10]

---

8. Bahendwa, 2004 "Kusimamia Neno na Sakramenti" Seminar Presentation.
9. Ibid.
10. Ibid.

According to the two constitutions of the ELCT and of the SD I have discussed above is no doubt resembles to the statements and emphases of Bahendwa. Those statements and emphases are strongly accepted and practiced in the SD and in the ELCT as a whole. However, the two constitutions that I have analyzed and discussed are silent about the call procedures.[11] Though it may not be easy to bear witness of one's own inner motivation for pastoral call, I can recall my personal call into pastoral ministry. Since I grew into a Christian family, we used to go to church according to the schedule. I once was a choir singer in children's Sunday School choir, in youth choir, and in other parish choirs in the church. I was also happy to involve myself in many of the church programs. For example, sometimes evangelists and pastors appointed me to teach in the classes of Sunday School children and Christian education in primary schools.

In my attendance in the church for personal spiritual growth, without my knowledge some church leaders were observing and discussing some names of Christians who can be recruited for church ministry. Surprisingly, my involvement in various activities in the church convinced them that I may join. Then, one evangelist made an appointment to talk to me as to whether I would be ready to leave my job in the government and join the church ministry as an evangelist or a pastor. After several conversations, I accepted the call. Now it became my own will to work with the church. Hence, several councils from the substation level to the diocesan levels discussed and approved all who were ready and qualified including my name. Thereafter, our diocese sent all appointees to colleges for pastoral training. This is the way the ELCT/SD calls and recruits individuals for church ministry.[12]

The application of the ELCT/SD constitution as it was practised during my call confirms and supports the arguments and emphasis of Bahendwa in his speech that nobody should enter into pastoral ministry in the church without passing through two stages: first, internal or external call, and second, the preparation. When Bahendwa names the two calls as internal and external, others use different names to mean the same. I will discuss the 'preparation' in the forthcoming step, that is, the 'training' subsection. We can site at least two examples: first, Gerhard O. Forde is interested much on the internal, as he calls it a 'private or inner' call. He supports that a person may have private or inner call. Forde argues that this inner call is of course of prime importance both in the church and for the individual. That is, for the church, it helps to sense an expression of commitment candidature; and

---

11. Ibid., KKKT, *Katiba*, 6.
12. Cf., Mwombeki, *Uongozi wa Usharika*, 6–7.

for individual it guides to sense an expression of contemplation candidacy for the public call.[13]

Second, James H. Pragman puts as two types of calls: first, 'immediate,' in which God directly calls, example that of Paul and Isaiah, and second the 'mediate,' where God works through the third party, for example a congregation brings an individual into the Church ministry. The Church has this mandate due to the fact that "God has given the whole church . . . the authority to call and fill the office of the public ministry."[14] The ELCT uses the two kinds of call and stages in the process of calling people to become pastors or other ministers in the church.

Pastoral (Pastor's) Training

Pastoral training is one of the activities the ELCT as a whole practices. It is among the significant steps for preparing pastors. In order for one to become ordained as a pastor, the process of training is to be undertaken first. The candidate attends a seminary or college for theological orientation. Similarly, according to the past practical experience, the ELCT, with all its constituents trains pastors at Kidugala Lutheran Seminary, at Makumira and Iringa University for a Certificate, diploma, and degree levels. The ELCT/SD hardly sent candidates to other non-Lutheran Tanzanian theological institutions, such as the Moravian college where they obtain certificates in theology. After their completion, the General Diocesan Council decides about their ordination.

The ELCT is among protestant Churches that do not ordain a person to become a pastor before attending theological education in a recognized theological institution. The Tanzanian pastor Fidon R. Mwombeki states that many years ago, pastors received training in all educational disciplines so that to be professional advisors of agriculture, livestock, health, politics, and so forth. A pastor was among the highly learned people in the community. Mwombeki argues that at present the church is hardly practicing that tradition to pastors. He sees the need to resume the practice due to changes in society. I will discuss in detail on this issue in chapter seven.

Pastor Mwombeki reminds me on this issue. Since it is not easy for me to list all sociological courses or subjects taught in all theological training institutions, however, I can try to mention some of them. There were sociology—among its components were agents of socialization (among them were: religion, school, family and workplace) and social problems (for

13. Forde, "The Ordained Ministry," 130–136.
14. Pragman, "Ministry in Lutheran Orthodoxy," 69; cf., Forde, 130–136.

example, poverty, crime, and deviance). Moreover, psychology and philosophy were also among the disciplines. Our lecturers told us that the addition of those courses into core subjects was due to realities in people's present life situation. Lecturers described that a pastor is a leader and servant of society. This pastor ought to know the characteristics and issues of society that he or she serves. Fihavango contends that the above description is an impression that came out when there was an exploration on the Christian responsibility toward areas of rapid social change. He expands his descriptions that in 1962 there was a signifying process of rapid social change in Africa.[15]

Pastor's Oath and Ordination

Two words are important for a coming pastor, the oath and the ordination. With regard to a person to become specially set apart for the church ministry in the ELCT, the two concepts bear a substantial sense, function and status. There is an important ceremony involving a new person who agrees to become a pastor. My aim here is to describe and show the emphasis that put on the oath and ordination when a pastor becomes an ordained person for the ministry in the church and society. I will discuss the two concepts in three steps: the oath, ordination, and then the 'ordination oath.' In the third step, I will concentrate on the sample of a formulated document as an example on how the ELCT/SD entrusts the pastor into church ministry.

First, the term oath refers to the pledge the pastor makes when contracting the priesthood role. The pastor pledges before the public. It is a solemn or word of promise. It is a formal or legally binding pledge to do something, such as telling the truth in a court of law. The pledge is formally formal and often naming God or a loved one as a witness. This oath portrays one's loyalty into the call or role and is between the caller and sender.

The second is ordination. The concept ordination can be defined as an official investiture upon a person to become a Christian pastor (or called: priest or minister) in the Christian ministry. It is also a ceremony during which somebody is consecrated as a priest or minister. Forde combines both oath and ordination to express the fulfillment of call and order.

> Ordination is the act by which one is placed in the public office of ministry. . . . [It] impinges upon, invades, the order of this age. . . . Ordination means that the church through its ordered structures calls and orders qualified members into the public office. What are these ordered structures? Lutheranism has never been dogmatic about this . . . the structures will no doubt vary

---

15. Fihavango, "Leadership and Family in the New Testament," 184.

with time and place. . . . Sometimes more Episcopal, . . . of a state church or folk church, . . . sometimes more congregational, and so on. The exact determination of the structure is not crucial so long as the public nature of the office is upheld and enhanced.[16]

As we can draw some more similar definitions, operations, and arguments from Forde about the concept ordination, the ELCT strongly holds that: "Ordination means both ordering in the sense of calling, and ordering in the sense of regulating or establishing order. In confessional Lutheranism . . . ordination involves at least four operations: the call; the examination; the laying on of hands; and prayer. All of these belong to the regular call . . . of ordination and . . . for . . . the public ministry."[17] Forde outlines interpretation of ordination and the necessary operations to be followed that according to the confessional Lutheran traditional doctrines for a person to become a pastor there are several processes. The aspirant has to have a call through and by defined church structures, qualified, and then ordained for the public ministry. However, the type of a structure set for this task determines the time and place. It implies that the Lutheran Church has flexibility in exercising some matters in order to fit with the time and context of society.

From my personal experience, I was engaged in the above expressions about oath and ordination to new theologians into pastoral ministry under the practice of the ELCT/SD. For example, after completing our theological training, we were gathered together, oriented with the oath and the way ordination will be performed on the next day. In the day of ordination, each one of us was called to come in front of the altar. Then the question and answer started. Finally, there was the laying on of hands by all ordained pastors who had attended that consecration day.[18]

Pragman asks, "But what is the meaning or the necessity of ordination?" Then he states that, it was assumed for theologians that:

> Ordination to the pastoral office was necessary for . . . [the] reason . . . that all things must be done decently and in order in the church. . . . Ordination is related to the capacity of the one called to assume the responsibilities and duties of the pastoral ministry. . . . Thus, ordination is ecclesiastical attestation of the ability to the candidate to accept and exercise the call extended by the church. . . . [Also, it is a] public testimony that the call being extended to the pastoral candidate was legitimate and

16. Forde, "The Ordained Ministry," 128, 129.
17. Ibid., 130.
18. Mwombeki, *Uongozi wa Usharika*, 6–8.

> that the one called possesses the necessary aptitude for the office.... Nevertheless, no one could be ordained without being examined to determine his [sic] fitness for the office and the thoroughness of his [sic] theological preparation for ministry.... Ordination should not be conferred if an individual does not possess a legitimate call to function in the church as the pastor of a specific congregation.[19]

Similar to Forde, Pragman emphasizes that no one should enter into pastoral office without passing through all necessary ordination operations. The candidate must be attested publicly of his or her necessary aptitude to exercise the call for ecclesiastical responsibilities in the church. In addition, the ordination legitimates the candidate called for pastoral office.

The third aspect under the oath and ordination is about the sample formulated and used to ordain candidates called for pastoral office. Again, the ELCT/SD stands affront to be used as a sample for other churches in Africa. As stated and emphasized above about the significance and processes of confirming the aptitude and legitimating the candidate into pastoral ministry, the ELCT/SD adopts and uses the "Ordination Oath" during consecrating some persons as a pastor for church ministry. Why does the ELCT/SD formulate and implement the ordination oath as other Churches might be doing? The above expressions and processes of oath and ordination are important because they define the candidate's ability to assume the responsibilities, devotion, aptitudes for the office, and commitment of the pastor for the ministry. During ordination, the candidate pledges before the bishop and the public. To use it as an example, during my research I came across the following 'ordination oath' that the ELCT/SD uses when new theologians are ordained as pastors. It may not be surprising that ordination oaths differ from one period to another, as this differs from the one that our bishop used to ordain us in September 1999. It contains some new features. Whereas the candidate kneels down, the following questions and answers are usually asked:

> **Bishop (1)** *In the Name of a Triune God, will you be ready to receive the Holy pastorate, to the extent that you will keep it up, so that God may be given thanksgiving, and people may be served?*
>
> **Candidate:** *Yes I will, May God help me!*

---

19. Pragman, "Ministry in Lutheran Orthodoxy," 70; cf., Strohl, "Ministry in the Middle Ages," 38–41.

Bishop (2) *Do you accept the WORK of being a PASTOR of the CHURCH AND TO PERFORM IT, so that God may be praised, and His church may be built and nourished?*

Candidate: *Yes I agree, May God help me!*

Bishop (3) *Will you be faithful in the parish, while being ready to serve God through Exhortation, un-tirelessly have a worship habit, even to care for the poor and the sick and those who have no one to assist them, and with the accord to the grace that you will receive from God to console those who have encountered problems and those with sorrowful hearts?*

Candidate: *Yes, May God help me!*

Bishop (4) *Will you be ready to control your moral behavior so that it becomes a model to all human beings?*

Candidate: *Yes, May God help me!*

Bishop (5) *Will you be ready to work wherever you will be sent?*

Candidate: *Yes, May God help me!*

Bishop (6) *Are you ready to serve God's congregation according to the church order, in the Sacrament, in Baptism and the Lord's Supper as Jesus Christ had established in his praise and in for the salvation of God's nation?*

Candidate: *Yes, May God help me!*

Bishop (7) *Are you ready to keep confession confidentiality, to preserve confidentiality in your pastoral ministry, even though you may be forced or tortured? And so are you ready to announce the absolution and forgiveness of Christ to all who asks for forgiveness in faith?*

Candidate: *Yes, May God help me!*

Bishop (8) *Do you trust that the Bible, that is, the Old Testament and New Testament is the basis for the faith life of the church?*

> *Again, do you agree that the Augsburg confession that is unaltered and the Small Catechism of Dr. Martin Luther are correct explanations of the word of God?*
>
> **Candidate:** *Yes, I trust and accept!*
>
> **The Candidate be provided with:** *BIBLE, AUGSBURG CONFESSION AND CATECHISM*
>
> **Bishop (9)** *Do you agree to FOLLOW and to OBEY faithfully the CONSTITUTION of the SD of the ELCT?*
>
> **Candidate:** *Yes, I agree to FOLLOW and to OBEY faithfully the CONSTITUTION of SD, May God help me!* [20]

The ordination oath of the ELCT/SD above signifies the sealing of the pastor's commitment made to the church ministry. The oath and ordination obliges the candidate to go into the world to help people both, in spiritual and secular dimensions of life. For example, pastors stand as the head confessors of the church and as leaders of the community of God.[21] The ordained agrees to bind his or her call within the church rules and principles. During the process of ordination, the new pastor receives the necessary Lutheran doctrinal books in and from which the ELCT builds the basis for its Christian faith foundation and practices. After the performance of ordination, the new pastors receive confirmation with their work appointments. I discuss this in the following section about work allocation.

Like the rest of the ELCT dioceses, the SD follows the doctrines of Martin Luther as the founder of the church. In the above ordination oath, the candidate is concerned with the Lutheran traditions and doctrines only. Robert Kolb in his article *The Doctrine of Ministry in Martin Luther and the Lutheran Confessions* states that the founder of the Lutheran Church, Martin Luther, set some foundations on priesthood of all believers as well as some specialty of offices. Kolb describes that, considering both the pastor's call, and the oath and ordination, Luther once stated that all Christians are of the spiritual estate. There is no difference between them except of office. However, Luther himself made and emphasized two important comments regarding the pastoral office in the Church. He used the biblical references from Apostle Paul when he states that Christians are all one body, yet every

---

20. KKKT-DKu, *Kiapo cha Uchungaji*. No specified year (translation into English is mine).

21. Kolb, "The Doctrine of Ministry," 59; cf., 56–58.

member of the body plays own role by which that member serves the others (1Corinthians 12: 12–13). Another comment is supported by a reference from Peter's Epistles (1 Peter 2: 9) that; even if all who believe in Christ are priests and kings, but some of them will be set to perform special tasks. Therefore, Kolb concludes "although we are all equally priests, we cannot all publicly minister and teach. . . . [There is] a special position to which some are called to make possible the formal and public use of God's Word."[22] Kolb shows how specially ordained people within the Church should do some tasks. This includes the formal and public pronouncements.

Work Allocation

After the pastor has been ordained, the appointment follows. Now the diocese provides the pastor a parish or an institution to teach or perform duties, as the diocese may want this pastor to do. In relation to the oath, ordination and the call, it is by the church and by God that a pastor of the ELCT is called and sent to minister in the church and in society. The oath made and the ordination performed upon the pastor does not allow him or her to select the place for ministry. Neither is a pastor given freedom to select a particular cultural background to be sent for service. We saw this in the fifth ordination oath that reads: **Bishop (5)** *Will you be ready to work wherever you will be sent?* **Candidate:** *Yes, May God help me!* This oath demands the candidate accepts that there will be no one who will have fixed or special station to work in. It also means that there is almost no room that a pastor plays in the allocation for a work place, neither are the parishioners given a primary role to choose a pastor for their parish. Only a few lay Christians who are members of the diocesan council participate in discussing the work allocation for all pastors. However, some special requests can be allowed if there are genuine problems, for example, health issues, or if the parishioners have completely rejected their pastor. So, it is only in rare instance that the respective pastor can participate in the allocation process. It remains as an opportunity if there is a special case.

The formal and informal relationship between the pastor and parishioners require sensitivity and commitment. It is rare to see a pastor demanding certain services from parishioners or complaining too much about something. For example, if the parish's house is not furnished, has slight cracks, due to low salary, and life hardships; this pastor is not expected to express such complains to the congregants. Otherwise it will imply that their pastor has less commitment into church ministry. On the other hand,

22. Ibid., 53, 54.

parishioners are allowed to express their feelings to and about their pastor. The community has wider chances to question or comment on their pastor than vice versa. Why is this happening? Mwombeki witnesses that: "The time has come whereby Christians are starting to reject pastors.... A pastor who fails to fulfil his or her responsibilities as a spiritual leader; people reject him or her. This has started to happen in a wide range. One bishop told me that he was facing a problem with some pastors because they the parishes rejected them. To date, parishioners tell the bishop, we don't want this, your pastor; take him/her out."[23] Mwombeki continues to argue that with the contemporary society, rejecting the pastor is becoming a normal practice in Tanzania, as we shall see in some of the interviews. Christians have their own criteria regarding the role and status of their pastor. It seems that, to date, competency and constructiveness are among informal principles set by parishioners for a pastor to be accepted or rejected. Parishioners are spotlighting to the roles of their pastors.[24]

ELCT/SD PERSPECTIVES ON THE PASTOR'S ROLES AND MINISTRY IN THE CHURCH

Exposition and Analysis of the Pastor's Roles from the SD Constitution

I now turn to the discussion of the roles that a pastor of the ELCT/SD is to perform. I stated in the introduction of this chapter (see 3.1 above) that, the constitution is an important document that ascribes the roles of the pastor. As a basis for pastoral ministerial roles, on the day of ordination each pastor of the ELCT/SD normally receives the Bible, the Constitution of the Diocese and the Augsburg Confession. These three serve as the crucial references for Lutheran doctrines that the pastor pledges to follow. Other items that are not central include the Book of Liturgy; and clerical gown, stole, black shirt and a white collar. These serve as tools that the pastor can use daily.

The SD constitution spells out eighteen functions of the pastor. In their expanded form, they are the following:

A. To proclaim the Word of God to believers (Christian) and non-believers together with administration of the Holy Sacraments.

B. To teach/instruct with the baptism, confirmation and all that are related to Christian Education in the parish.

23. Mwombeki, *Uongozi wa Usharika*, 10. Translation into English is mine.
24. Ibid., 10–11.

pastoral ministry in the perspective of the ELCT-SD 79

C. To administer the parish spiritually through warning, teaching, rebuking and to lead Christians both, confidentially and publicly as the Word of God directs.

D. To visit Christians and all who may need any spiritual or bodily assistance.

E. To lead worship and prayer services in the parish.

F. To be a model of moral life while recalling his or her call

G. To be in-charge of everything in the parish.

H. To call, run and be the chairperson of the general meeting of the parish, executive committee, finance committee and other committees that he or she will be elected as a chairperson.

I. To oversee that principles and procedures of the diocese are observed in the parish.,

J. To conduct meetings of church elders,

K. To visit the parish,

L. To prepare and present monthly work report to the district and diocese,

M. To prepare and present an annual work report to the general parish and district meeting, a

N. To install ministers of the parish,

O. To receive work reports from other fellow pastor(s) who is/are under his or her supervision within the parish,

P. To present his or her work plans to the district pastor,

Q. To officially open church buildings in his or her parish, and

R. To be the overseer of all parish, district and diocese's possessions in his or her parish.[25]

These eighteen functions are organized into groups, in a bit different ways. Festo L. Bahendwa, Harold Taylor, and Jackson W. Carroll have similar categorization that I find more useful for this book. Their arrangement is similar to that of Pragman and Cook. Bahendwa finds that pastors perform four main important tasks. Functions relating to: first, 'Discipline and Leadership [*Nidhamu na Uongozi*]; second, to preach and administer the Sacraments [*Kuhubiri na kugawa Sacramenti*]; third, to Instruct and Evangelism

---

25. KKKT-DKu, *Katiba*, 21–22; cf., Parker, *Mke Aliyechaguliwa na Mungu*, 42, 43. Translation into English is
mine.

[*kuendesha Mafundisho na Uinjilisti*]; and fourth, Pastoral care and Counseling [*Utunzaji na Ushauri wa kichungaji*].[26] Even before Bahendwa had presented his analysis, in 1989 Harold Taylor presented the four essential roles of an ordained church leader - a pastor in a congregation as have been instructed by the Church Father Chrysostom. He names them as: the sacramental, disciplinary and administrative, teaching and evangelistic, and the pastoral functions.[27] For Jackson W. Carroll the roles are: celebrant of the sacraments, preacher and teacher, overseer of congregational life, and giver of pastoral care. Cook also supports this arrangement.[28]

Thus, as I enter into discussion of those roles, I find it to be clearer if I categorize those roles as Bahendwa, Taylor, Carroll, Pragman, and Cook have tried to compile and arrange them.[29] However, I will not start as Bahendwa did with 'discipline and leadership'; rather I use the models from other theologians I have mentioned above, which start with 'preaching and administering the sacraments.' I also recall my ordination day whereby the bishop, in all his speeches, he emphasized the pastor's ministry in the Church and in society by starting with the responsibility to preach the Word of God for the salvation of all people and the administration of sacraments. Then, other roles will proceed. I call this first role to be 'expounders, preachers of the Word of God and administrators of Sacraments.'

Expounders, Preachers, and Administrators of Sacraments

Explaining and preaching the Gospel is a primary task of the church and for the pastor. The pastor always has a duty to give detailed descriptions and explanations of a written text from the Bible. It is an everyday responsibility.[30] The SD perceives and puts this role first among many other responsibilities. For Evans, when the pastor performs the named tasks, he or she is doing "a ministry of proclamation, release, healing, freedom, and hope to the poor, the prisoner, the blind, and the oppressed.... (Luke 4: 18-19)."[31] It is not a plain and significant service for God's sake.

26. Bahendwa, "Uchungaji Leo," 94–102.

27. Taylor, *Tend my Sheep*, 2.

28. Carroll, *God's Potters*, 97–98; Cook, *The First Parish*, 30–32.

29. Bahendwa *Uchungaji Leo*, 4; Pragman, "Ministry in Lutheran Orthodoxy," 68, 70–71; Taylor, *Tend my Sheep*, 2; Cook, *The First Parish*, 30–32, cf., 25–29, 33–117.

30. Carroll, *God's Potters*, 97.

31. Evans, *The Pastor in a Teaching Church*, 52; Kolb, "The Doctrine of Ministry," 54; Strohl, "Ministry in the Middle Ages," 40, 42.

There is no doubt that society seems aware of the fact that religious leaders perform the role of proclaiming faith. However, among the problems that a pastor faces is how much time should be for fitting people's interests. Fidon Mwombeki observes that: "Days have passed where a pastor could preach for the whole hour expecting that people would fearfully remain seated in the pews. Nowadays even the bishop himself, if he prolongs the worship service, soon after the offering session, in a silent way, people leave the worship service for their homes. This also happens even in rural villages . . ."[32] Mwombeki points out about time management and the way in which the contemporary society observes. The present society prefers short preaching in worship services. Prolonged sermons and services are discouraging both, in urban areas as well as in the rural villages. On the one hand, it is true that long and non-motivate worship services do not keep people in the church. On the other hand, sometimes it might be due to corrupt behavior in people. This is because; the same people remain too long in other leisure clubs. In those clubs, they can stay even the whole day. In there they do not complain. Overall, the Church with her pastors ought to plan some more attractive and constructive programs. This should go with the varieties of preaching and teaching styles.

Teaching and Evangelism

It is the responsibility of every pastor of the ECLT to teach and perform evangelism to all people, to defend against false doctrines and to build Christian believers into good knowledge of the Gospel before other people. David Evans argues that the pastor is the instructor of the people. As people become the faithful in their knowledge and understanding of the gospel, they in turn can proclaim the good news to other people with whom they live and communicate to. The pastor is also a theologian, a teacher and evangelist. According to Saint Paul, " . . . some should be . . . pastors and teachers" (Ephesians 4:11; 2Timothy 4: 5). Teaching is in the Great commission that Jesus commanded to his apostles (Matthew 28: 19-20a). For Evans, Cook, and Carroll, 'teaching is the whole life of this special community called the church. Pastors are the leading actors of this task. Christian Education and Bible-study in churches, in schools, and in other social events or gatherings

---

32. Mwombeki, *Uongozi wa Usharika*, 10.

is the role of the pastor of every church."[33] It is the way a pastor perceives, ministers, and enables the people.[34]

Furthermore, Evans continues to state that the teaching role has lasted for centuries. It is during teaching processes that faith teachers attempt to distinguish between what they think is true and the false teaching. Since many years ago, teachers have become even more important as it grows necessary to discriminate between true and false teaching. Ever since the founding of the church, pastors as well as nearly everyone who is a teacher of Christian faith are all seen as processors and communicators of the life and stories of Jesus. They are recognized and appreciated increasingly for their importance. Even the church history informs us that: "As the church grew and developed, teaching became a full-time responsibility so that the local congregation was held responsible for (a teacher's) livelihood."[35] From Evans contention, it shows also that, teaching is beneficial to both, the church and to the ministers themselves. When teaching, a pastor orients with the local congregants to realize and participate in taking care of their minister.

Evans goes further to declaring that, "The early church's concern for teaching the faith is clear. I believe it needs to remain the contemporary church's concern also."[36] The truth may stand firm even in the twenty first century. The teaching responsibility seems to be the most important one because since church history, the significance and magnitude of the teaching task of church ministers had great emphasis. Teaching imparts more knowledge into people than preaching. In teaching, people ask questions, and or respond to questions raised. We have been noticing Christians being comfortable when they are taught rather than being preached to. Teaching gives more clarifications wherever it seems unclear.

Discipline and Leadership

The pastor is an administrator or manager and organizer.[37] Harold Taylor underlines that this role comprises all disciplinary and administrative functions. In this role the pastor maintains the purity of the church; administers

---

33. Evans, *The Pastor in a Teaching Church*, 13–15, 17, 22–25; Cook, *The First Parish*, 31; Carroll, *God's Potters*, 97–98.

34. Evans, *The Pastor in a Teaching Church*, 52, 59.

35. Ibid., 13.

36. Ibid., 14.

37. Cook, *The First Parish*, 31, 32.

discipline to unworthy members; judges disputes among Christians; and administers the church property.[38] Similarly, the ELCT and SD perceive pastors as persons who "have been set over the church by the doctrine of Christ to instruct the people to the true godliness, to administer, the sacred mysteries and to keep and exercise upright discipline."[39] The pastor has to exercise the office in accord with the church's public theology, the Holy Scriptures, the Creeds, and the Lutheran confessional writings. This is a task of overseeing the Christian moral life and administrative functions, for example, to oversee the ethical principles through warning and leading meetings;[40] as stipulated in SD constitution. Strohl concludes that pastors should try as much as possible to be nurturers of the church and society. They should observe by example the purity and significance of this role in the church and for the salvation of all people.[41]

Pastoral Care and Counseling

Among other duties, the pastor is also a servant of God's command and of people's needs. Pastoral care and counseling is among essential roles of the ELCT/SD pastor. Harold Taylor emphasizes the importance of this role because it calls for:

> Helping people to meet the various crises and changing situations which come about their lives. It is likely to involve: healing people . . . both physically and in their personal relationships; sustaining people in times of difficulty, frustration, and sorrow; guiding people as they seek to clarify their thinking and decide on the way to act in different situations; reconciling people, challenging them to face the weakness and guilt of their broken relationships and find reconciliation and restoration both with God and with other people. In all this work of helping people, counseling will play important part.[42]

For Taylor, 'care' and 'counseling' mean giving advice or instruction to someone who needs help. It includes teaching, or admonishing, warning or correcting people, exhorting, comforting, encouraging, to as far as

---

38. Taylor, *Tend My Sheep*, 2.
39. Strohl, "Ministry in the Middle Ages," 41.
40. Forde, "The Ordained Ministry," 130, 191–192.
41. Strohl, "Ministry in the Middle Ages," 41.
42. Taylor, *Tend My Sheep*, 72.

strengthening people (compare John 14: 16, 26; Isaiah 9:6).[43] Cook and Evans use stronger words to emphasize and elaborate the significance of this task. Cook gives his analysis of the activities that a pastor undertakes in this role: "[T]he pastor is the care giver, the feeder of the flock, the spiritual overseer. . . . pastors do shepherding things."[44] He or she is both a teacher and a pastor who has to perform the " . . . shepherding, guidance and protection. . . . to all the flock . . . [pastors are] overseers [and] care[rs] for the church . . . (Acts 20:28–31a)."[45] Due to the value and enormity of this task, Bahendwa reminds that, to every pastor, to perform this role requires relationship with people. 'Relationship is essential because in this role the pastor works by relating to all people. The pastor participates in various daily events or occasions that people (society) encounter with them.'[46]

The main four roles I have so far analyzed and discussed above are among the general courses which are regular part of theological education in the respective training institutions of the ELCT.[47] However, it may imply that the training institutions may not be providing an in-depth knowledge and skills as the SD analyzed the roles, the 'clinical' pastoral training, and other related functions. This may be because of the difference in the nature and approach of each institution from which churches prepare pastors for Church ministry. In addition, it might have been due to the difference of each individual diocese as the ELCT constitution gives a room for each diocese to have some particular analysis of the pastoral roles.

CONCLUSION

In this chapter three, I have presented and discussed the pastoral ministry in the ELCT and SD. The main concentration was on the ELCT and SD's perspectives on pastoral ministry in the church in terms of how the pastor is perceived, set apart for church ministry, and the roles that this pastor has to perform. In general, we have seen how the church authority emphasizes the significance of pastoral ministry and binds pastors into its prescribed guidelines. Nonetheless, the guidelines show that it is s hardly possible for a pastor to enter into church ministry before the approval of several church councils. After the approval of the councils, then other processes of training, oath and ordination, and at last the work appointment that take place. Being

43. Ibid., 76–79.
44. Cook, *The First Parish*, 31.
45. Evans, *The Pastor in a Teaching Church*, 13.
46. Bahendwa, "Uchungaji Leo," 54.
47. Taylor, *Tend my Sheep*, 78.

in the appointment, the pastor has to perform the stipulated roles in the constitution(s). It means that, the pastor's role is strongly committed to the specified tasks in the church documents. Additionally, it is seen in both the church document and the witness of lived experiences that, the ELCT pastor is not fixed to one appointment. The diocesan organs have the mandate to re-allocate ministers according to the needs of the Church. Therefore, it is expected that any pastor of the ELCT has to commit himself or herself to those set guidelines as they (guidelines) are argued to reflect the church's way of life. Failure to follow those guiding principles is a sort of waywardness. Moreover, failing to abide to and follow, the pastor is perceived to be attempting to impose other new or unapproved principles in the church.

Thus, as I stated before, in the forthcoming chapter, I perform my analysis, presentation and discussion of the lived experiences from my interviewees. The analysis and discussion will mainly provide some of the characteristics of social change and their effects when pastors implement the above prescription of roles as I have discussed in this chapter three.

4

THE SOCIAL AND CULTURAL CONTEXT IN WHICH PASTORS WORK

INTRODUCTION

As I HAVE POINTED out in chapter three above, I have already analyzed and discussed the four roles of a pastor according to the ELCT constitution. Those were, first to expound and preach the Word and administer the sacraments—in which a pastor communicates by interpreting the meaning of the biblical text to the present context. Parallel to expounding and preaching, a pastor also administers baptism and the Lord's Supper according to the Lutheran tradition. Second, undoubtedly a pastor is described to be a teacher and evangelist who instructs in faith and Scriptures to the faithful regular (church goers), to new converts (together with those who are backsliders) as well as to all people in order to protect them from relapsing into their former lives and thoughts.[1] Conjoined in the teaching task is the responsibility of evangelism whereby a pastor visits church members and spreads the Christian faith to all people. Third, the disciplining and leadership role deals with exhortation, showing a good example, and influencing people to behave according to desired expectations of the church. Fourth, pastoral care and counseling in which a pastor facilitates the process for a client to find a solution to a problem. I would like to state earlier here that, I found out that the church documents are silent about the persistence of

---

1. For detailed information see Evans, *The Pastor in a Teaching Church*, 13.

the social and cultural context in which pastors work 87

rapid social change. Nor do they allow room for some precaution if such a thing happens in future. The documents are authoritarian.

In this chapter, I present the first part of the analyses. Accordingly, my main aim is to explore how pastors implement the above roles and the practical experiences of ambivalences and tensions that pastors encounter in a changing society. The main questions to be addressed by informants in this chapter are two: first, what are the characteristics of contemporary society? Second, what types of social changes are rampant and how do those changes affect the role of the pastor and hence the mission and life of the Church? This second question is central to the aim of this chapter. This chapter seeks to give a contextual understanding of the current experiences of pastors, society and the church in the prevalence of social changes.

It is of paramount to highlight the background of the name for this chapter and some concepts that deserve be defined earlier. I adopt the title of this chapter from Carroll in his book *God's Potters: Pastoral Leadership and the Shaping of Congregations*. The title was originally: "The Social and Cultural Context in Which Clergy Work."[2] I take 'Social and Cultural' to reflect the interactive life of people in their groups. Although one can agree that the concept 'cultural' includes an element of education; however, there is a separate chapter that analyzes and discusses the educational context and its effects on the role of pastors. The respective chapter five has the title: 'The Pastor in a Cognitively Changing Society' in which pastors work.

The term 'cultural' illustrates the main impression of how the pastor lives and works in a social and complex multicultural, or more precisely, as Lartey calls it, an 'intercultural' characteristic. By using the concept 'multicultural and intercultural', Lartey portrays an image of how society is mixed. Then he is convincing pastors and all theologians " . . . to move from a multicultural to an intercultural community . . . to a dynamic recognition of interaction, mutual influence, and interconnectedness."[3] Lartey views the pastors to be working in an intercultural community where cultures are interconnected. Cultures are very dynamic, interactive, and influential to each other. He invites pastors and theologians to move into this context so that their roles are effective and realistic.

In this chapter four, I open the analysis and discussion by exploring the features of social changes along with their effects/impacts[4] on the role of a pastor. As a consequence, the effects again do control even the mission and

---

2. Carroll, *God's Potters*, 31.

3. Lartey, *Pastoral Theology in an Intercultural World*, 2006: front cover.

4. In this chapter, I use the terms 'effect and impact' interchangeably to mean the consequence they bring onto pastor's roles and to the life of the church at large.

life of the Church. I call it the 'characteristics and effects of 'social change' on the roles of the pastor and mission and life of the Church.'

CHARACTERISTICS AND EFFECTS OF 'SOCIAL CHANGE' ON THE ROLES OF THE PASTOR

Before I enter into the presentation, analysis and discussion of the findings, it appears important to start by highlighting the meaning and implication of the concept 'social change.'

What is 'social change'? In an investigation of encounters between the Dii people in Cameroon and Norwegian missionaries over a period of many social and religious changes, the Norwegian theologian Tomas Sundnes Drønen summarizes that "social change refers to any alteration in the social arrangements experienced by a group or city."[5] Relevant to the theological importance of this examination, Drønen describes the relationship between religion and, social and cognitive change. By using the theory of paradigm shift in science as Thomas Kuhn proposes, Drønen compares it to some theories of both sociological sciences and theological perspectives. The two aspects of change, that is, social and cognitive seem to emerge due to "certain patterns of human behavior."[6]

While leaving aside the aspect of cognitive change in his work; Drønen argues that social change both enhances and affects the religious conversion and life of people. That is, most of the time, social change brings religious change.[7] As it may have happened in other places around the world, African people are currently experiencing "turbulent social change related to the arrival of external . . . forces."[8] For Drønen, social change is both an internal and external force that members of society find themselves inside it. This condition of social change requires both African pastors and all other people around the globe to make some adjustments in life and suit it. The forces from realities of life enforce people to try to make life suitable to their needs, demands, and interests pertaining to their contemporary life in a group form, religiously form, intellectually, and in terms of material welfares. Society, whether religious, secular or both, may alter such facets to meet its wishes and wills.

Furthermore, Church ministers cannot escape the encounter of varied changes in the individual life and in their ministry. Harold Taylor repeatedly

5. Drønen, *Communication, Conversion and Conservation*, 88.
6. Ibid., 27, cf., 26.
7. Ibid., 26–28.
8. Ibid., 27.

comments that, for example, when pastors undertake their care and counseling role, they need: "To recognize that there are different sorts of change, and to understand the difference between *social* change and *individual* change. By 'social' change, we mean change and development in the *general* cultural and economic conditions experienced by society as a whole, from which no one can wholly escape. By 'individual' change we mean the *particular* changes which occur in the individual lives of each separate person or family."[9] Considering the above definition and its kinds; it implies that change is one of the greatest characteristics of society. Moreover, change appears to be an imperative condition. It cuts across general socio-cultural life and also the economic conditions in life. This change happens both to an individual and to communities of people. Regarding the group of people; for example, social change relates to population change, religious life, and marriage and family context, to economic, political and to people's intellectual life. Again, Harold Taylor and Xenia Chryssochoou argue that social changes influence and cause individual change. Once it is in whirl, in most cases social change has great control over the role of that individual.[10] As data will show us, there are many features of social change. Each condition has some impacts on life and work. Now, I turn to my analysis and discussion of some characteristics of 'social change' and the way in which they affect the role of the pastor and the mission and life of the Church.

DEMOGRAPHIC CHANGE: DECREASE AND INCREASE OF CHURCH MEMBERS DUE TO MIGRATION

The concept 'Demographic Change' as I draw on in this analysis was noted by two group informants anonymized as H and I. For these informants, it reflects the increase or decrease of the number of people or of the number of worship services, of birth or death rates, and of marriages. Therefore, in this discussion, together with the above understanding of the informants; I employ the phenomenon to reflect the exploration of human populations in terms of size, growth, distribution, and mass. Similarly, for Carroll, demographic change relates to "changes in characteristics of the population."[11]

Among essential things that church ministers need to know in their given ministry and context is the population of people and their characteristics. For example, demography may help in planning religious or social

9. Taylor, *Tend My Sheep*, 261, 260.
10. Taylor, *Tend My Sheep*, 261–266; Chryssochoou, *Cultural Diversity*, 166–174, cf., 132–134.
11. Carroll, *God's Potters*, 33.

programs of preaching, of teaching, of evangelism and mission, of administration, and of care and counseling. As discussed in chapter three above (in 3.3) about Pastor's Roles and Ministry, to a serious minister, the task of preparing the service observes and considers many factors. Carroll states by suggesting that, for example, when a pastor prepares sermons or teaching sessions normally sets the time to be used in relation to the congregation ahead. However, Carroll pinpoints one of the dilemmas that pastors encounter when preparing for pastoral services. He highlights that, there are times when a pastor finds himself or herself to spend more time in one role, for example, in administrative tasks than in other roles due to increasing size of social population and of the increase in size and complexity of local church structures.[12]

Certainly, clear and correct knowledge and realization of demographic features as one of the social changes can be one of the useful tools in evaluating the church growth or decline. As a tool, it helps plan many other policies, resources, and activities in the parish. For example, when a pastor intends to carry out evangelism task, he or she must first think about the population to be visited. Thereafter, he or she plans the resources in terms of evangelists, transport, and other materials necessary for that task in a respective area. The same plan will be done when arranging for administrating the sacraments.

As I stated above that, social change relates to population change, thus on this feature, I wanted to know how it was changing and affecting the pastor's role. In the following discussion I start by describing some changes that happened, thereafter we will have a look on some consequences in various areas of Church life and on the pastor's responsibilities.

Migration

Migration is one of the factors for demographic change in society. During my survey, I asked how and why there was a population change. The informants pointed out that in general, demographic change was due to people's migration. In an interview with evangelists, which took place when Evangelists gathered for their monthly meetings of the parish, they stated that there was a rapid tendency of people to move from remote areas into an up-coming rural community and into centers, such as urban areas. They said: "*The organization of our society is changing also. People are migrating and immigrating into up-coming towns, substation of the parish. With this, the population of society is growing in other villages and decreasing in rural*

12. Ibid., 99–106.

villages. The same is for Christians. Most of them are moving into growing towns and urban centres.[13] To substantiate and correlate the arguments of evangelists, I had to discuss with some pastors. In another interview with an urban pastor from my focus group, the same features were vivid. First, he acknowledges that there was a similar behavior of people to move from one place to another. Then he describes the contrast, urban church ministers used to receive a lot of Christians and other people from countryside compared to the number of people who were moving out. This was his testimony:

> *Today there is much movement of people from one place to another. For example, many are moving from rural areas to urban centers. For a pastor or evangelist who is working in towns like these can testify the truth of what I tell you. We always receive many Christians from rural parishes or villages who tell that they have immigrated here. Nevertheless, we have less of those who are moving out into rural areas. Normally, only those who are appointed by the government who move for work in those rural places. The businesses people go and return to towns after their businesses are over.*[14]

The quotations above imply that urbanization is one of the reasons for people to move into other areas. Urbanization has become more attractive to the majority of people who live in rural areas. Urbanization causes movements and alterations. In supporting the above descriptions of the informant, Andrew A, Kyomo writes: "There is an increase move from rural areas to urban areas. . . . Urban life is . . . the impact of social change."[15] Additionally, George M.D. Fihavango claims: "Urbanisation is another great factor contributing to the changes in family structure."[16] Here, I asked a question: why did people move more into urban centers than into rural areas? I will come back later to this question.

Second, however, even in urban areas people appear to move from within, that is, they move from one street to another within a town. The same urban parish pastor comments by arguing that: *There is people's behavior of migrating from one street to another street within our parish and substations. They move as they like, today they (Christians) are members of this place but tomorrow they move into another street. The same is done from*

13. Informant E.
14. Informant B.
15. Kyomo, "Pastoral Care and Counseling to Families," 201, 202.
16. Fihavango, "Leadership and Family," 187.

one substation to another.¹⁷ Practically, it seems the movements of people share two characteristics: first, there is a movement from villages to towns; and second, there are movements within towns – from one street to another. Certainly, there are some movements within villages and also from one village to another. Kyomo has much description about how rapid social change is a serious issue. He shows that urbanization is one of the factors for social change and vice versa. He perceives urbanization as one of the causes for movements of people and it brings some more effects and challenges on the role of a pastor, especially, regarding the 'pastoral care and counseling.'¹⁸

But why there is movement of people from one place to another, especially, from rural to urban areas? This is one of my follow-up questions. The respondents described that this trend toward urbanization adds the number of church members in urban parishes. Even if for others the mobility of people would be an expected action; but still the question remains: why are people 'so' mobile? When I probed with such questions, informants responded by highlighting some of the reasons. First, they pointed out that people like to live in the growing (developing) areas. Second, people believe that in urban areas there is availability of jobs and life that is more comfortable. They dare to argue that *There is a growing – up of small urban centers. Some rural villages are growing into urban life statuses.*¹⁹ People move in search for job, for money, and for better life. I came across this description: *People are very mobile today in search for jobs, a pleasurable life and modern social services.*²⁰ It means that people were very mobile with reasons. They search for jobs and better life. The third reason relates to the availability of social services that can help them attain better living. Both two informants above describe that sometimes people moved into urban areas due to development, search for jobs, and accessibility of social services, for example, the availability of good infrastructures for better public services and life. Such public services or systems include: good roads, public communication and transportation, health services, water supplies, educational centres (such as schools and colleges), electricity, and telecommunications. Fihavango supports this when he writes, "There have been a move of many; they come into the city ... People have become more and more mobile because of searching for money and better living."²¹

17. Informant B.
18. Kyomo, "Pastoral Care and Counseling to Families," 193–216.
19. Informant E.
20. Informant C.
21. Fihavango, "Leadership and Family," 187.

Nonetheless, in the course of their movements, some people are also mobile from one religion or denomination to another. When they move to those urban areas, some change even their religious affiliations. I will show this in the next analysis and discussion about another feature of social change, that is religious pluralism and its effects.

During this research, I learnt that the people's need for employment, better life, and social services was a high priority. One could also continue asking other questions, does it mean there is no work in places where they are living? What types of employment are those people searching for, self-employment or employment by other people and organizations?

In the above discussion about the demographic change, migration has been the focus. Most informants and other scholars acknowledge that most of the time people moved from rural to urban areas. However, a few people immigrated into countryside areas. Most of those who move to rural areas are the employees in both, the government as well as in some private sectors. For example, the schoolteachers, health doctors, and other expertise from the institutions of secular government, business people, and those who were privately searching for jobs.

The discussion shows that population change is primarily a result of that movement. I witnessed the movement of people even during the time of my research for this book. Most people have been moving into urban or rural areas depending on the motivation. Now I turn to the discussion of the consequences of migration on the role of the pastor and of Church's life.

Consequences in various areas of Church Life and Pastor's Responsibilities

During conversations on the consequences of migration of people, church ministers continued to complain especially on some massive movements. Most of the time pastors grumbled that the movements are disturbing and bringing some tensions in their church programs. Informants expressed at least two main effects that seem to bring tensions as pastors carry out their tasks.

Growth in Individual Freedom, New Social Forms of life, and Leadership

This first consequence is drawn from the general ideas of the Church Elders, other Lay Christians,[22] and youth. All members in these groups were non-theologians. I name this group as 'informant F.' My interview with Church Elders was done on Sundays when I went for both, the worship services and for research. Together with it, since I was both a participant researcher and a pastor; sometimes the parish pastor was requesting me to help in administering the worship services. In some substations, sometimes, we could go together. During church announcements, the parish pastor or Church Elders announced my need for the parishioners to help me get relevant data for my project. Those who were willing could come back. Thus, soon after the worship services; interview sessions took place in the located office. Then I held an interview with the youth during their three-day Youth Gathering. Having talked and got the consent of the youth group itself; both, the parish pastor and Youth leaders set a time for my interview with them.

During interviews with church elders, Lay Christians and the youth emphasized that the life of society is in constant change due to freedom in people. For example, in all sessions they testified that *each one has a freedom of moving and proclaiming his or her faith.*[23] As I will discuss it in detail in the forthcoming sections, at this point it seems that a person moves with his or her religious ideologies. The freedom that rests upon each individual as well as upon society is an opportunity for each person to move from one point to another. Usually, when a person moves into new context, he or she can share his or her ideologies with natives. His or her ideas, whether secular or religious, may be influential to or influenced and hence affect their lives. For this informant, individual's freedom of movement can also modify the shape of people's social and religious life, and vice versa. In trying to elaborate their descriptions, my informants noticed that the interaction and integration of the population changed its form of life. Now it was in another outlook. They said: *the form of social life has changed. Yet, it is still changing as people interact and integrate.*[24]

When asked about the implication and effects that the changed and yet shifting form of social life was bringing on the roles of leaders, this informant responded that, the social life of the people has to be the guideline for leaders in tasks they want to plan. This lay Christian informant argued that:

22. The concept 'Lay Christians' as I use it in this book refers to 'Christians who are not trained as theologians.'
23. Informant F.
24. Informant F.

Whatever the government and society would want to plan or perform has to focus on the social life of the people.[25] According to this informant, both secular and religious leaders are forced to undertake all their leadership tasks prior to their realization of the situation or needs of society. As people interact with each other, they share some life experiences. This interaction and sharing of life experiences result into some mental and emotional changes. As they said: *Due to this interaction of the people, society's attitude and mode of thinking, feeling, and attitudes toward life have changed.*[26]

One could ask: is it possible for a leader to plan or perform his or her tasks by focusing only on society's status and needs? On the other hand, is it possible to rely only on the stipulated roles from the Church when planning and undertaking the pastoral office in the Church and society? If people are so mobile, is it possible to have a stable and an everlasting guideline for use by a pastor in all varied contexts and generations?

The experience I got from the lay Christians (informant F) concluded that the growth of individual freedom and the interaction that people have bring new social forms of life. Social forms of life change due to new social life resulting from new styles of life that is constantly emerging when people integrate. Then I held another interview with some theologians in one of the training institutions. Those theologians stated that Tanzanian people move and used to move from one place to another, though today the behavior is too rapid compare to some years ago. According to this informant, people's movements have been bringing the following effects: first, the movements disturb or reform the image or form of society and the Church in all settings. The movement makes one group different from the other in terms of size and structure. When I asked as to how the movement alters the formation of society, this informant state that:

> *There are many social changes in this society. The first is its formation. It changes as the life settings change. For example, if some members of the group move from one point to another, then the form of those two groups will have new appearances. One might become bigger than the other. Other more structural forms and differences will happen. There will be new types of leadership, interests, attitudes, and related things. Due to demographic change, the number of people either increases or decreases. Even in Tanzania, the number of people is rapidly increasing daily, but with little decrease in number.*[27]

25. Informant F.
26. Informant F.
27. Informant H.

From the quotation above, the second consequence is more or less of internal change. This informant calls for the need for different "structural forms", that is, "new types of leadership." The contemporary formation of society, its needs, interests and opinions bring up a requirement and emergence of new forms or types of leadership.

Following the above arguments, some questions seem important here: why should there be a new type of leadership. Can the present leadership suit the new form of society? What are those new types of leadership? I am convinced that it is because of the need for new characteristics or qualities of leadership that matches and can help the pastor to respond to the contemporary forms and problems of the contemporary society. Charles Taylor argues that the present society needs leaders who focus on three areas: first, the leadership that considers the need to help people improve their economic status; second, leaders who communicate issues with their followers and act according to the common opinion; and third, the leaders who invent society, that is, leaders who guarantee the voice of the people.[28] Walter C. Wright in his book *Relational Leadership* conforms to my informants and the arguments of Charles Taylor. Wright argues that society of the twenty-first century prefers a relational leadership because it considers both the leader and the followers during all processes of planning and accomplishing the mission and goals of an organization. It also considers the life of the followers. Once society does not meet the required social needs, it will always complain against leadership. Relational leadership is the only model that matches with the realities of society.[29]

Therefore, on the one hand some movements of people decrease in number or destroy the structural formation of the group. On the other hand, the movements have been increasing the memberships into areas where people have moved in and they do reform the existing social structural forms. One may agree with the above explanations that, if the contemporary society in Tanzania, as well as in Africa at large, creates some new appearances and hence new phases, then this appears to be the effect of social change resulting from demographic transformations. Consequently, new phases of society may also demand new leadership structures. The same image might be true for the Church and for the ministerial tasks of the pastor.

Furthermore, the arguments in the above paragraphs show that, due to the growth of freedom in individuals, the new social forms constantly emerge. The interaction and integration of people causes the emergence of new forms as the society enters into new requirements for leadership.

28. Taylor, *Modern Social Imaginaries*, 143.
29. Wright, *Relational Leadership*, xi, 40.

Therefore, the life of the Church must undergo a constant transformation as well. This means that the movements, the changing images or forms, interests, needs and outlook of society will forcefully change the expression of the Church in terms of population size, religious ideology, and on the roles of the potential Christians as pastors. To conclude, it presupposes that the church authorities have to do the following: first, there is a need for inventive and constructive types of leadership. Second, the new forms of life call for a need to invent society in almost all issues that affects it. Third, the prescribed church policies and strategies that are in place need revisit in order to see whether they respond to the demands at hand or not. Fourth, new type of leadership implies the need for new and reframing of pastor's roles. Finally, a pastor seems to be in the midst where pressures are coming from the tasks analyzed by the church and from society. The problem is that, both the church and society are optimistic upon the pastor as the changes emerge amid fulfilling the pastoral office. Thus, both the Church and pastor ought to re-plan their policies.

Effects upon Church Life and Pastors' Work

All pastors who participated in this discussion acknowledged that the movements of society cause some depressing consequences upon worship services. As we noticed above, if people move in or out, the movement affects the number of participants in worship services, and with regard to worship schedules. Fluctuating attendance does mislead the plans of a minister. Plans will always be minimal or over-estimated.

Migration also brings great changes when pastors plan for home visitations, and even for care and counseling sessions. From their parish experiences, their descriptions about the effects of movements and migration go as follows: *This affects the churches programs and increases the pastor's roles. If he or she had allocated a 'one day' for home visitations, now the schedule will change according to the number of people. The same problem holds for worship services, increase of people's problems, counseling sessions and many more.*[30]

The descriptions above point to the prevalence of unstable programs due to unstable residences, number of people, as well as Churchgoers. It means that unrealistic plans affect the basic functions of a pastor. Consequently, there might be ineffective service to the people.

Expressing similar views, other pastors state that the changes occurring in society is one of the criteria for church ministers to decrease or increase the number of worship services. Most urban parishes are facing the problem

30. Informant H.

of increasing the number of worship services. This problem leads them to a call for parish pastors to increase the number of Christians who can volunteer to help lead and preach in worship services. On the other hand, due to social influences, some Christians are becoming faith backsliders. Thus, pastors have to perform some more tasks of evangelism. Sometimes, the worship service sessions have to be reduced if there are poor or decreasing attendances. One informant expresses the effects in this way:

> *Sometimes the structure of society causes change in attendances in our parishes. We increase or reduce the number of worship services. If it is due to backsliding of Christians, we try to visit or arrange public preaching in villages or streets with such problems. In addition, we increase volunteer Christians to help us establish other worship services in the streets of our substation's. Therefore, the challenge here is to increase evangelism and increase or decrease the worship services.*[31]

Another pastor who at that time was serving in a rural parish expressed that the problem of movement brings some great discomforts. When responding to my questions, that pastor said: *There is free movement of people from one place to another. This change is causing the migration and immigration of people into different villages, towns and cities. People are very mobile today. This problem leads to the lessening of the population of Christians in villages.*[32] The quotation above shows that, freedom of movement increases the migration of people from one area to another. To this pastor, the mobility of peoples is a problem. It depopulates churches, especially in rural substations. However, to the urban pastors perhaps this could be an advantage because it indicates a Church growth in terms of the number of Christians. There are some observations from the above descriptions of informants. It shows that there is a difference between a rural and an urban pastor. The urban pastor seems to have many tasks due to big population than the rural one. However, urban pastors have the advantage of the availability of social services. It seems that rural pastors have less tasks in terms of the number of worship services, but those pastors are disadvantaged with the inadequacy of social services.

Moreover, informant B added some effects resulting from demographic changes in society. This informant holds that demographic change also creates some problems when pastors prepare and report the statistics of their Church members. There is a daily fluctuation in the number of participants. Likewise, the movements of people cause some problems, especially,

31. Informant I.
32. Informant C.

when pastors plan to carry out their tasks of home visitations, evangelism and mission, and sacramental services. This pastor acknowledges this way: *We fail to have an exact number of our Christians in each street or substation. Thus, we fail to follow our home visitations schedule as well as in doing evangelism and mission because we do not know who are already Christians and who are not.*[33] In addition, for the pastors who, in the time of data collection, were serving in urban parishes could also face some other difficulties in managing all Christians. The increase of Christians demands for an increase of other church ministers. One of them accounted thus: *We have to devote much time in one street or substation while delaying to go to another preaching point. How will a pastor know each of his or her flock in this kind of ministry and time? Is there any pastor who knows clearly his or her sheep in our Church of today?*[34] At last, another effect of migration of people relates to 'family structures' and nurture. Some spouses, especially men who move into towns in search of jobs or other activities neglect their families hence remarry or remain irresponsible with regard to their home families.

The above discussion has been on the general characteristic and some effects of social change due to demographic change. I now present some reflections on how pastors implement the prescribed roles in the church constitution. The aim of this section is the same - to discover some effects and ambivalences that pastors encounter when they perform the analyzed roles (see chapter three). In conversations, the following issues carried an important room: What are other major issues that characterize the contemporary society in which pastors live and work? What is the efficacy of the prescribed roles in the church constitutions, and what effects do pastors encounter as they implement those given roles? Thus far, how do pastors deal with the emerging effects? The main themes in these discussions include: pastors as religious leaders and teachers of the community in the time of religious pluralism, diversity and Similarity; the pastor as worship leader; the pastor as moral leader; the pastor as pastor; and the pastors as Community leader.

PASTORS AS RELIGIOUS LEADERS AND TEACHERS IN THE TIME OF RELIGIOUS PLURALISM

In the previous section, we have noticed that there is people's freedom of movement. That freedom was also in religious proclamation and affiliation. One informant held that: *each one has a freedom of moving and proclaiming*

33. Informant B.
34. Ibid.

his or her faith.[35] Due to the integration of ethnic groups, freedom and movement that happen in society; migration into any street becomes open to people from around the nation. This freedom brings a growth of great freedom of people's migration from one faith to another. That is why one informant could confirm that there was a *daily migration and immigration of people from one denomination or religion to another.*[36] This happened after the time of strong emphasis on villagization. If people are allowed to migrate into or practice any religious life; then it is likely that even the society's religious identity can also undergo dramatic changes.[37]

It means that religiosity is openly becoming a form of social life. Thus, starting with the impression "there are many religions and denominations" above; in this section I will discuss seven issues. Those are: religious pluralism, relations between denominations, problems in ecumenical collaboration, renewal movements, confusion over true way to salvation, faith wanderers" and increase of syncretism, and some reasons for people to move from one religious community to another.

Religious Pluralism

It seems that religious pluralism is becoming a form of social life. In relation to a village to village or street by street observations, religious pluralism is growing more and more. The discussion above showed us how people move and influence each other with all their culture, religious belief, and other life knowledge and experiences. It meant that just as *society moves a lot from one village to another or one town to the other*[38] so it does in the faith. However, some pastors pointed out that some years back, in places where there were big and strong Roman Catholic Church, other denominations could not go into those same places. Other denominations perform their Christian mission and establish churches where there are no such Christian services. At present, the case has changed to the extent that one denomination or religion can establish a preaching point closer to the other. However, they argue that Christians practice this much more than Muslims do. One pastor in the focus group observed: *Society is in a multicultural life in a sense that, first; it is in a multi-religious life. There are many religions and denominations. It is a time of pluralism of faith, and other forms of social life. In the multi-religious life of society: there are Christians who have old faith that is*

35. Informant F. cf., Fihavango, 186.
36. Informant B.
37. Cf. Chapter two about Ujamaa and 'villagization 'in Tanzania.
38. Informant I.

a conservative faith and old traditions.[39] The quotation above brings up the question of religious pluralism and the ambivalence, pressure or turbulence that pastors encounter when they undertake their responsibilities according to church authorities. In the Tanzanian society; religions with their denominations appears to multiply and challenges the old and conservative faith and practice.

Consequently, this entails the fact that at present, the villages, districts and the nation are experiencing enormous expansion in global religions, denominations and cultures. This expansion is the result of immigration, integration and the freedom that people have or the respective government constitution guarantees them. During the time of my research, almost in every village or town I went, informants listed to me the presence of Muslims with their denominations alongside Christianity and African Traditional Religion (ATR). Furthermore, there were Christian denominations such as Pentecostal churches and Seventh Day Advents (SDA) alongside mega and mainline denominations of Lutheran and Roman Catholic.

Hence, as informants asserted, there is little doubt that the number of religions and denominations has increased considerably from the time mono – cultural life started to change into a rapid growth of multicultural life of society. Pluralism and diversity seem to bring implications and effects upon the churches, pastors and society in general. In my view, despite the problems that may prevail, religious pluralism can create opportunities for pastoral offices and for society to opt for or learn from each other. Yet, to other church ministers and to some members of society, religious pluralism might make difficult both for the pastors to lead and for the church to pursue the goals and purposes. Then, what effects does religious pluralism bring on pastoral roles and on the mission and life of the church in general? In trying to answer this question, I look at the relations between the denominations.

Relations between Denominations

The society's religious pluralism also creates some differences in doctrinal emphases and practices. Based on experiences in religious issues; any denomination or religion can be established due to several and varied reasons and goals. For example, it may be due to certain conflicts between church leaders. In such case, it would be obvious that each religion or denomination might have its own spiritual worship services and practices. That is why it appeared that each denomination was teaching and emphasizing its own faith doctrines.

39. Informant A.

On this issue, when I held an interview with a pastor who was also in my focus group, that pastor argued that, sometimes other denominations preached and taught doctrines that brought many problems between their fellow Christian denominations. Besides, their doctrinal emphases were causing denominations to have bad relations between each other, but bringing instead conflicts. The teaching task became tough to all church ministers. For this reason, it was hardly possible to teach and convince those who had moved out to return. This pastor observed: *We are also facing problems and challenges about the mushrooming of denominations. They (denominations) come up with new emphases and bring conflicts between one denomination and another.*[40]

Other differences that make the denominations enter into conflicts are forms of worship services, multiplication of teachers and preachers of the faith, and the differences in convincing power. This informant as a pastor points out that:

> *Today there are many forms of worship services depending on the denominations or religions. I call it a time of pluralism in faith or religions and of worshipping styles. The society in which we live and work is full of free faith teachers and preachers. Therefore, the religious life of our society is of mixture and full of varied and challenging doctrines. The mainline churches and all non Pentecostal Churches faced the influence of Pentecostal and Muslim doctrines in their Christians' life. This has led to daily mobility of Christians from one denomination or religion to another resulting from our emphases of Christian doctrines and other problems.*[41]

It seems that other denominations use different forms in their worship services. In addition, the *free faith teachers and preachers* seem to have been powerful in convincing people to join into their faith communities. This implies that the powerful wins. When I wanted to know what they are doing with those problems, some pastors responded that: *we try to adopt any traditions or customs cultural background or denominations into our Lutheran practices if we think it can be useful. Nevertheless, it remains a problem in the whole church.*[42]

The above descriptions, thus, underline that the rapid multiplication of the religious life of society and the increase of difference in doctrinal emphases and religious practices is also a result of the persistence of freedom of religious expression and of movements. Another problem that religious

40. Informant C.
41. Informant B.
42. Informant I.

pluralism and relations create is the loss of identity. For example, the adoption of doctrines and worship practices is losing the Lutheran identity. One informant complains: *Our Lutheran denomination in Tanzania is losing its identity due to imposition of almost all new practices from other denominations, such as Pentecostalism teachings and loud prayers.*[43] For this pastor, religious pluralism and Pentecostal influences are not bringing good relationships between the denominations. The Lutheran denomination appears to dilute its traditional doctrines and practices. Consequently, the church itself is losing it real identity. Moreover, pastors and other church ministers are encountering hard times for them to preach and teach people so that there is a harmonious relationship between the denominations and the Christian teaching. As stated above, each denomination claims to hold all truth about faith. Almost the same problems exist on the whole issue of worship practices. I will come back to discussion of worship services later in its separate section.

Problems in Ecumenical Collaboration

Some mainline protestant churches practice the ecumenical cooperation. Christians gather and share songs of praise, listen to gospel preaching, and give some offerings for their ecumenical tasks. According to my parish experience, usually, before the session closes on that day, they carry out some special prayers. The leader who controls the session asks the participants to mention some issues that they would want to be prayed for specifically. After the prayers are over, they disperse until another Sunday at another denomination. Sometimes the ecumenical collaborations are fruitful. They build and strengthen unity among leaders and their Christians. However, sometimes-ecumenical gatherings cause pastors to get into competition for members. This hence, can bring some conflicts between leaders of the denominations and sometimes between their members. There was the following illustration: *We fish each other's people, collision on our emphases of Christian doctrines and other problems.*[44] Competition for the same Christian members leads them to fish from the basket.

Competition for members can lead some preachers, teachers to be tempted to abuse the preaching and teaching of the gospel done by others. The informants (especially pastors and evangelists) appreciate while complaining that Christian religious preachers introduce and perform public meetings and ecumenical gatherings as they can. On the one hand, they

43. Informant B.
44. Informant B.

build their faith. On the other hand, the collaboration also causes some Christians to move into other denominations. Moreover, there are some rumors from informants that some preachers condemn other faiths or religious communities.

Renewal Movements

The fourth effect of social change is on the birth and multiplication of renewal movements,[45] public meetings, and other Christian gatherings. The group is very mobile. Once they commence their gatherings for their preaching and teaching of the gospel, most people leave their churches to the designated village. Since its arrival in the area where I took the sample for survey, it is growing fast. Many Christians join it for their spiritual growth. Aneth Nyagawa Munga dates the beginning of renewal movement in East African countries as far back as to the late 1920's and early 1930's. The same, 'revival movement,' to use the words of Munga, is not young in Tanzania.[46] As well, Fihavango confirms: "Charismatic groups are common in the Protestant Churches, and only some Christians from the Roman Catholic Church participate in charismatic groups."[47]

During interviews with pastors and lay Christians who were leaders or participants in renewal movements, in public meetings and in other related gatherings, they described that the primary goal of renewal movement is to preach the Gospel of Jesus Christ to all people that they are saved in His name. Second, besides the gatherings of renewal movement, the group aims also at helping people share and strengthens their spiritual life and experiences. On the one hand: *There is a rapid growth of 'Christian religious groups for preaching the Gospel within the same denomination.'* For example, there are *New Life Crusade* and *UWATA-Uamsho Wa Kikristo Tanzania (Christian Revival in Tanzania) and so forth.*[48].

On the other hand, as I stated above, since they belong to varied denominations, sometimes during those gatherings and worship services, their religious preachers are competing for members. I noted from some informants that despite the advantages of preachers in the renewal movements, other preachers attempt to get some popularity and empires for

---

45. In this book, the expressions 'Renewal,' 'Revival,' and 'Charismatic' (in Kiswahili *Uamsho*) are used interchangeably.

46. Munga, *Uamsho*, 69–71. For further details, see the whole work of Aneth Nyagawa Munga.

47. Fihavango, *Jesus and Leadership*, 98.

48. Informant B.

dominion. For example, I came across the complaints that famous and influential preachers within renewal movements want to monopolize the members whom they serve. They started strongly to preach around the parish hence capturing and taking over the office of the Church. This is one of the evidences from the interview:

> *As a result, it is happening that Christians and society are becoming captured and monopolized by those who are not specifically called and sent into Church ministry. Congregants have become slaves of those who are not to be their ministers. The intended ministers are outside, uplifting their life standard and economic situation. For example, many of the renewal movements have taken over the church, and become the main teachers and servants of the Church.*[49]

The above evidence from the informant above shows us how the spiritual groups and other lay Christians in the Church can be more influential and overpower or take over the role of a pastor. This is evident especially to pastors who forget their congregants or are busier with their individual life struggles than of their role of spiritual care.

Once more, other informants complain about some members of renewal movements who pretend to be good preachers and teachers of Biblical scriptures. Those people claim that they do not belong to one Christian denomination, but to all. So, they declare to have a neutral affiliation of faith to all denominations. One could notice this mostly in those who were good participants and leaders in renewal movements. Most of those members of renewal movements do mix the Church traditions hence endangering the identity of the mainline Lutheran denomination. *"Moreover, there are examples the New Life Crusade and Christian Revivalism in Tanzania and so forth. These groups belong to all denominations. Questions: how is this pastor handling these people while preserving the traditions of their denominations?"*[50] The pastor stated that although the issue was not to have a negative attitude toward renewal movements, yet, there were two problems: the first was on how to lead those Christians, and the second related to the tension regarding the ambiguity in preserving the Church identity. Pastors complained of the difficulty to lead those Christians by using the Lutheran constitution. Some Christians have been asking for freedom from strict rules of the Lutheran denomination. They feel comfortable to free expression of their Christian faith.

49. Informant A.
50. Informant B.

Some advantages that renewal movements provide to members and for the church is the spiritual health. Despite those advantages, sometimes groups show to identify themselves in separate categories within the Lutheran denomination. Two pastors witnessed that they were experiencing this problem in their parishes. It happens that, within the respective denomination some parishioners register and remain strict into any of the three kinds of groups: *A pastor undertakes his or her roles in the midst of three divided groups: a conservative group, a liberal group, and a revival movement.*[51] This informant complained that those groups bring pressures upon most parish ministers on their doctrines. Each group has a tendency of influencing the pastor to perform his or her tasks while recognizing its presence and the contribution it makes to the church. Each group attracts the pastor to bend and favor it. Sometimes those groups attempt to create classes of people's spirituality in the church and in society. Munga confirms that pastors have been encountering those tensions since its beginning. She reports that apart from many advantages of renewal movements, "The beginning of the *Uamsho* movement was a time of tension between the congregation pastors and *wanauamsho*. . . . Antagonism was also expressed within the movement, mainly due to doctrinal differences."[52]

It is also surprising that antagonism prevails, even within the revival movement itself. Sometimes antagonisms emerge because of human natural differences. The difference in needs, demands, and interests may put the group members into antagonism. Each participant has his or her own wills and wishes that he or she expects to meet. Once they are not met, this member will obviously not be comfortable. In general, we can learn that there are variations in spirituality and doctrinal emphases. However, renewal movements have both positive and negative effects in society as well as to the role of the pastor. For example, the group engages very much in preaching for people to join Christianity. It is strongly committed to doing mission and evangelism. Another emphasis is on purity in life. On the other hand, some members are somehow living with no clear denominational identity. This is especially to those who emphasize that what matters is being in Christ, other issues are minor. It may be very difficult to identify a person with no clear faith affiliation.

The second problem is on full autonomy. This study has discovered that in some congregations, followers do not listen to their leaders. Unfortunately, there are stories that some of them have even separated or divorced their marriages. They neglect their families because of doctrinal emphases

---

51. Informant A, cf. informant B.
52. Ibid., Munga, *Uamsho*, 71.

or because they are too busy in the programs to the extent that they do not have time to think for their homes and other socio-cultural and economic activities. Nevertheless, it is important to ask this question: why and how do these groups emerge in the Churches as well as in society as a whole? Why and how does this group survive and perform its programs amid pastoral roles while there are potential theologians and leaders both, in the Church and in the communities in which they live and serve?

Fihavango seems to have some insights to start with in responding to those questions. He states that,

> These groups emerge at a time when the values of society seem inadequate for addressing social issues and the Church seems to be too lax and lacking spiritual dynamic activities. They are groups formed within established institutions. Niwagila refers to them as *ecclesiola in ecclesia*, because they do not start as separate movements outside the Church. They start as revival groups which have experienced spiritual renewal. The renewal enables the individual members to change their behavior. These individuals distinguish themselves from the rest of the Church members (non-charismatic Christians) by their ideology and ritual behavior.[53]

Fihavango describes the emergence of these groups and their survival. Furthermore, he shows the moral stands and the psychological tasks of influencing other people to change their behaviors. In that sense, for Fihavango, these groups belong to the same mega and mainline Churches.

Thereafter, Fihavango goes on to pointing the reasons and rationales of the survival of the charismatic groups in the Church. He argues: "The group is held together by a strong belief system and a high level of social and emotional cohesiveness, and, the members are deeply influenced by the group's behavioral norms."[54] On the one hand, these groups impress pastors and some other leaders in society. They welcome and use them as tools to enhance the ministry and spread the gospel outside Church circles. The moral stance of those members encourages other people to view them as good and helpful in both religious and ordinary life of the communities. However, to some leaders and other people, charismatic groups are a threat. They would not even want to hear about them. There are varied reasons for this denial to appreciate and make them useful in their life and ministry.

Furthermore, Fihavango highlights some background experiences of the charismatic group members. He pinpoints that "one finds that most

53. Fihavango, *Jesus and Leadership*, 98.
54. Ibid.

of them, not all, come from some oppressive condition. Some have had trouble in their marriages. Some had chronic diseases, and others especially women, are feeling the threat of HIV/AIDS because of the behavior of their husbands."[55] In this kind of experience, for me, charismatic group becomes a refuge for them in all dimensions of life, that is, their spiritually, physically, and mental healing and growth. The charismatic groups aim at protecting their life on earth as well as being faithful to their creator, savior, and sustainer of their lives.

Additionally, Fihavango, illustrates and locates the group into the larger social system. Too, he mentions some positive and negative characteristics of individual members in the renewal movements as they relate to other people and their Churches. He states,

> The charismatic group operates as a close social system to assure its stability. The members of the group consider themselves as family members, brothers and sister [sic!] and parents. Some have rejected their non-charismatic parents and relatives and adopted spiritual parents. They refer to the Bible . . . The group is socially active, helping each other in times of need, but most of the time in the boundaries of the in-group. . . . The group members possess a high capacity to define themselves, and make their presence felt in social life. . . . women are attracted to the movement and then draw their husbands and children with them. . . . this happens because by their biological and psychological nature women are more open and friendly than men.[56]

From the above quotation, one can realize the merits and demerits that the group has. On the one hand, it is fortunate that; it has strong ties amongst its members; members recognize their spiritual belong; members can help each other in times of cries and joys; the group is socially identifiable; besides, members especially women have the capacity to convince other people to join their group. On the other hand, the group contains some unnecessary biasness and segregations. The group puts unpleasant and unbiblical boundaries. This is especially when members reject others who do not belong to their group; when they deny their birth and parental origin; when they do not show humbleness. I personally recommend appreciating whatever good in those groups and discouraging all show-offs from members or the group itself. Such kind of behavior is unchristian neither should it be encouraged in life, nor should will leave them teaching other people.

55. Ibid.
56. Ibid., 98–99.

As well, in most cases, such boundaries destroy the aims and goals of being charismatic in Christian perspectives.

Finally, just as the interviewees testified above, Fihavango supports also that there are times some members of the charismatic movement attempt to monopolize the group. This is especially for leaders.

> The group leader accumulates the whole authority, decides for the members, sometimes he/she threatens that what he/she decides is the only will of God. . . . Normally, the charismatic group leaders are lay Christians who sometimes work closely with the clergy or work against it [Sic]. It depends on the Ideology of the charismatic group and the attitude toward the institutional Church and its leadership, or on the relationship of the clergy to the charismatic movements.[57]

The tendency of attempting to accumulate authority is perceived as one of the motives for them to join the groups. It is in the categories of power monger. If a person missed some leadership positions in the ordinary series, he or she may attempt to try to fulfill or restore the lost ambitions in the mother Church or substation, and or in the secular community. That is why, since they have no legal registration as separate institutions, they have to honor their mother Churches. The kind of relationships established and enhanced between leaders from both sides might not end-up conflicts because of varying missions and visions, programs, leadership qualities, doctrinal understanding and emphases, liturgical practices, as well as the external social and political influences into each Church and between the clergies with the prescribed rules and principles in which they ought to abide to. In my view, the exclusion of leaders of charismatic groups in the official structure of the Church increases conflicts between them and the leaders of the mother churches.[58]

Confusion over the True Way to Salvation

Religious pluralism is another problem that happened to bring some confusions and dilemma to society on the true way to salvation. Informants stated that Christians are getting confused with the bulks of varied religious doctrines. In the interview with the lay Christians in my focus group, they verified thus: "*We are in a time of globalization and confusion because each person has a freedom of moving into religious affiliation and proclaiming his*

57. Ibid., 99.
58. Cf., Fihavango, *Jesus and Leadership*, 99–100.

*or her faith."*⁵⁹ Since each religious preacher convinces people to join their religions or denominations, both Christian communities and society become confused as to which religion or denomination is directing them to the true salvation. As a result, this pluralistic preaching and teaching of faith leaves parishioners into dilemma.

Moreover, this behavior makes people think that even their own denomination does not hold all truth to salvation and to God. The same confusion exists as society thinks about the true denomination that can help it attain the true salvation. This also affects the preaching and teaching role of a pastor. Confusing preaching and teaching resulting from religious pluralism and freedom of proclamation cause pastors to have constant deranged programs for Sunday school teachings and evangelism to close down the problem. For example, if the pastor had planned to preach, then in a few days he or she must prepare a teaching against what other denominations are inducing into people.

Faith Wanderers, Increase of Neutrality,⁶⁰ and Syncretism⁶¹

Given the social integration and the multiplicity of religious perspectives and practices, some Christians are wandering from one faith to another. Those people affiliate to more than one faith. For example, such Christians are good participants in both the Christian faith and ATR or in Islam traditions. One informant noticed:

> *There is also strong prevalence of syncretism. The interaction of religious life makes people mix their faith traditions without being selective. There are people who worship in all religions or denominations. Some members in the Christian group called New Life in Christ (a renewal movement) have this kind of faith practice. Some know what they are practicing while others do not. This dilemma is a result of people's search for spiritual health and peace in heart from many problems they get; although to others it is due to their conversion into Christianity. Society is in a freedom of worship and religious affiliation. This freedom is growing rapidly*

---

59. Informant F.

60. I use the term 'neutrality' to mean a person's unclear affiliation, the state of not taking sides, especially in religious life.

61. In this book, I use the term 'syncretism' to mean the combination of different systems of religious belief and practice.

> than in the previous years when society was not in great multicultural like of today.[62]

The quotation above testifies that people belong to more than one religion or denomination. For this informant, the mushrooming of denominations with their varied doctrinal emphases is among the major sources of making people become faith wanderers. Furthermore, doctrinal variations create the increase of neutrality and prevalence of syncretism among Christians and other members of non-Christian religions.[63] As we noticed in the discussion about religious pluralism, each denomination is convincing people to join into it. Another pastor remarked: "*They cause Christians to move into theirs or become faith wanderers.*"[64] As a result, pastors argued that in such a situation, it is very difficult for them to lead such Christians who are faith wanderers and have neutral faith and affiliation. It would not be easy for the pastor to meet them.

Why do People Move from one Religious Community to another?

In the quotations above (see footnote 6),[65] it seems that there are varied reasons why some people might affiliate with more than one faith or religious community. The interviewees suggested some of other reasons as follows: first, it may be due to lack of theological knowledge. For this informant, sometimes people think that every religion or denomination resembles one another, and has the same faith doctrines. Second, there are people who comply with almost all faith communities in search of spiritual health. The third reason seems to be a search for alternative solutions to their problems.

The fourth reason is on their exercise of religious freedom. Fifth, according to informant C above, there was a difference in convincing power. The preacher or educator who had strong influence could attract more people to follow his or her religion or denomination.

We have seen that religious pluralism is one of the most affective social changes regarding the pastor's role. Religious pluralism seems problematic to the contemporary religious leaders and teachers in society. People's freedom of worship and speech enhances the problem. As a result, pastors as religious leaders and teachers in this era encounter numerous problems that bring pressures upon them. The diversities of religious teachings sometimes

---

62. Informant A.
63. Munga, *Uamsho*, 85.
64. Informant C.
65. Quotations from informants A and C.

bring conflicts between denominations, reduced Church members, and sometime they cause confusions and dilemmas to people. Due to confusions, some Christians affiliate with many denominations. We may ask ourselves, how can one lead and manage such society? Certainly, all people around the world have the freedom to exercise their religiosity. It is very unfortunate that, the freedom seems to have given people an opportunity to establish denominations; furthermore, the impacts are pressing the leaders and their fellow religious communities to live and work according to interests of society.[66]

The issue of religious and denominations pluralism is one of the things that Charles Taylor discussed in his reflection on the spheres of the contemporary society. For Taylor, this pluralism can be traced as far back as to the nineteenth century. He writes:

> The early nineteenth century was the age of the second Great Awakening, the spread of revival through itinerary preachers all over the public, to the most remote frontier. The new religious fervor, most often outside the old establishments, in the rapidly growing denominations of Methodists and Baptists, was itself a reflection of the ideal of independence. Individuals broke away from ancestral churches and sought their own forms among the rapidly multiplying denominational options. At the same time, they sought the strength to live this new independence, to beat back the demons of fear and despair . . . This is a pattern that has become familiar today, in the rapid spread of evangelical Protestantism in many parts of the globe: Latin America, Africa, Asia . . .[67]

In his quotation above, Taylor argues that religious pluralism is a result of people's practice of independence. People practice a freedom of expression and of options. Carroll agrees with Taylor and states that the pastor is now living and performing in an age whereby "consumerism and a culture of choices" characterizes society. He states deliberately that:

> Consumerism encourages people to view religion as a commodity like any other, from which they can pick and choose those elements that best suits their sense of self or identity. . . . the available options from which consumers may choose in almost every area of life have increased exponentially over the past half-century. Educational and occupational choices have exploded. . . . Each

---

66. Knitter, *No Other Name?* 1–22.
67. Ibid., Taylor, 149–150.

generation is freer to make its own choices regarding cultural and religious practices from the options they encounter.[68]

Both Taylor and Carroll emphasize that religious leaders need to know that people are practicing their freedom of belief, of expression and of preaching and teaching their faith. For those scholars, the contemporary society has its own freedom to make some choices that suit its needs and interests. However, in the process of making choices and suiting its needs, it affects the roles of pastors.

THE PASTOR AS WORSHIP LEADER

As I stated in chapter three and in the introduction of this chapter, worship is one of the primary tasks of a pastor. In performing this responsibility, the pastor uses a liturgy. How did society respond to the way worship services were? In this section, I discuss the way the community perceives and responds toward the use of time (time management), liturgy and the time spent by a pastor when delivering a sermon.

Informants stated that church members complained that the church did not use time well especially regarding worship services. The church has a conservative and long liturgy. As a result, worship services seem to be too long for most people to stay to the end. When I probed all informants to give their detailed descriptions on how and why the worship services were too long; they responded that the church had a common and well-written liturgy in the hymn and liturgy book called *Mwimbieni Bwana*.[69] This liturgy is not used faithfully in worship services. The present liturgy provides some basic processions of worship services according to the types of services. All informants agree that, normally, one Sunday service has to take at least two hours. Out of those two hours, at least fifteen to forty minutes are for the sermons. During my interview, Informants could tell that society claims for a liberal liturgy and worship services.

However, most of the time, church ministers go beyond two hours in one worship service. To some leaders on duty to administer the worship services, this was not a big problem. Most informants argued that, to some people it is a very long time, while to other people it is not so. Some informants stated that on several times society has been requesting all preachers and teachers to make short sermons, not to exceed two hours. Long services become boring. Then I probed on with the question "what farther actions do congregants

---

68. Carroll, *God's Potters*, 48–49.
69. KKKT, *Mwimbieni Bwana*, 267–530.

express if services happen to be long?" The informants responded that people who could not tolerate to stay in the church decided to leave the worship service. Such people usually ask those whom they sat next to give their offerings and donations while they have gone for their personal programs.

All the same, some church members confronted church elders about such long worship services and sermons. Church elders take people's claims to evangelists or pastors for further discussion and resolutions. Conversely, during the time of research, I came across lamentations from some Christians who explained that most of the time their evangelists and pastors have been rigid to adjust or reform the liturgy. Rather, they are just stressing that it is hardly possible for a pastor or evangelist to adjust the Church's liturgy. Pastors and evangelists condemn on the cry of congregants to spend fewer hours in the church than in other personal activities. Pastors and their evangelists also complain that, after all, their Christians can spend longer time in the pubs and recreation centers than with their creator. Therefore, those church ministers decide to remain faithful to the liturgy as they per their training and ordination. Consequently, even so, the church elders have been suggesting that one of the alternatives to minimize the problem is to buy a big watch and fix it on the church walls so that leaders of worship services can control their services at least not to exceed those two hours. This would help leaders to keep time in liturgy and during delivering sermons, and to minimize some complaints from congregants.

In my parish ministry and interview sessions, the cry for short liturgies and sermons was also expressed during wedding administration and burial ceremonies. People could express their feelings, murmur or shout out against ministers if preaching and liturgical processions were long. Most of the time, especially during wedding and funeral ceremonies; we witness society complaining about poor time management from Church ministers. Moreover, society claims that it wants to go fast so that it can go for personal and communal socio-economic programs. Among such activities are to open their business shops, going to their office works, travelling, and leisure issues. Society desires, enquires, and pushes for some changes in church ministers about time and flexible liturgy.

The situation implies that when society is constantly changing its understanding on time management, the church, some pastors and other ministers remain faithful to the prescribed time in the constitution or to their own plans only. When I asked pastors about this problem of time management during worship and sermon delivery, I got two varied responses. Some pastors and evangelists acknowledge that long liturgies and sermons are not comforting even themselves. Normally, they try to adjust the time for sermons and advertisements while abiding to the prescribed church procedures. In addition to that response, pastors said that, there are times when they skip some of the sections of the liturgy so that congregants may not get tired with worship services. For example, the shortening is present especially if there are baptismal and confirmation ceremonies.

In contrast, pastors argue that some people are tired staying only two hours in worship services, but God had given them more than two hours to do their personal activities. Now it was for them (society) to use at least those two hours to adore their savior for all that He had done for them in the whole week. It appears that it was very difficult to alter or postpone what in the plan. May be it could be possible to make some adjustments during preparation before the respective day. However, others argued that sometimes certain service alterations could work prior to the start of worship services or during sermon delivery.

As discussed above, within the same issue of worship services, informants stated that including themselves, there are several Christians who cry for flexible and liberal liturgies to give room for public prayers. Informants noted that according to the ELCT worship liturgy, there are no specified areas allowing all people to perform loud prayers during Lutheran worship services.

The issue of liberal liturgy is subject to discussion in the whole diocese by all pastors during their meetings. Generally, there are varied opinions on regarding Lutheran tradition. During my research period, I happened to attend a pastors' diocesan meeting[70] where we also discussed about liturgy. Some pastors observed that the current liturgy of the ELCT that pastors and other church ministers use does not provide any room for people to come in front and confess their sins after sermon delivery. As a result, other pastors argued that the liturgy is too conservative and rigid. Some pastors and other ministers, caused by that conservatism and rigidity, suggest that it is high time for some sections to be included in the worship liturgy, especially the sections that would allow a freedom of spiritual expressions and people's conversion soon after sermon delivery.

Other pastors have had different opinions. This second group argues that such changes would not distinguish the ELCT from other denominations, especially the Pentecostal Churches that have a tradition of public and loud prayers in any worship service. As the discussion continued, I discovered that other pastors are against conservative styles of the liturgy and sermon service. The first group favors the accommodation of the contemporary people's spiritual expressions during common worship gatherings, while other pastors want to preserve the identity of the ELCT. This variation

---

70. Cf., Informant I.

of ideas and feelings bring some misunderstandings between church ministers themselves, and hence between them and society.

In that long discussion about the inclusion or exclusion of spiritual expressions in the present liturgy, I came to realize that the issue had its importance, especially in the time of rapid social change. The contemporary society seems to claim the need for brief but attractive worship services and sermons that respond to problems of the people in that particular society. The discussion revealed to me the pastors' personal and spiritual interests and needs. Additionally, the discussion demonstrated to me on how society was in need of the pastors' understanding and realization of time, of the doctrine of liturgy, and of the whole theology of worship. In addition, the pastors' differing understanding and realization of society's claims, interests and needs illustrates the complexity of the context in which the pastor and society live while serving each other.

In general, the contemporary society is crying for a change in worship services (from the traditional to a postmodern one) in terms of the forms of spiritual expressions, and in the methods and approaches of sermon delivering. In spite of the antagonisms among church ministers, the pastors' meeting as well as from all informants, acknowledge that change is inevitable in any aspect of life. Some of the reasons that informants gave was that society, Church and the pastor are living and working in new times. That is, if society has been transforming, so also the church ought to be transforming into another faces. Certainly, that is why both, the pastors complain about the pressure from society, and in turn, society complains over strict and rigid: roles, guidelines, doctrinal contradictions, liturgical expressions, and methods of delivery. Due to the liturgical and methodological discrepancies, society is confused; hence, it attempts to put its stand and pressurize ministers to abide to it. This may term it to be immoral. That is why another role that a pastor plays is to be a moral leader for both for all ethical issues in the church.

THE PASTOR AS MORAL LEADER

It is clear that pastors work as moral leaders. My leading questions in this level are: What are the critical issues that come up as pastors perform this role? How are such issues bringing effects upon the role of a pastor and upon the life of the church? In responding to these questions, pastors and some other informants pointed out at least three critical issues in relation to social change. Those are the following: intermarriages, moral crisis, and secular influences. Therefore, in this section, I discuss such issues to see their scope and how they affect the role of the pastor as a moral leader and how they affect the life of the church.

Intermarriages and their Ambivalences

The persistence and growth of intermarriages in Tanzania and Africa, alongside demographic change and religious population prove the features of social change. The informants added this aspect of marriage and family structural change to be one of the features of social change. It means that as the population growth increased in most parishes, also the intercultural, cross-cultural and interfaith marriages were increasing. One pastor from my focus group who had greater experience with intermarriage issues commented on the moral dilemma of intermarriages: *Contemporary pastors are facing a big dilemma due to inter-religious, inter-tribal, intercultural, and cross-cultural marriages. The present society exercises freedom of choices and actions. During our time it was hardly possible for one to marry to or from other cultures or religions. The situation has completely changed because of people's interests, integration and close interactions.*[71] According to the above experience, pastors have been facing some moral problems related to intermarriages. Although marriage practices are old, most intermarriage practices appear to be of recent times. The great freedom of the society's integration, interaction and flexible religious emphasis on marriage give rooms for people to select partners to marry to or marry to whoever and wherever persons feel interested. That pastor described that in the past whoever wanted to marry usually had to find a partner within the same religion, and tribe, with similar cultural backgrounds. The informant above acknowledged that situations have changed compared to the past times. Other informants support the above descriptions:

> There is an issue of the mixture of marriages whereby limits of where and whom one can get married to is extremely free. In previous times, parents and faith communities could have enough room to give some advice, but now it is the partners who are decisive others remain as listeners who come at the last stage for other assistances and marriage administration. Then, it becomes a difficult work for a pastor to give some advice and counseling sessions to such marriages or those in the process to wed. Therefore, there is much prevalence of many interfaith and cross-cultural marriages.[72]

---

71. Informant D.
72. Informant B.

Apart from bringing effects upon family structures informants stated that intermarriage patterns also bring both positive and negative effects. On the one hand, those new features of society give wide opportunities and choices for one who would want to marry. Some pastors and informants admitted that it is now easy to teach or give some advice that one can get a spouse even outside his or her cultural boundaries. On the other hand, others hold that it is problematic if the choice goes outside one's own religion, denomination, or cultural background. But what effects do such marriages bring on the role of the pastor?

First, as moral leaders, pastors and other co-workers experience a lack of control. During the research, lay Christian informants complained about the recent changes in marriage processes and administration. They said:

> *The type of intermarriages existing today cause problems and challenges to church ministers. The problem starts during the time of early counseling processes. This is especially when partners are from different denominations or religions and tribes. Each one comes with his and her traditional backgrounds that they need to receive honor. Therefore, there are difficulties on how to administer and to handle such marriage sessions and their worship services. For example, two pastors have had been having a joint administration of worship services in one of the churches. This is mostly done if a Roman Catholic (RC) member marries to another Christian denomination.*[73]

The citation above describes the problem relating to early counseling for marriage decisions. It is hardly possible to undertake early counseling for marriages because to date partners make own decisions for their marriages. Church ministers get information very late. Another problem that lessens the leaders' control and decisions over marriages is the administration of worship services and the liturgy used in those marriages. This problem exists if the partners belong to different religions or denominational or cross-cultural backgrounds (for example, if one is an African and the other is European). In these kinds of marriages, some cultural differences are not easy to counsel. More descriptions that are similar come from another pastor:

> *Other changes are due to increase of marriages. There are so many wedding ceremonies today. The kinds of marriages we experience in our parishes are the intercultural and interfaith. There is much freedom for one to marry to wherever he or she feels. There are no longer boundaries of tribes, religion, denomination or race. . . . For intermarriages, the challenge is 'what kind of counseling can*

---

73. Informant E.

help in intermarriages? What wedding liturgies should pastors use to accommodate all religious or traditional backgrounds of the partners who want to wed in the church or society?[74]

Most descriptions above admit that although there is a growth of both organized and non-organized marriages (cf. informant I above), however, the latter seems to grow faster than the former. Partners arrange their marriage process and later can share it with their parents and the church for further actions if need be. If parents, relatives, other church leaders, and or pastors seem to have different opinions and thus would want to change; the partner are more decisive. They can agree or disagree. Sometimes partners decide to live with unofficial marriage.

As stated above, people's migration influences the unofficial marriage life. Many people have cohabitation marriages. According to the informants, this is due to the sharing of values and customs, freedom in the selection of marriage partners and the sharing of religious practices and experiences. Pastors and evangelists hold that society has entered into a time of great family, religious and cultural complexities and ambiguity. Too, pastors as moral leaders encounter those marriage complexities and ambiguity. Today it has become very difficult to control the marriages due to their natures and processes they use to enter into it.

The second effect resulting from intermarriages is the break with traditions. Most of those who want to get married do not follow the traditional marriage culture of their parents, nor do they start with their religious marriage procedures. Therefore, partners start by creating their own ways of life. This pastor remarked: *We have interfaith and cross-cultural marriages where Africans marry to Europeans, other people wed into the government's court and thereafter they come to confess.*[75] This kind of a marriage procedure does not reflect an African way of marriage and family life that existed before. However, informants recalled that, despite all those ambivalences and some changing processes and practices in Tanzania and in African context marriages remain a society's property. This is because at last parents and other social institutions will be informed and have to get an opportunity to bless it in any way. For example, parents sit together and talk to their married children or through receiving at least a small dowry.

On this second effect, J. N. K. Mugambi laments that social change has broken down the traditional norms for marriage, rites of passages and human sexuality in Africa today. Mugambi states that transformations disturb

---

74. Informant I.
75. Informant C.

the norms, breaks down the social cohesion and cultural identities hence causing everything become difficult to sustain. He writes:

> When society is in flux, the dominant norms are undermined, and social cohesion breaks down. Cultural identity then becomes difficult to sustain, and society rapidly deteriorates into behavioral anarchy. . . . When a society undergoes rapid transformation owing to various factors –political, economic or technological, these norms are disturbed, and cultural education becomes difficult to sustain. . . . The norms that used to regulate human sexuality have largely broken down, without effective alternative norms to promote responsible behavior.[76]

The third effect of intermarriage relates to human sexuality. Both the informants and Mugambi agree that there is a change in sexual morality. Informants confirmed while claiming that in the contemporary society, there is many people engaging in sexual activities outside wedlock (that is in prostitution and adultery). They do not start with the church, rather cohabitation comes first and then they come to churches to confess and then register their marriages for pastoral blessing. The practice signifies that it is likely to become a custom to the extent that the church is becoming the last to perform its wedding administration. It means that to date there is a high rate and rapid growth of pre-marital life in our society.

The fourth problem related to changes in social customs. The change in social customs is in new forms of intimacy discipline between children and their in-laws. Both pastors and non-theologian informants agree that they get surprised by the way society is no longer behaving in the way it is expected. For example, as I stated above, there was a change on how they greet each other. According to their observations, at that time there was a small distance from the in-laws. Parents and their children were now closely interacting. People from varied cultural backgrounds lived in the same villages or streets and even in the same apartments. However, why is this growing larger than reducing?

One of the results of this research is that people are behaving in a different way than it used to be during the mono-cultural life. In mono-cultural life, there was strong sharing of respective ethnic backgrounds, knowledge and other experiences. Today people share almost all cultures and customs surrounding them. People are under influence of cultures and values; and thus, they continue sharing almost all values and customs that come before them. They enhance while transforming other values and customs. This is a socio-cultural change of a society.

76. Mugambi, "Rites of Passages and Human Sexuality," 228–229.

On marriage and its ambivalences, most pastors and evangelists from my focus group gave me a similar example on effects and ambivalences of intermarriage and its complexities. For example one informant said:

> *In this generation we cannot avoid intermarriages. Christians report to church ministers that they feel free to get married to whoever enters into their feelings. It is innumerable and rapidly becoming a great practice that parishioners (especially the youth) tell that they have partners from outside Lutheran denomination, from Islam or from African Traditional Religions. In most of the denominations and or religions, there are varied and different traditions and customs. After getting married, if problems arise, each spouse would want to be helped with counseling services according to one's faith, customs, and or own traditional backgrounds. In such a situation, if it were you, how could you do? Similar problems are prevalent in the raising of their children. People raise and orient children with unclearly defined faith, culture, or specific customs.*[77]

The above quotation shows how difficult it is to avoid and prohibit intermarriages. Christians claim for complete freedom when they want to enter in marriages. It implies that marriage is becoming more of a private decision than of the community. The youth want to have complete decision before other social agents are involved. This now becomes difficult for church ministers to control people when it comes to wedding processes and ceremonies. The same problem emerges during raising their children. Children are likely to have no single direction of nurture because they belong to intercultural marriages. It is even of more difficult to help the couples with moral care and counseling.

The fifth change is due to differences in marriage teachings, especially, on varied emphasis regarding polygamy. During this study, I came across some explanation about the impact of religious pluralism toward the teaching and practices of the Christian marriage. Some pastors argue that in the same Christian denominations, there exists a different marriage teaching which favors polygamy. This informant expresses one of the differences that exist: I*n my parish some of my neighbors have started accepting women who are married as 'second wives' to work as any other woman who is in her marriage. They (denominations) teach that, they (second wives) have to continue praying while asking the Holy Spirit to tell them to leave those marriages or not. The voice of the Holy Spirit will be the last answer; otherwise, they have to remain into their marriage.*[78] This appears to be very attractive to most

---

77. Informant E.

78. Informant A. By 'second wives' I refer to those married after the first wife, while

of the second wives and to polygamous husbands. This pastor was on the opinion that if the marriage teachings will have an emphasis in the way those Christian denominations were doing, then, many people might run into that loose and attractive emphasis. On this teaching, this informant commented that in future there might emerge another church, that is, a denomination comprising of those who are polygamous. However, he concludes by admitting that, still, it was very difficult for him to view the future image of the Church due to the varied teachings about the Holy Spirit and the varying practices of marriage within the Christian denominations. To wait until the Holy Spirit decides, makes one remain in the same state of marriage without learning the reasons for him or her to be in that marriage and hence find the last and better Christian life alternative.

As I wanted to know, how this would affect the church, he stated that the expression of the Church keeps changing as its members change in attitudes, in views and practices about marriage and Christianity, in social structures, in their needs, interests and hence in spirituality. At last he concluded that he himself and other people, especially Christians from his parish, experienced a dilemma as to which type of the Bible and texts were those fellow Christian denominations using when teaching about marriage. In my view, society through some Christian religious communities brings another marriage doctrine that accommodates polygamy. Therefore, we have to acknowledge that *Pastors encounter difficulties in performing marriage counseling, administration and reconciliation when couples get problems. In addition, there are new types of marriages.*[79] Hence, the informants concluded here that pastors encounter great problems due to intermarriage ambivalences when they try to control some moral issues in the church as well as in society in which they live and work.

Again, Knight in his same book *Ecology and Change* describes that intermarriages have been highly practiced in Tanzania since the operation of *Ujamaa* Villagization in 1974. Knight combines migration and intercultural marriage patterns. He accepts that this is one of the sources of the society's change. Society can change its shape of natural balance through this aspect of life. To him, the society's migration and intercultural marriage patterns have either positive or negative effects on personal and social ways of living and working. Migration and intercultural marriage bring considerable knowledge in life where the spouses share both positive and negative experiences from each other.[80]

---

the first is still alive.

79. Informant D.
80. Knight, *Ecology and Change*, 170–171.

the social and cultural context in which pastors work 123

Drønen highlights that due to social change the youth are seeking social and spiritual reorientation to escape from other traditional and dominating religious family teachings. In addition, the youth want to escape from several forms of paternal control on marriage. They do not want to survive under their parents' traditional marriage formulas and viewpoints. Then, Dørenen adds the social transformations have been evident for many years from the family level. He states that in some African societies, "for many families the old family-structure was in transition."[81] Social integration, interaction and religious influences cause this transition. Due to those social characteristics, there is also " . . . images of social mobility."[82] Dørenen finds that " . . . social change . . . moves society toward new plausibility structures."[83] Therefore, social mobility and intermarriages transform traditional marriage and family patterns, structures, practices and moral behavior that relate to marriage in society at large.[84]

Together with the mission to preserve their traditional life, the youth have been among first members of society to alter their life into new styles. This is rampant to date. For example, the youth are adopting and practicing many styles of life and music. They learn from their neighbors. Tribes with their cultures have been mixing with and influencing their African beliefs and morality into the church. The church has been encountering streams of cultures that can enrich or transform it, This remains a challenge to pastors as they undertake their pastoral roles.

Kijanga argues that, however, "in spite of all cultural adaptations and diversification, the Christian church remains the same and one body of Christ."[85] For him, adaptation is a model set by the Lord of the Christian church through His Incarnation. With this, he emphasizes that Christianity through pastors and other ministers has to become incarnate in each culture. Incarnate in the sense that it should observe contexts, people's ways of life, needs, time and embarking into new methods of doing theology when undertaking mission and evangelism in the contemporary society without distorting its message. Which new method and how can it be useful in doing such theology today? Why is this important in the time of rapid social change? The first question remains un-addressed at this level.

For Kijanga, cultures are very dynamic in Tanzanian and in the world at large. Cultural dynamism has "shaped and even changed the outlook of

81. Drønen, "Communication, Conversion and Conservation," 119–120.
82. Ibid., 121.
83. Ibid., 115–116.
84. Ibid., 192.
85. Kijanga, *Ujamaa and the Role of Church*, 86.

the church as an institution."[86] He suggests that pastors' approach and attempts into "understanding the fact of change and adaptability may help the Christian church in Tanzania to create suitable atmosphere in the church for a sound cultural integration."[87] The consciousness of both, the pastors and the church about people's culture and their dynamics that are now changing as the society changes help find suitable responses to problems facing society in a particular context and time.[88] Culture contact and spread of ideas make one change his or her dimensions of life.[89] This then depends on how strong the two will be.

Moral Crisis in the Society

Morality relates to decent conducts. Therefore, in this book I use the term 'morality' to mean the ways of behaving and interacting expected by society. Others may simply call it an ethical trait. Informants note that the postmodern society seems to have entered into moral failures. Some pastors are complaining that at times it is becoming very difficult to teach Christian ethics and give pastoral counseling to this society. Pastors, evangelists and other co-workers state that the moral behavior of the Tanzanian society is complicated. One pastor confirmed:

> There are values or moral changes whereby society has adopted and adapting in; either from Western culture or it has created own moralities in order for it to sustain in this age. Society is constantly changing its morality. Social morality challenges Christian moralities. Society is influencing pastors to change the doctrine of our "Christian ethics" and form another "social ethics." They ask this question when we teach Christian ethics in the Church and in schools.[90]

The quotation shows that the church expects that people will behave according to the moral guidelines analyzed by the church and secular authorities of society. Nevertheless, it is surprising to see that society seems to change the moral behaviors. As a result, the contemporary society is behaving different from the teaching and expectation of the church. This problem is especially the case with most youth Christians. They appear not to abide

---

86. Ibid., 87.
87. Ibid.
88. Ibid., 86.
89. Knight, *Ecological Change*, 170–171.
90. Informant C.

with the prescribed and preached Christian ethics by the church.[91] Another pastor noted:

> *Today it is very difficult to understand the type of Christian moralities in the church. Society is daily formulating dynamic moralities that are very situational. Society changes them to fit the interests as it likes. The church is greatly undefined because people change or mix their Christian faith with the surrounding influences. The surrounding communities are very powerful that they even drag the church outside its track into the society's interests. Contemporary pastors have to discover new morality.*[92]

Consequently, society is convincing pastors to change their doctrine of church ethics. Due to those changes, society has been attempting to take the role of its leaders. On this take over, church ministers encounter a lack of esteem in almost all age groups of society - in children, youth, and in old people. Church ministers express their views that the future morality of the church and of society is unpredictable. All the same, even the image of the church and society portray an appearance of flux. Then, what should pastors do on this problem? There are some proposals that pastors and churches have to find some new moral conducts that suits the contemporary society.

The above discussion about the moral life of society shows that while church ministers are holding some prescribed moral guidelines, society is adjusting, formulating and implementing some other moral guidelines that suits its interests and needs. This is leading pastors to perceive and feel that they are not listened to and obeyed by the youth and by the general public. Pastors seem to lack authority over the moral guidelines in society. What does it imply? It seems the church with her ministers are either slow, or late or do not feel some of the moral dilemmas. One question that remains unresponded is this: what morals or ethics are the good, right, correct and common for the whole society? I will return to this question in my discussion of the challenges facing pastor's role and the church life at large.

Secular Influence in Religion

In chapter two, I stated that during the time of Villagization, politics was the main force for people to move from their scattered and tribal life into 'socialism villages'. The social amalgamation and integration of religious life took place simultaneously. The Tanzanian and African societies possess

---

91. Dørenen, "Communication, Conversion and Conservation," 190–193.
92. Informant D.

both the secular and the religious life. Likewise, society has certain interests and opinion that are pointing to fulfilling ordinary life that differ somehow from the ones that are for people's spiritual affairs. In this section, I present and discuss the secular influences that both influence and bringing forces into religion. I point out at least two secular influences to serve as an example of how society is very influential on religion. Those are the secular music and politics. Let us start with secular music.

Secular music such as *Hip Hop, Twanga Pepeta, Bongo Flavour, Taarabu, Kiduku, Makanga, Kwaito* and other secular styles are rapidly penetrating into the Church. These are kinds of poetry and dances. Most of the agents of these styles are the youth. The kinds of styles used by secular choirs outside the church now are adopted in the church. They said:

> *The present society has formed another culture with its new and varied values. For example, the styles of clothing, music inside and outside the church are more secular related. The church music, especially to the youth has an influence from secular practices. They dance a lot when singing Christian songs. If you ask them as to why they dance in that way; this is their response: "this is a style of the new generation—the liberal and free generation. We do not want to sing while standing still." Therefore, a new form of music that is in practice nowadays in the church is a result of social change. As society transforms its style of music tune; its renovation becomes very influential to the youth and young adults in the church, hence they adapt that form into the Church.*[93]

Another pastor supported the above descriptions in this way: *Even the type of music is a reality. For the youth, the Hip Hop, Bongo flavor, 'Taarabu, Kiduku, Kwaito' styles are among their contemporary interest. They have brought them and many others into the church. Pastors need to know this and teach them instead of just rebuking publicly or arguing that it is a sinful music.*[94] My question to my informants was: what is wrong with that imitation of styles from those secular rhythms? There were varied opinions about the kinds of music rhythms as depicted above. To some Christians, there is nothing bad, while to other Christians the styles are not good. Largely church ministers and Christians, especially the old or those who have intact commitment to Lutheran traditions, seem uncomfortable with these styles. They feel unhappy because, to them, usually secular music styles are associated with sin. When singing the gospel songs in their choirs, normally they dance. Some of the singers have extreme imitation. Christians

93. Informant G.
94. Informant F.

perform songs with too much twisting of their waists. It seems that people are worried that these types of performances cannot differentiate faithful Christians from unfaithful ones, and there can be no difference between gospel music and secular music.

Things are changing in the Church. Secular music styles do alter many of the traditional music styles of the church. As narrated above, the youth groups and other church choir singers leave the church if they forbid that imitation. As I stated in the early chapters of this book; all African pastors in the Christian religion encounter some effects of social change regarding their roles, such as, this of moral leadership. This problem is also prevalent in the Roman Catholic Church. The Tanzanian Roman Catholic Priest, Laurent Magesa observes that:

> Catholic youth choirs have played a big role in introducing new ideas in Music. 'They are the most inventive group and offer their services freely', . . . this group which has 'set aside' the 'secular words' from the rhythm of the *twanga pepeta* and replaced them with 'religious words.' A similar process took place with hi-pop music . . . 'Pop music is fashionable in the parish. Young people have simply substituted the secular words with religious words and they are making an impact. Their songs have an important message to everyone in the community and they are liked very much. . . . 'you cannot forbid them from using it. They are so good that even if the parish forbade them, the people would keep on listening to them.'[95]

Magesa gives his witness on how the Catholic youth invent new ideas in music. They replace secular words with religious words. Magesa credits this kind of music style. He argues that this rhythm of music has positive effects in the church of today. Their songs bring important messages to the community. In addition, the community itself likes it very much. At last, he recommends that the styles should remain because people keep on listening to it. It implies that, this can be a useful tool in teaching and preaching the gospel. Nevertheless, what effects does this bring to pastor's roles and to the life and ministry of the church?

On the other hand, some informants completely discredit the imitation of gospel music style from secular styles. Together with some informants, there are Christians who argue that secular music styles promote evil behavior. For them, it is unchristian to imitate something from outside the church. Taking an example of the songs accompanying dances during wedding celebrations in the Tanzanian Iraqw society and Church, Snyder

---

95. Magesa, *Anatomy of Inculturation*, 42.

states that the Church has been in war against some songs and dances that some Christians borrow from traditional and secular practices. They are *'backward tradition[s].'* She reports:

> The Church, in its war on 'backward tradition', targeted dancing in . . . District. In justifying this position, the Church claims that dancing encourages drunkenness, laziness, and promiscuity, which all lead to HIV/AIDS. In addition, it proclaims that dancing . . . is a health hazard, . . . Often, the priest came . . . to make sure that dancing ended. In several instances, the rule was disobeyed, and the dancing . . . started up again when people believed the priest was not nearby.[96]

As noticed above, Snyder observes that the Church associates dancing with evils. She argues that the Church claims that dancing encourages evils such as drunkenness, laziness, and promiscuity that lead Christians into HIV/AIDS. It means that the Church perceives dancing to be hazardous. As a result, pastors have to make sure they stop Christians from dancing. However, people never obey the priest. Once he or she is far away, they continue. People repeat this process now and again until this pastor gets tired to end their interest.

Sometimes, if pastors continue to prohibit the Christians from dancing the Christian songs in the church, some church members propose to remove such a pastor out of the parish. It means that Christians do not easily accept the pastor's authority if he or she is against modern music. Certainly, there were some differences from church music over "secular" music. Therefore, it appears very difficult to stop dancing because many people prefer singing while dancing, especially the youth.

When I was undertaking this research, informants, especially pastors, described that the Tanzanian society had entered into an arena of strong political outlooks. It is in a state of interconnectedness. This is an outcome of ethnic integration and powerful political influence. Politicians who hold leadership positions play a great role to reformulate the social and religious life of people whom they lead. Since they also belong to some religious communities, they also become very influential in those religious congregations. We may have a look on how politicians affect the Church as well as the roles of pastors. First, church ministers argued that, for example, during church councils sometimes politicians could convince pastors and evangelists to arrange church programs and policies by following the nation's policies. Sunday Worship Services were one of the examples that political influences

---

96. Snyder, *The Iraqw of Tanzania*, 83.

affected them. One pastor illustrated how politics had developed and its effect on the role of the pastor and on church:

> *The Tanzanian society has entered into multi-party system. From 1990's there are many political parties with their varied political ideologies. The pastor is leading these same people who also belong to political parties. This type and change of social structural life brings many challenges to the pastor and the church. For example, both strong, enthusiastic and influential political leaders and Christians bring politics into the church. We always see politics penetrating into the church hence affecting the true interpretation of our Christian faith, administration and management of the church. In great percentages politics has penetrated into the church such that it affects the true faith while making some of our fellow church ministers become trapped by it, to an extent that they preach it even by lying to Christians. This problem brings chaos especially during election of political leaders in society.*[97]

Moreover, secular social leaders have been arranging village meetings to start at ten o'clock in the morning. This is the time when most of the Christian worship services start. Informants told that the state largely knows that most Christians attend their worship services in those times. Therefore, it seemed that some politicians used churches with their worship days to fulfill their goals.

Second, some politicians can infuse their secular politics into Christians during worship services. As noted in the previous sections above, some politicians who are members of the church can also use the worship services, especially during preaching and church announcements, to infuse their political philosophies to people. Since Tanzania is a multi-party nation, even church members belong to varied standpoints of secular politics. Sometimes the infusion practices bring conflicts among Church members and hence make divisions. As a result, if a pastor or any church minister is biased, he or she can face a great pressure. I noted in the interviews, for example, sometimes it happens that strong politicians pressurize Church ministers to move pastors out and send them into other workplaces or appointments. This force is applied upon ministers who are openly showing their interests in certain political parties that are not dominant in the contexts in which a minister is serving. In order to avoid those tensions, some pastors would just remain silent about secular politics. These problems are prevalent especially during national elections.

---

97. Informant A.

Third, another effect is the pressures that secular leaders put even on issues that are controlled by church ministers and other respective church authorities. One example is divorce among Christian marriages. How do secular political standpoints affect marriage issues? I asked my informants. Most pastors complained that secular policies are sometimes making some decisions on divorces without consulting Christian religious leaders under whom those marriages have been administered and nurtured.

On those pressures, Stephen Bevans states that currently, Christian theologians need to be aware that they are doing theological reflection in the postmodern world. In this time, society is full of several and varied forces and influences that may seem to disestablish the Christian religion. He notices thus: "the single most far-reaching ecclesiastical factor conditioning theological reflection in our time is the effective disestablishment of the Christian religion [world] by secular, political, and alternative religious forces."[98] Then he recommends those theologians that they must be humble when articulating the Christian truth. This is important because they do their role " . . . in a world of many religious [and secular] ways."

At last, before concluding our discussion in this section, I want to know the attitude of church ministers toward secular politics. Although church ministers seem not to be very much comfortable with those secular effects, however, they admit that the most important thing today is: first to live and work by observing the realities of life. Second, it depends on each one's perceptions and approaches. A note is that despite the prevalence of political differences, society claims to consider and involve in most decisions. However, secular issues should not be one of the major strategies or criteria when undertaking the pastoral roles. Neither their influences are they supposed to be overemphasized and used in religious gatherings. By avoiding some secular political problems to dominate the church, there can be none or minimal unnecessary conflicts. Even so, some cooperation with secular leaders is necessary for all church ministers.

Charles Taylor is aware that the contemporary society is in a secular time. He states that the underlying social practices bring a number of other changes with them.[99] There are several secular influential changes that have been taking place, and which might continue even in future. In addition, he mentions politics to be among secular aspects that characterize the contemporary societies around the world. As the informants above have given their testimonies, his arguments seem to apply to what was happening in the ELCT/SD. Taylor describes that since the whole society is within a secular

---

98. Bevans, *Models of Contextual Theology*, 83.

99. Taylor, *Modern Social Imaginaries*, 155.

time, it is hardly possible to escape from such an environment. We all belong to a secular time. In this secular time there are so many happenings, of both secular and religious events. Thus, he suggests people to understand that:

> As long as secular time is interwoven with various kinds of higher time, there is no guarantee that all events can be placed in unambiguous relations of simultaneity and succession. . . . A purely secular time-understanding allows us to imagine society horizontally, unrelated to any 'high points,' where the ordinary sequence of events touches higher time, and therefore without recognizing any privileged persons or agencies, such as kings or priests, who stand and mediate at such alleged points.[100]

Taylor is trying to make an emphasis that we cannot escape from secular time and its secular events in our social forms. Therefore, in my opinion, I would suggest that we ought to understand that secularity might remain in our places in spite of our religious and moral boundaries that we may have set. This implies that, since the same people act as both religious and members of the secular world, social secular practices are likely to persist in religious and secular settings. It is a matter of understanding and hence taking some measures to deal with them. Certainly, we cannot prohibit them from coming, because they come with those members of the Church.

THE PASTOR AS PASTOR

Another role that a pastor plays is the care and counseling. Informants held that this role was widening and increasing in its demands. Society seemed to have high expectations and demands in the pastor. Moreover, the increase was in Church members, in worship services, in marriages, and candidates for baptism. Another widening responsibility was due to 'social problems'. Such were diseases and death rates. As a result, the counseling sessions and burial services had increased and widened. In the time of this research, one pastor who was in the rural parish described how the role of pasturing was daily becoming tough and widening:

> *The work today is very tough because there is lots of work to do. Today a pastor has to perform many roles due to the society's needs and problems. The change of social life and formation or structure has increased the tasks. For example, the role of counseling widens due to varied problems within society. Such are people who need special care and help, like the HIV/AIDS patients. In*

---

100. Ibid., 157, cf., 185-189.

> addition, there are many orphans, widows and widowers, increase of schools that need teachers for Christian education, increase of worship services and so forth.[101]

Again, when I conversed with another pastor from an urban parish, this pastor described that there were a widening and an increase in worship services from one to three. This was also a common characteristic of most of the urban parishes. As I listened to him, he seemed to complain when testifying that: *There are added tasks such as frequent visitations in health care and home—based care centers, and many counseling sessions.*[102] Furthermore, almost all informants acknowledged that society was now encountering a high rate of diseases such as malaria and sexual transmitted diseases.[103] Those problems also widened and increased the pastor's role for frequent: of home visitations, counseling sessions, and confession liturgies during general worship services. Most informants mentioned Malaria and HIV/AIDS to be the prominent problems that increase the pastor's roles in the area. Therefore, due to that increase of responsibilities there were also a need for the church to increase other ministers, that is, pastors and evangelists.

Another widening and increasing role was on burial ceremonies due to increase of death rates. People had high expectations and demands that their pastors were the ones to participate in those tasks than other co-workers such as evangelists. Then, I asked them as to why the society had that great and difficult expectations and demands upon them (pastors)? They responded that, frequently people explained that they felt honored if their pastor attended to their problems rather than someone else. This could probably signify that pastors had a certain special status that put them over other church ministers.

Therefore, all church ministers described their roles and ministries as tough, challenging, with a constant and high expectations and demands from society. In spite of some pastor's satisfaction on pastoral and church ministry, some found the whole work of pastoral ministry difficult to the point of despair and became prime candidates for dropping out. However, other church ministers might have left due to other reasons such as economic problems.

---

101. Informant C.
102. Informant B.
103. Ibid.

THE PASTOR AS COMMUNITY LEADER

We have so far looked outside individual religious organization, especially Christian denomination. Now we need to turn and look inside individual church institution itself to find other characteristics of the social world in which pastors perform their tasks. The intention here is to hear how economic statuses of society and of the pastor could either lead to failures to provide supportive environment for pastoral ministry or bring alternative opportunities for pastors to achieve a set goal through their roles. However, neither the characteristics should they be regarded as of old nor are they necessarily of recent origin. Especially important at this level is the high and low standard of life to society and the church ministers.

The Society's Economic Status vs. Pastor's Low Economy

One of contemporary characteristics of Tanzanian society is its economic status. In most cases, Tanzanian society is much more of agricultural based activities than of other activities. During my survey, there was an expression that most of the people were improving their living through that agricultural economic resource, as they said: *"People improve their standard of life by building modern houses."*[104]

Though, in general, the Tanzanian society was said to improve its economic situation, yet, during this research informants could confidently describe that most of the church ministers in the area in which this research was undertaken) had poor economy compared to most of other people around them. Among the testimonies said: *"The pastor's poor economic status in the changing society does not make him or her be their modeling figure. Hence, they run away from him or her. Neither have they listened as they could do if he or she was as economically well as they were or at least if he or she would be in a growing situation. So as society changes its economic status; it expects the pastor to change as well, otherwise, he or she is seen as a burden and an obstacle of social development."*[105] Another one added: *"The salary is too small. This makes the minister to leave a full involvement in church ministry and run into other places or have very minimal timetable of spiritual service to the people so that he or she goes to get something that will help him or her to fight against this tough life]. That is why you may also find that almost all pastors are complaining about the society's claims and the situation of their*

---

104. Informant F.
105. Informant B.

ministry in the church."¹⁰⁶ The quotations above tell that poor or very low economy lead pastors into inferior voice, poor offerings, weak contribution in social affairs, and standard of living. Hence, they may become not models to the community. Even so, if they can try to improve their economic status, still, the speed is not as equal as to that of the community. Then, I asked, why is it becoming very difficult for pastors to improve their economic life? Several responses come out. They state that among the reasons for them to have poor economic status are the following; first, it is due to low salaries. They express that the church is paying them very little salary that cannot meet most of their needs. The second reason is due to *high cost of living*. Therefore, the little pay they receive is not satisfactory them to get most of their living requirements. The salaries are unsatisfactory even to establish some small economic business as society is doing.

During interview with informants F and G, they added other two more reasons; third, some church ministers are too busy with church programs and not with economic activities. They spend most of their time doing church work only than in economic dealings. They seem to have no time with such secular oriented entrepreneurships. Fourth, sometimes some church ministers, who would want to try to carry out some economic activities, also appear to fear the forces that are could accompany business activities such as witchcraft. Therefore, they have doubtful feelings and attitudes upon most of the economic businesses that society is involved in.¹⁰⁷ In such perspective, most of the pastors are suspicious of the dishonest trading projects. Therefore, church ministers, especially pastors have less confidence toward business activities. As a result, they remain with what they can earn or make at that time.

Then I probed with another question: what repercussions can their poor economy bring onto their reputation and as church ministers in society? Almost all informants could acknowledge that society has a better economy and improves life standards compared to that of church ministers. One of the effects that informants try to express in common is the saying that 'Pastor's economic life status is not of a model to society.' For example, one of the informants testifies: *"The pastor's poor economic status in the changing society does not make him or her become the modeling figure."* As a result, *"Society runs away from him or her. It (society) expects the pastor to change, otherwise, he or she is seen as a burden and an obstacle of social*

---

106. Informant A, C, E and G.

107. Informants F and G. Most of the informants are non-theologians, nor are they church elders.

development."[108] From the highlights of informants, it hurts in the heart to hear that a pastor has bad role model, and or he or she is a burden to society. Worse enough, it hurts more to be termed as obstacles of development in society that he or she has been called and sent for service.

When I reflect my parish experience, I can remember some incidences that humiliated my evangelists as well as my personality and profession. Apart from my own experience, one pastor who was serving a nearby parish once shared with me his experience that church ministers including pastors can testify that in society they are not well listened to especially in matters concerning economy. Though good at emphasizing about self-reliance and entrepreneurship, pastors themselves have become neither model factors nor strong advisors of economy in the community. Furthermore, one of the impacts of this problem is that most of the church ministers argue that poor economic status decreases and lessens confidence over and from the followers. The same problem of less confidence occurs to pastors when they preach or teach about Christian stewardship or about material wealth from God as a blessing for all people. The pastors have less authority due to their poor economic statuses. Parallel to the problem of economy in pastors there emerges the fifth problem consequently to them. This is their lack of fast and up-to-date communication and transportation means. Little involvement in economy causes this problem. The next section provides more details about communication and transportation in pastors.

Charles Taylor states that economy is the first social sphere or form that characterizes the contemporary Western world as well as other nations around the globe. He argues that most people are busy with economic activities in order to sustain and make their life enjoying. We read that the contemporary "humans are engaged in an exchange of services. The fundamental model seems to be what we have come to call economy. . . . We can see here how much importance the economic dimension is taking on in the new notion of order."[109] Furthermore, Taylor describes that historically, apart from economy, there has been a time that emerged some change in self-understanding in relation to several levels of life, including the political and the spiritual. However, economic occupation became an essential activity for most people whether professional or ordinary people: "If ordered life became a demand, . . . for the mass of ordinary people, then everyone had to become ordered and serious about what they were doing, and of necessity had to be doing, in life, namely, working in some productive occupation. A

---

108. Informant A.
109. Taylor, *Modern Social Imaginaries*, 71.

truly ordered requires that one takes these economic occupations seriously and prescribe a discipline for them. This was the political ground."[110]

The sample of society that I use in this book seems to adopt the emphases of Taylor. It envisions that people were trying to fulfill this demand of becoming serious about economic occupations. "The new kind of highly interested economic activity is seen as the cornerstone of a new ethic."[111] In this case, pastors cannot escape from involving themselves in serious economic occupations. Serious involvement and discipline in economic occupations will make pastors become and work as 'economic advisors'[112] to society.

Communication and Transportation

Improvement in economic status of society can also help society improve some ways of communication and transportation. Better communication and transportation make people share important information and can travel as part of interaction. In the area where I carried out the research, I noticed people discussing about the importance of good infrastructure. Good infrastructures help both; secular societies and religious institutions perform their tasks effectively. Therefore, people keep busy with economic occupations to improve their infrastructures for better networks in life. One among informants states the way in which society struggles about it: *People improve their transport and communication facilities and traveling to learn what and how others do things in other places.*[113] Better transport and communication necessitates the travelling in search of new knowledge, new skills, and new opportunities.

In the conversations with my interviewees, they spoke about people's need for new and up-to-date communication and transport means. They further responded that society is in an era of science and technology that urges people to struggle for better communication as well as struggle for better standard of living. This is a time where the life of society is improving. Society is constantly transforming into better and more suitable conditions. Society is striving toward getting its needs and interests even through ways of communication.

Almost all informants had similar descriptions that in their parish and church district, society is in rapid change from old and slow methods of communication to new, quick and improved ones. Among the indicators

110. Ibid., 73.
111. Ibid., 151.
112. For further details see chapter six in this book.
113. Informant F.

for this rapid change is in the growing use electronic instruments: mobile phones, computer usage and other useful modes for fast communication with their pastors. This is especially rampant in urban societies. The urban pastor confirms this argument: *They use mobile phones, internet, motorcar, and other modes that make easy and fast communication and good life.*[114]

I witnessed that to date, if Christians have a problem that requires the minister's attention, they just call him or her by using their mobile phones. Nevertheless, if their pastor does not have a mobile phone they have to go and communicate the problem face to face with him or her. With the face to face, most congregants and the community at large feel uncomfortable with such old kind of communication. Commenting on the need for pastors to use new, modern, reliable, and fast modes of communication, informants recommend pastors to be aware that their society is in global communication. Therefore, there is also a need for every pastor to enter into that global perspective of society. Consider the following observations in a tandem: *Our Christians and society are in a global point in time.*[115] *We need to have new communication and transport systems. Pastors and other church ministers are very backward on this. You may hear almost all pastors complaining on how Christians interact and communicate with church ministers. Christians feel undermined if their pastor lives a primitive and conservative type of life.*[116] If a pastor has no mobile phone or does not use fast ways of immediate communication, he or she undermines his or her church members. He or she also perpetuates primitive and conservative living. Such kind of life humiliates his or her people because they perceive it as old and degrading. Christians feel uncomfortable. Another pastor also emphasized:

> People no longer use much time to make each other informed of what is happening around the world. In this kind of new ways of communication, society wants pastors and all church ministers to be in that kind of life, otherwise they may ignore you. People also tell their friends that our pastor is still in the old life – in the time of primitive life. He or she does not have a global communication. If this leader has no cell phone and the way he or she communicates with people; they are not comfortable.[117]

This informant acknowledges that pastors, as leaders of the community, should have reliable and available communication. By using modern ways of communication signifies that the pastor has global attachments. Then he

114. Informant B.
115. For further details, see chapter six.
116. Informant B.
117. Informant A.

recommends: *To have mobile phones to date is something very important, otherwise you will be moving a lot to follow Christians and other people while in turn they can just call you through your neighbor who has got a mobile phone. Society has changed the methods or means of communication. We also need to enter into that world of new ways of communicating with Christians and other people.*[118]

From the discussions above, we can draw the some implications. First, it implies that one of the statuses and qualities of a pastor, as leader of the community, is the ability to communicate with people. As a community leader, people do not expect the pastor to miss the necessary qualification that enhances his or her roles.

The second issue that all informants expressed is the fast and reliable modes of transportation in contemporary society. The discussion introduces the fact that pastors need to travel easily and fast to reach their people and provide them with pastoral services. One can notice that most of the church ministers hardly have reliable means for transportation. The situation is contrary to contemporary life of society. They stated that *Christians and society use motorcar, and other ways that make easy and fast communication and good life.*[119] The contemporary society feels happy and proud if its pastors and evangelists have new, fast and modern transportation.

In the above analysis and discussions, a person can learn that for the contemporary societies the use of bicycles is outdated. Parallel to that there are widening and increasing roles of a pastor. Society can pressurize a pastor to work according to the existing requirements at hand. It can instruct him or her to perform some un-prescribed tasks. Far more, the contemporary society likes an "express" pastor with modern and fast means of communication and transport. People want their pastor be communicative and reachable. But what does society do toward empowering their pastors to manage and work under those conditions of fast and improved communication and transportation ways? Some informants have been silent to respond to this question. Others parishes provide their pastors with the mobile phones, motorcycles. Sometimes Christians may help pastors with cars whenever especially if he or she to travel into substations that are very far from the headquarters of the parishes.

It seems that if a pastor has a mobile phone for communication, it would help in the following ways: First, it is a sign of being in a new and postmodern world. It would also be a sign of one to have It signifies that their pastor belong to a new fashion of communication. People now perceive

---

118. Ibid.
119. Informant B.

this church minister to have a global communication and global perspectives. Second, it saves time, especially in times of great need for fast help. On the other hand, it appears that if a pastor does not have a mobile phone and no fast transportation such as motorcycle, both that pastor as well as parishioners would feel like working and living in a primitive and conservative era. Hence, they might experience inferiority. As the society changes its ways of communication and transportation, so it demands the church and all leaders to change into that new world.

For Charles Taylor, communication through media is a means for society to meet together. Taylor is aware that communication is one of characteristics of a free society under the public sphere. It is a central feature of modern society. Communication unifies individuals and associations. It seems that, for Taylor, fast and reliable communication helps society get informed of what is going on around the globe.[120] Even if the society mentioned in this book had not yet reached the communication standards like that of postmodern Europe, communication is becoming among essential modes of life of contemporary society.

As I approach the end of this chapter, I would like to use the summary from Jackson W. Carroll about the contemporary social world in which pastors live and work. He states that this current social world has so many characteristics that affect the role of the pastor as well as the life of the community itself. Carroll highlights six of them to demonstrate the special importance for the work of pastors and for the life of the Christian community.

1. There is demographic change: This is the first and the greatest effect of all since it brings change in the characteristics of the population. In most of the time it shifts people from a rural society to an urban society. This change has five effects in itself: first, it depopulates the countryside and enhances the trend toward urbanization. Second, it moves the educated from rural areas into urban centers. Third, the educated society demands and pushes for pastors with better education. Charles Taylor emphasizes that society desires its pastors become as educated as itself or above. The educated society puts much trust on educated pastors. He writes: "Simply put, educated laity generally expects more of their pastors."[121] Fourth, demographic change causes a dramatic increase in life expectancy. This contributes to the growth in the number of responsibilities to pastors; such is of care and counseling. Fifth, demographic change causes a: change in labor market especially in the current century, sharp increase in the number of women

---

120. Taylor, 83, 89, 91
121. Carroll, *God's Potters*, 35.

in the labor force, 'demographic change' transforms and brings new forms in marriage patterns while reducing the availability of women for church work.

II. There is secular state's permission and protection for religions to proclaim their faith. It means that the government allows people to practice their religiosity. There is a general and religious climate in which the church does its work today deemed supportive of religion and religious institutions. Due to this liberalism and convincing environment, some churches have a declining number of members while others multiply because of competition for members.

III. There is a considerable increase in religious diversity that new immigrants bring, both within and between faiths. This emerges the inter-religious dialogue and collaboration, especially between Christianity and other religions.

IV. There is a growth of religious conflict due to the prevalence of special interest groups.

V. There is a growing impact of consumerism and choice on churches and church involvement. People choose the Church or faith they want.

VI. Finally, there are growing implications of the "de facto congregationalism" on religious participation and the pastor's work.[122]

CONCLUSION

We have seen that despite some opportunities and challenges (as I will discuss in future chapters), there are some great external and internal forces that press or prevent ministers from performing their prescribed tasks. To some pastors, due to such severe pressures and obstructions, sometimes they cannot tolerate longer. Consequently, they would speak back to their society with emotional responses. It happens also that in some parishes members of the community dare to pronounce that their pastor is out dated. Hence, they attempt to refuse the opinions and interests of their pastor. Besides, members of the religious societies ask very complicated questions even before the mass in test of the competence in their pastor. Most pastors have been uncomfortable with the criticisms from the community, especially when they are teaching the parishioners about important concepts from the Bible and also in schools.

---

122. Ibid., 33, cf. 34–56.

The persistence of free will that leads to movement, to choice and faith expression in people, brings both the opportunity and ambivalences to pastors when they implement their given roles. Other features include, the increase of religious life in terms of an increase of denominations, growth of mega and small religious groups with their denominations – especially in the Christian denominations (for example, revival movements, New Life Crusade group). There are also some changes in marriage practices and patterns, in morality, and in some worship-songs that youth tend to adopt from secular practices.

In addition, the analysis shows that people involve themselves in economic activities in order to improve their standard of living. As in other issues, pastors are expected to be models in economic status and in standard of living, although, in reality it is not so. Most pastors have less status, both in economy and in life standards as compared to society around them. Consequently, poor economy lessens the pastor's authority, hence making his or her roles difficulty. The pastoral roles (see chapter 3) is affected by being obstructed, or insufficiently performed because church ministers work under tensions and pressures of anxious conditions resulting from the pressures that society imposes upon them. All these bring some difficulties for pastors to lead or perform care and counseling, and other pastoral tasks.

Furthermore, in this book, we realize that the roles prescribed by the church authority seem too static, too individualistic, and too old-fashioned to meet the demands of contemporary society. Both, the roles and rules do not define social change, how pastors can work comfortably, and ways in which they can respond to the demands, needs, and interests of changing society. The roles and rule of the church do not show how a pastor ought to respond to the reality. Then one can ask, what should pastors do in order for them to work and meet those needs and interests of the changing society? What should be changed, the church authority or the personality of the pastor or society, and how? Charles Taylor states that the contemporary society has reached the last phase of patience whereby it no longer tolerates the old social forms of interaction, of leadership, of relations and subordination. Moreover, the present society wants equality to replace hierarchy. Taylor shows this query from society:

> Servants and subordinates can't be inducted into an imaginary that gives them a place among those equal individuals who make up society unless the social forms of subordination tying them to their betters are transformed. There has to be a break with these old forms, in which equality replaces hierarchal, and in which at the same time a general and impersonal recognition

of equal status dissolves and replaces the personalized, particular relations of the old dependencies.¹²³

In this quotation, Taylor emphasizes further that contemporary society is tired of old social forms, old rules, and old systems of relationships. Society is calling for a freedom that realizes the "impersonal recognition of equal status." Now society desires transformations in all traditional ties.¹²⁴

Throughout this research, I came to learn that Taylor and Carroll's observations seemed to illustrate what was happening in the society that I studied. Most of the time the community and the church authority seemed to have varied attitudes and interests. That was also a reason for the pastors to find themselves in situations of tensions. The fact was that when pastors tried to emphasize the prescribed principles, society demanded what it wanted from their pastor. Nevertheless, I will highlight that, the analysis in this chapter does not mean that all pastors experience the same effects of social change. Most of the consequences depend on the work appointment, type of people and the era in which that pastor performs the given tasks.

Second, the analysis does not serve to deny the significance of church authorities, nor do I wish to suggest that everything from society deserves acceptance. But as I stated above, the prescribed pastoral roles contain inadequate responses to the needs and interests of the contemporary society. In this manner, the analysis aims at depicting some characteristics of the changing society and the way in which those changes affect the role of the pastor. Third, I agree with Carroll that the analysis in this chapter does not necessarily emphasize that the contemporary society is "a more difficulty one in which to be a pastor. But it is a different world, one that offers pastor's . . . challenges peculiar to this time in history and different from the social world in which many pastors and lay Christians first became part of the church."¹²⁵ There are some changes on the ways of doing ministry. The aim of this analysis is to understand how the ways have changed and how it is of signal importance for pastoral roles and for the church to take the age seriously.¹²⁶ Taking the age seriously involves the recognition of the mind-sets of both, society as well as of the pastor himself or herself. This is the concern in the proceeding chapter.

---

123. Taylor, *Modern Social Imaginaries*, 147–148.
124. Ibid., 149.
125. Carroll, *God's Potters*, 56.
126. Ibid., 56.

5
THE PASTOR IN A COGNITIVELY CHANGING SOCIETY

INTRODUCTION

IN CHAPTER FOUR, I have presented my analysis and discussion of the first part of social change and the effects it brings as the pastor undertakes the prescribed roles of the Church that I discussed in chapter three. Additionally, in the same chapter four, I extend my discussions of those effects to show how they are also bringing certain consequences in the whole mission and life of the Church. In this chapter, I present the second part of my analysis and discussion of data in relation to the changes in the mind-sets of people. In chapter two I presented the educational and religious status of the Tanzanian society. One of the essential aspects that I want to refer to again is the way the mind—set (an intellectual or cognitive state) is connected to the *Ujamaa* ideology. I want to use it in opening the whole process of my discussion of the educational change in people and its effects on the role of the pastor and on the mission and life of the Church at large.

My main interest here is to show how the mind-set and the knowledge that society attains through formal education links with the practices and behavior of people. For example, after attaining a certain formal education, a person reads the Bible with a critical mind. In that process, people can be able to criticize pastors or ask critical questions about certain theological concepts also found in social science subjects. For example, the stories of creation in the Bible and in biology bring some challenges to both, theologians–the pastors and social scientists. As I pointed out in chapter four, interaction and the change in people's attitudes have some influences upon rethinking about their progress. When people interact, they share important knowledge and skills for their survival. We can recall a little: *The form of social life has changed. Yet, it is still changing as people interact, integrate and improve their standard of life by building modern houses, transport and communication facilities and traveling to learn what and how others do things in other places. Due to this interaction of people, the society's attitude and manner of thinking have changed.*[1]

Charles Taylor states that changes in a society happen because of both the practices and the understanding in people: "the relation between practices and the . . . understanding behind them is therefore not one-sided. If the understanding makes the practice possible, it is also true that it is the practice that carries the understanding."[2] Taylor maintains that knowledge and practice appear to be inseparable. It is likely that the way people understand things influences their practice. Therefore, every one's own experience becomes a major force for change. This experience seems to be among the features of society in the ELCT/SD area where I have drawn the sample for investigation.

In addition to Taylor's, Kijanga has similar descriptions about social change. He states that social transformations attributes to the intellectual part of an individual and thereafter to the community as a whole. Below, as an example, let me try to expand his (Kijanga) exposition in detail on the way understanding and practice can change the system of life. Kijanga once examined the way in which *Ujamaa* as an attitude of mind influenced the social system of Tanzanians. From the year 1974 and back, Tanzanians lived in scattered areas. But soon after *Ujamaa*, people changed into living close in villages.

I pointed out earlier that some prominent and influential politicians tried to link *Ujamaa* (socialism) with the mind-set of the people. Kijanga highlights that when introducing *Ujamaa* in Tanzania *Mwalimu* (teacher) Nyerere maintains "that *Ujamaa* is an attitude of mind."[3] For Nyerere, once a person changes his or her attitude of mind, certainly, that person can also change even certain conditions of life. In order for society to understand and practice the concept of *Ujamaa*, it was necessary first to help every individual person to transform his or her mind-set toward the thoughts and practices for the wholeness of human development.[4]

1. Informant F.
2. Taylor, *Modern Social Imaginaries*, 25.
3. Kijanga, *Ujamaa and the Role of Church*, 4.
4. Ibid., 5.

the pastor in a cognitively changing society 145

To me it means that the intellectual part of a person plays a significant role in life, both as an individual and in the community. Society becomes very inquisitive in issues and things that the church through pastors and other ministers do and induce into the people. As a result, society questions any hierarchical formula of the guideline and role that a pastor undertakes. It questions even the personal life of that pastor. Kijanga maintains that an increase of consciousness in the minds of people is among the characteristics of human development. Now people cannot allow their ministers to take things and responsibilities for granted. Society requests to revisit and reformulate all principles, programs and practices for the betterment of the contemporary community.

As I will discuss below, Charles Taylor also emphasizes that if the church or its agents are not willing to change, then society may even attempt to organize a constructive and peaceful demonstration against the ruling class, or as Charles Taylor calls it "the established order" in order to achieve and sustain a democratic order, and system in doing things. Furthermore, Taylor describes clearly that society can take a peaceful demonstration when it fights for freedom in political elections, for human rights, economic right, social and individual expressions, and even in religious expressions. In all those aspects, contemporary people want to show that they are in a different 'space and time'. Even the present 'moral order' is almost different from that of the pre and modern society.[5] It means that society may seek freedom and inclusion of all members of the contemporary community in all processes to save their social and religious life.[6]

Kijanga describes that some rapid changes are already happening in the areas of politics, socio-economic, and in other social-religious affairs in people. These changes signify the coming of fast social changes in the Church. Hence, the Christian Church had to think as well about changing the attitudes toward that social development in the whole nation of Tanzania. How then was the Christian Church paying attention to the wholeness of a human being? Kijanga has some good responses:

> It is paying more attention to the concept of the whole man [sic] than ever before and discussions are still going on as to how the biblical view of the whole man can be understood in Tanzania. An involvement in this socio-economic situation of the nation is given a theological justification. Human development is viewed as socio-economic, intellectual, moral and spiritual. With this understanding of human development, the Christian Church

---

5. Taylor, *Modern Social Imaginaries*, 25–33, 28.
6. Ibid., 24–29.

contends that an increase in economic efficiency in a nation is indeed both a moral and spiritual progress. It is a positive movement toward a better state of affairs, a knowledge of and feeling for life.[7]

Kijanga states that since there were movements of people into *Ujamaa* villages and later on, from one town to another; then, the Christian Church was predicting that, including education in people, various things would probably change. The changes may in turn affect the ecclesiastical structures and many pastors as they perform their tasks in the Tanzanian society. Thereafter, Kijanga proposes that the following questions be considered: "What will the role of . . . pastors who live in *Ujamaa* village be? Can . . . pastors earn their living by their profession as clergymen?"[8] Furthermore, Kijanga, observes that most of the existing administrative structures of the Christian denominations in Tanzania have had a tendency of inheriting and emphasizing numerous roles and guidelines from the past structures only. For Kijanga, those denominations could keep reformulating or formulating the new ones according to the contemporary societies, where most people have become more educated.

What then have been the influences of the contemporary society upon the church? Some denominations and perhaps some preaching points hardly managed to maintain the elaborate administrative structures of the church. Sometimes, certain learned individuals may seem to influence some immediate church leaders to explore new models of simple administrative structures and new models of ministries or even methods that they think are appropriate for pastoral ministry in a changing society.[9] Society takes some own initiatives like "revolution" for the sake of reforming some ecclesiastical structures so that certain prescribed roles may be renewed. He defines the word 'revolution' as "repentance" and "the turning up of the whole church."[10] Why do some church leaders feel that they should enter into that radical change strategy? It may be because of the changes in all aspects of the life of the contemporary society, in both its secular and religious parts. Cognitive change is dominant.

Thus, in this chapter I also present the second part of my analysis and discussion of data in relation to the cognitive transformation. It is changes in the mind-sets of people; the change in people's knowledge and experience through cognition, and the way those changes affect the role of the

7. Kijanga, *Ujamaa and the Role of Church*, 66.
8. Ibid., 67, cf., 66.
9. Ibid., 67.
10. Ibid., 67, 68.

pastor. This is important in this thesis, because first, social change connects with the mind-sets of people. Thus, it is difficult to separate a person from these social changes, as this testimony states *the mind-sets of people today are rapidly changing with many demands for their present life.*[11] My interest in this quotation is on the *mind-sets* and *many demands* that change brings to a person. Once the mind-set alters, it calls and pushes one to think about the contemporary life. Second, the contemporary pastors are to be leaders of an educated society. Third, there are some vivid indications that the society under research has been constantly learning and increasing knowledge and experiences. Thus, fourth, it appears that these changes have some pressing implication on the role of the pastor and on the mission and life of the church. Now let us have a look on each of them.

THE PASTOR AS LEADER OF AN EDUCATED AND CHANGING SOCIETY

Before the informants described to me about the scope and development of educational changes of people in the whole society; I wanted first to know the position of the pastor in society as one among other leaders of society. Almost every pastor confessed that he or she serves in the midst of a learning community. This community is cognitively changing. Secondly, I wanted also to explore how that learning society, throughout its change process, perceives of and needs the leadership role of a pastor. The leading question in this section is this: how society perceives a pastor in relation to its cognitive changes?

I noted that, despite some shortcomings that pastors appear to have (as I will discuss in the forthcoming sections within this chapter) society regards a pastor as an important leader among other leaders in society.

> *Christians and society of this time see a pastor as being a significant, dignified, and liable person. Therefore, in this generation; he or she has to be very careful, competent, visionary, and an innovative person. A pastor is at the same time a leader and a manager of the church and the community. Christians and society expect him or her to carry out multiple functions and help them in wide spectrums of people's lives. Due to his or her position as a significant and potential person: he or she may become a change agent toward development of society or vice versa. People may sometimes*

---

11. Informant G.

> depend upon, respect and feel proud of him or her. They would not feel good if they were miss-represented.[12]

And according to the following evangelists:

> A pastor is an important person in society. He or she is a leader of all people. He or she has many people who listen at and follow him or her. Therefore, Christians and society strongly claim that a leader must be a model in many things such as good life standard, morality and education because people imitate from him or her. However, it is very difficult to be a model in all things in the way people would want.[13]

Even if pastors are primarily employees of religious institutions to work as spiritual leaders, the above informants confirm that pastors are also among important leaders in the community. They work as mentors of society. As the quotation above states, the pastor *has many people who listen at and follow him or her*. Pastors seem to be very important persons, specially, when people encounter problems such as sickness, marriage conflicts and when people need some prayers for them to succeed in their jobs. Not only that, but also, the pastor is seen as an agent of social development. In this sense, he or she is a change agent. Due to that significant image that society views and bestows to the pastor, people admit that they expect to imitate him or her as a leader. Subsequently, it implies that he or she ought to be at high role model in most of his or her life and ministry experiences. Otherwise, people ignore this pastor and his or her profession(s) and jeopardize his or her leadership titles.

In my view, therefore, any leader who is to be a model, he or she is also required to possess certain essential qualities in order to live and work courageously and effectively in society at hand. Indeed, good education - in terms of more knowledge and skills is among necessary attributes that society expects him or her to possess. However, not only are the pastors perceived as leaders of society, but also other church ministers, such as heads of parish departments and evangelists are expected to play this role. Those ministers also need to possess certain similar qualities whilst the criteria may probably be less relevance for some co-leaders such as church elders and choir leaders.

As highlighted in some descriptions in the previous sections and chapters, the respondents were quite open that in most cases pastors are leaders of the educated society. He or she is leading the learned and learning

---

12. Informant G.
13. Informant E.

the pastor in a cognitively changing society

community. Far more, most of the people have and are constantly attaining formal and higher education. Taking Tanzania as an example, in this book we consider formal and higher education as from secondary school to university level. Many people send their children and or go for formal and higher education. This is among the reasons for society to become educated. The growth of education in people is due to accessibility of schools and colleges into which most of the people can enroll themselves and their children for formal education. This is especially the case with the increase of secondary schools in many of church and government district wards in which I conducted the research. One informant argues:

> *Currently there is a rapid growth of schools and colleges. This has led many people to go to school. Many Christians nowadays are educated or becoming educated to the level of secondary school education or more in all villages. It is good that we get more people who are literate than it was in the previous years where many did not go to schools, especially secondary schools due to several reasons, one of them being the scarcity of schools. Today every district ward has one or more secondary schools. The level of education in people is constantly changing from being uneducated or primary level to secondary level and above. This is also another change within the society's life. From 1990's to date there is a rapid growth of people who up-grade their level of education. Children and youth are of the majority. This means that we are living and leading the educated society.*[14]

Undoubtedly, the quotation above shows the practical experience of educational context in which pastors carry out church ministry. The situation relates to what I discussed in chapter two, based on literature. I have noted above that the government of Tanzania and other sectors have been committed to educating the majority of Tanzanians.

We can briefly recall about the three great enemies of a nation – a Tanzanian. Both religious and government leaders of Tanzania mention that there are three major enemies: poverty, ignorance and diseases. Brilliantly, even some institutions in the country have been conducting surveys to trace the success and the present status of these enemies. The issue VI, January 2010 of *Maendeleo Dialogue: Democracy in Tanzania* when making follow-ups about the economic status of the nation describes the persistence of the enemies and the vision for eradicating them. *Maendeleo Dialogue* confirms that: Soon after independence, Tanzania started to implement various programs and policies, and "declared total war against three development

14. Informant E.

problems: poverty, ignorance and disease."[15] One can obtain other details from the political philosophy of some influential politicians within the Tanzanian context. Most of the philosophies that proclaim a fight against those three enemies of people can easily be reflected from the political stands of (the late) Julius Kambarage Nyerere. "During the years of political struggle, Nyerere had developed the outlines for the policies which his economically poor country should follow. With the motto of *Uhuru na Kazi* (Freedom and Work), he at once mounted a major attack on what he considered the three major enemies of his people - poverty, ignorance, and disease."[16] In the political campaign rallies, contestants to try to polish their policies with the strategies for helping people get out of those problems.

Since then as in this respect, most sectors have been fighting against the second great enemy of people, ignorance. Not only that, but also both, the secular government as well as religions have been constantly declaring publicly that those three enemies are the biggest of all, especially in the Tanzanian society. Every human being notes it and fully engages in the fight against them. That is why people are responding to that call as those authorities are declaring and emphasizing.

UNDERSTANDING THE MIND AND THE NATURE OF HUMAN SOCIETY

Many years ago, Phil L. Snyder edited a book called *Detachment and the Writing of History*. This book explores the contribution of Carl L. Becker on historical facts. The book purports that the way in which mind-set works within people causes some transformations. Its functions affect human society. We can read from this book:

> Mind is thus a union of memory, which binds man to what he [sic!] has done, and of intelligence, which restates and reconstructs the past suitably to the present and in the prospect of what he hopes to do in the future. Since this is essentially the nature of mind, it is also essentially the nature of human society, or of the culture upon which a human society is built. From this point of view there can be no point of radical separation of intelligence from feeling and purpose, or of mind from behavior and action. For intelligence is a capacity to use the means at hand for a purpose, to adapt old ideas to new situations, to solve the problems set by an ever changing environment, and to enable

15. *Maendeleo Dialogue*, v.
16. Nyerere in *Britannica Concise Encyclopedia* (Online) (Emphasis is mine).

> conduct to deal effectively with a future which can be neither arrested nor stereotyped. Its work is perennially destructive and constructive: destructive because it must restate the formulas of a past that has become outmoded; constructive because it must seek restated formulas adequate to the purposes and aspirations of the future.[17]

In the quotation above, Becker argues that people use their minds to build human society. They use their mind in whatever way they think can help them fight against the problems in their respective environments. People can change formulas of their lives depending on the needs and interests— that is, depending on their purposes and aspirations. It means, as their environment keeps changing, so do they. Therefore, the way they act reflects their intelligence, feeling, purpose and force from their environment.

In those years, Becker also observed that due to intelligences that people possess, they formed the so-called "climate of opinion." "Climate of opinion" is one of the characteristics of human society.[18] It is "a constellation of related ideas largely inherited but constantly undergoing change under the impact of new conditions which set new problems and demand new solutions."[19] It is time when human society decides to argue, emphasize, and opt toward what favors it. It also reminds all people that every age has its own opinion. Becker believed that people keep on editing whatever does not fit their freedom and responsibility. Human society edits the speech, actions and plans that do not respond to its demands, needs, and interests and human society uses its mind to transform the context.[20]

However, change in attitudes of mind definitely, transforms the ways of doing things. To my surprise; the interviewees stated that some religious leaders remain stationary in fighting against this enemy, ignorance in them, that the nation considered being detrimental to people. I thought that all churches with their leaders would stand in a frontline to eradicate the problem in them, but it is the reverse. There are church ministers who harmonize the problem while complaining over the social transformations taking place.

An interview that I held with lay Christians confirmed the issue of cognitive change in people:

> *At this time, society is highly becoming an educated one. The pastor is in the midst and a leader of an educated society. Society is daily in a process of increasing its education. The pastor and the church*

17. Snyder, *Detachment*, x.
18. Ibid., xi.
19. Ibid.
20. Ibid., xii–xiv; cf. 6–7.

> are of the people within the same society. If society is changing cognitively, it means that also the church is changing cognitively. The number of learned Christians is multiplying. Thus, the pastor being the society's leader should also be changing cognitively.[21]

In addition, an urban informant stated: *Most of the people whom the pastor is leading, working and living with are educated or fast continue to getting education.*[22] The citations above disclose that the number of both Church members and as well as other members of the surrounding community who are becoming learned to a higher level is increasing. Certainly, almost every members of society is getting more education.

Based on his long experience in the church ministry, an aged informant who has already retired from parish pastoral responsibilities testifies that: *The present generation is an intellectual one.*[23] He contrasts with the time when he joined the ordained ministry. In those times, many Churches and the surrounding communities had a few leaders as well as other people with formal education compared to the contemporary generation. Primary schools, secondary school, colleges, universities, and other training institutions were few in Africa and in Tanzania in particular. Therefore, the situation has been very different compared to the present. Today both, society in the Church and in secular circles prefer and enquire for leaders who have higher or at least the same level of education with the community.

The pastor as a leader is now in that midst of a learned and a fast learning society, society that demands their leader is educated as equal as itself or above. A question may be raised: why and how is their pastor required to think about their intellectual status? One of my group informants responded in a lamenting and complaining way that: *Unfortunately, most of our church ministers are very little educated. Most of them are standard seven leavers.*[24] The information from this group may not be satisfactory until we hear another voice from ministers themselves, especially pastors. The pastors themselves admit and confirm that, first; there has been great development of formal education in people, from secondary school to higher education level. This pastor proved by stating that: *There is great development in education in Tanzania compared to the time of the nation's independence. Many people are learned and many more continue learning. However, there is less*

---

21. Informant F.
22. Informant G.
23. Informant D.
24. Informant G.

number in rural areas as in urban; but in both parts, there are people who are secondary education and degree holders.[25]

According to the quotation above from a pastor who has been ministering a rural parish, despite some variations on the number of people with formal education, nonetheless, the development of education in people has been growing in both, rural and urban areas. Second, most pastors feel less educated when they compare themselves with the level of education in their society. Again, a pastor from an urban area discloses that despite the growing number of schools and colleges for people's formal education, still there is great number of pastors who have never reached even the level of secondary education or above it. This informant recounts:

> *The emergence of schools and universities signify that today education is so essential. The increase of educated people in society means an increase of educated church members. Thus, we can say that it is the increase of an educated Church. If we come to the church ministers, the truth is "Many Christians and society are educated, but we are less educated." Most of the pastors are standard seven.*[26] *A few are form four and graduated in universities compared to the number of pastors in the church.*[27]

Thus, we can obtain and construct some insights from this discussion that may be necessary for concluding this section. The interviews show that, first, there has been great and rapid development of education in communities nearly in all areas of Tanzania as well as in the whole continent of Africa. Second, most of the church ministers have not yet been to secondary school education and above it. Even if some of them might be in harmony with the problem of ignorance, however, other pastors are complaining about the problem. The church ministers who complain do argue that it is unfortunate to them to lack such levels of education. In trying to clarify their statements, they respond that secondary or higher education is not only necessary for pastoral ministry, but also for their personal, family, and social life. For them, to attain a higher education is among important things in every one's life. In addition, higher education is for all leaders in society so that they counted upon among reliable resources in society.

It also seems that there are some pastors and evangelists who expect that since they have joined church ministry then their education can constantly be up-graded to qualify as leaders of an educated community. However, in

---

25. Informant A.

26. See chapter two for detailed explanations about the minimum education for every Tanzanian.

27. Informant B.

some ways it may be a different story. It appears that the Church is more or less reluctant to carry the burden of upgrading the ministers to the levels that each pastor or evangelist would want for constructive encounter with social, economic, political, cultural and technological changes. This is why some of those with whom I conversed with show that they are willing to leave the offices and go for further studies, though, it is unfortunate that they are unable to do so due to high educational costs. Consequently, they have to remain and wait for some time in their positions and use the knowledge and skills they already have while leading the intellectuals and tolerating the tensions of social change. They observe that: *We tolerate the situation; we try to teach and preach by using the little knowledge we have.*[28] They have been sharing their problems to their superior authorities on how difficult it is for them as leaders to control and teach or preach to the learning and educated community. Some superiors seem to understand while others delay to understand or to implement the suggestions from their parish pastors.

THE PASTOR AS COMMUNITY EDUCATOR

Apart from preaching, the pastor is also responsible to carrying out the task of teaching the community. Pastors and more or less all church ministers who have undergone theological studies have been responsible in society as Biblical scholars. Being committed to the Church and its constitution, they feel and try to work as scholars and teachers of Biblical Scriptures. It seems that the church authorities expect and perceive all ministers are competent enough to fulfil the ministry of educating people.

E. Harold Jansen illustrates clearly the task of education ministry. Jansen was among bishops of the Evangelical Lutheran Church in America who reflects and discusses the pastoral roles after discovering that pastors were reporting several tensions and challenges due to changes occurring in their society. I find his reflections useful in this work because the title that he dealt with is applicable to the role of an African pastor as stated in chapter three of this book.

He first agrees that a pastor is a community educator who starts to minister to the parish, and thereafter, extends the ministry to the whole public. For Jansen, this pastor is entitled to complex and extensive collection of educational responsibilities. Then, Jansen tries to list some educational tasks that pastors of the ELCT, as well as those of other Churches around the world, are likely to perform as educators of the community. According to Jensen: "Confirmation instruction, Sunday school supervision, . . . adult

28. Informant E.

the pastor in a cognitively changing society 155

classes and forums, [teaching] Bible [knowledge in] schools, orientation for baptism and first communion, orientation for worship leaders, various Bible studies, and orientation for council members."[29]

Jansen continues to highlight:

> Pastors will . . . realize that being an educator has to do with the entire enterprise of instructing, equipping, and enabling people for new levels of awareness, abilities, and participation in the extensive tasks and experiences possible for a child of God through the gospel. The pastor . . . also acts as the developer of the curriculum, the selectors of the materials to be used, the recruiter of the class members, the counsellor to deal with various problems that emerge, and finally, the person whose presence seems to convince the [society] that this is important.[30]

Jansen illustrates the scope of the task regarding the educational orientations. The pastor carries out lots of teaching people so that some may become aware, capable, and participative in enabling other people through the gospel. Other tasks that the pastor performs are to participate in educational forums, conceptualize and develop some policies and strategies for Christian education and for social growth. It implies that this pastor works as both, a policy maker as well as a policy implementer. These tasks show how important and busy a pastor is. Furthermore, it calls for a need to be competent and constructive by using his or her educational backgrounds and capabilities to manage and utilize the resources (skills and materials) available.

My informants confirmed that, as Jansen states above, educating society is among the primary tasks of pastors and trained evangelists. They carry out this role, for example, through teaching some topics during worship services, in Sunday schools, and Bible knowledge or Christian education in schools. Let us take at least three interviews as examples to show how pastors are responsible for this essential role of the church. The first is from a pastor, the second is from evangelists, and the third from lay Christians (elders and other Christians). The first said: *Among the roles of pastors and evangelists is teaching Bible knowledge in secondary schools.*[31] The second informant added: *In schools, we teach Bible knowledge, for example, we teach about creation stories in the Bible. In addition, we have to teach certain issues of the Bible in the church.*[32] Another pastor added to the next consequence of

---

29. Jansen, "The Pastor as Parish Educator," 57.
30. Ibid.
31. Informant D.
32. Informant E.

educational growth in parishioners to the above descriptions. He responded to the interview that:

> *As people get more education, they also bring many questions to church leaders. Some of them need secular knowledge in order for one to respond to them. We mostly meet with this problem when we teach certain issues of the Bible. For example, students ask difficult questions when we teach creation stories in the Bible. They relate with their studies as their teachers teach them. This has led some of the church ministers not to teach Bible knowledge in schools. Many of us who have never attended secondary school education or Bible schools do not attempt this task due to fear of tough and tricky questions, otherwise we will tell lies or humiliate ourselves before students and society. We also preach regularly in the church than more teaching. Christians and society at present are too speculative to be fooled. You cannot easily fool them. They are very inquisitive and critical.*[33]

Therefore, the effect from the quotations above (of informant C and E) relates to criticisms toward the teaching role of church ministers. When teaching of Christian education, Bible knowledge, or even in some councils and meetings, 'people ask tough and tricky questions.' This situation discomforts some of them. As a result, there are times when they attempt to diverge as they respond to certain tough questions. Why do they do so? As analyzed and discussed above (see the subheading: *The Pastor as Leader of an Educated and Changing Society*), the problem of deceiving may result from low knowledge or lack of confidence.

At last, lay Christians expressed that pastors carry multiple responsibilities including that of educating the community. They used the terms teacher, advisor and influencer. "*A pastor is a preacher, teacher, counselor, adviser, administrator, etc. He or she can easily influence people to change from one type of life to another better one. Society perceives the pastor as a knowledgeable person. Therefore, a pastor should show seriousness in his or her work.*"[34]

The above quotations from both Jansen and informants illustrate the comprehensive picture of educational tasks that a pastor of the ELCT/SD has to or performs in a week or in a year. The pastor performs those tasks during both, worship services and outside church premises. Even if pastors themselves admit that those roles are theirs and that they are trying to perform them; some pastors state that most of the time they face severe

---

33. Informant E.
34. Informant G.

the pastor in a cognitively changing society 157

ambivalences and that they sometimes feet like surrendering the ministry. The problem that most of them share with other fellows concerns their lack of academic qualifications when they compare themselves with those of most members of society. From their practical experience, they feel that it would be good for an educator of the community to have at least similar levels of education to most lay Christians. They deliberately express their complaints and the way those roles are becoming harder to perform in relation to the educational changes that going on in society. Thereafter, I got an interest to know the effects of what those pastors experience due to educational differences between them and community.

DIFFERENCES IN EDUCATIONAL LEVELS BETWEEN THE PASTOR AND COMMUNITY

The main question here is: what are the effects on the church minister when they performed their role amid a big gap in the levels of education from that of society? In their responses to this question, informants gave several effects and their impact. In this section I first of all start by an illustration from one lay informant who gives a wide description on how society perceives the church minister, especially a pastor, and some effects and impacts that emerges in that discussion. Thereafter, by support from almost all informants; I present some general effects and impacts to signify how most church ministers understand themselves as leaders of the intellectual society, especially, during undertaking their roles. Likewise, in turn, the same illustration may even confirm how society itself feels the situation.

> *Although they do good jobs; they get many challenges from Christians and society. Their difference of education from that of their people makes most of the pastors feel inferior, hence have less confidence before the public or if they may be required to teach certain issues from the Bible in the church, in schools or in academic conferences. It is important to bear in mind that one of the qualities of a church minister at this age is reasonable education. A pastor is needed to have wide knowledge on diverse things and disciplines – wide knowledge theologically, intellectually and in all other dimensions of philosophies of a human being's life. The difference between his or her level of education and that of the congregation should not have a very big gap as it is today. This is very important especially in towns. Many believers are government officials, business people and many others are highly educated. All those are his or her church members. His or her preaching and teaching should*

> *reach their level and respond to their problems; otherwise, they will not feel helped by their church and minister.*[35]

One important impression that one can appreciate from society is the acknowledgement that in spite of their low education, *they* [church ministers try to] *do good jobs*. This witness statement implies that Christians accept pastors as ministers at the level of their knowledge and experience. However, there are serious impacts from the big difference in levels of education between pastors and people they lead.

First, it may make church ministers feel inferior before the public because other members of the community have higher education than themselves. After a long discussion about the problem of feeling inferior and the way the situation is so serious that it touches their consciences; another informant freely described that sometimes there is even a feeling of withdrawing from pastoral ministry: *Following the level of education of society; today the church needs to be led by highly educated pastors. Therefore, I suggest that, either the contemporary pastors be up-graded or to resign so that the educated society is led by intellectual ministers. It seems that highly educated pastors will lead the future church better than it is today.*[36] In my opinion, withdrawal from work is perhaps not the first and best answer because; even an educated minister can face similar problems. For example, if the society does not accept one for other reasons, he or she can probably experience stress, burnout, despair, frustrations or related problems. Therefore, to me, withdrawing from work cannot be a solution to such a problem; rather, the best alternative is to upgrade one's education.

Second, lack of education may reduce confidence and authority in the minister and hence the community or certain influential individuals might possibly come up and take over the whole role of the leader, especially, during processes of decision-making. The following testimonies emphasize this aspect: *low education or lack of wide knowledge on some important secular issues also leads a pastor into less confidence in his or her tasks.*"[37] A pastor confirmed that argument by predicting and commenting that: "*It seems that society will have a strong decision making over their minister. It is good for pastors to be aware and get prepared to get off the control we have, and which is getting out of our powers and authorities.*[38] After a long conversation with him, this pastor appeared uncomfortable with some social changes and arguments from the people because they attacked his arguments or preach-

---

35. Informant G.
36. Informant A.
37. Informant F.
38. Informant A.

ing and teaching due to his low level of education. He also expressed that, there are times when the situation is very upsetting in the way that, some members of society are sometimes responding negatively to him, especially during parish councils.

Third, low level of education in a pastor can probably discomfort society. There is some witness that: *Learned Christians tell that they are not comfortable with the level of education that their pastors have.*[39] Fourth, low education may possibly hinder a leader from being competent in using technical instruments: *In this generation, many of the instruments for official or worship services are technical. For example, there are computer applications and electronic devices that the pastor needs to be knowledgeable.*[40]

Fifth, low level of education can possibly *diminish or debase the status of the minister* and consequently devalue the status of the church and of society. Lack of communication competence in terms of language proficiency seemed to bring this effect on one's role of confidentiality in pastoral ministry.

> *In terms of communication competence, the pastor today ought to know at least one international language, for instance English, language, for our country Tanzania. If there happens to come a guest; then is good if a pastor can easily communicate with that guest rather than asking an interpreter for him or for the congregation. This, on the one hand debases him or her, his or her church as well as society. It diminishes his or her status, ministerial value and confidentiality.*[41]

According to the above informant, the mode of communication that society wants from pastors is different from the one used other objects like mobile phones. Now it is an oral competence in communication, that is, knowledge of at least one international language is important. The reason that this informant is trying to show relates to confidentiality in some issues. If a pastor is ignorant in some international languages, such a problem cannot preserve some matters that require confidentiality.

Sixth, it may lead the minister into providing shallow education to his or her people. *Even the preaching and teachings that he or she will be making cannot reach the level of the society's level of understanding. You will provide shallow education due to your shallow knowledge.*[42]

Almost in line with the above effect, however, I prefer to discuss separately two more effects from the following informant:

39. Informant A.
40. Ibid.
41. Ibid.
42. Ibid.

> *Consequently, each one of them wants to be served or administered according to his or her level of education and life standard. Again, this creates a problem and becomes a challenge to the pastor if all his or her educational backgrounds (both theological and secular education) are low or not helping perform the ministry. For example, a person with form four or six or degree intellect expects me to reach him or her in that reputation. There are parishes or groups of Christians in society who reject or ignore some pastors if they know that he or she is not competent as they would want or expect. The situation is one of the reasons why most of the learned youth do not go to churches. They argue that there is nothing new they will learn in church. May be this is true in many places, though there are other bigger reasons than this. Even during meetings or when teaching some topics in the church, the learned ask tough questions that require secular knowledge in answering them. There is a tendency of diverging to explain in the way Christians may want so that you do not entrap yourself into a problem that is above your level of education.*[43]

The seventh effect relates to devaluation of the minister and the church, as well as losing the members. For example, the quotation above points out that sometimes society might ignore both the church and the pastor. This may hence lead into loss of church members, especially the learned and the youth. It seems that once there are unmet and unaddressed expectations and questions, some people may possibly reject or change their attitudes toward their pastors as well as even their church membership. Expectations such as that of their pastor to be competent in knowledge and skills are widespread. Nevertheless, how can a minister become competent without some relevant knowledge and training? Together with the suggestion on the requirement for a secular education that informants emphasized, we will reflect and discuss those questions in the last chapter where I discuss some implications and responses.

Moreover, as the eighth effect, the criticisms from the parishioners also seem to create fear, loss of confidence in pastors and evangelists, and hence some Church ministers become tempted to neglect the teaching role and concentrate only on preaching. *The contemporary Church members and society in general are very inquisitive. They have a tendency of asking questions about everything in life. Therefore, to encounter this, pastors need to go for more training. The society advises pastors are to upgrade their levels of education. Churches build education centers as part of alternatives for people's*

---

43. Informant C.

education.[44] Due to low education, pastors might enter into the danger of misinterpreting certain Church doctrines. It implies that the prescribed roles are too tough in some pastors and other church ministers to carry out. This also highlights how some church ministers are not able to keep up with social changes. As a result, they find themselves entering into daily encounter with severe tensions. Even so, some difficult situations could be manageable if at all church ministers received constant training through formal knowledge and skills relevant to social change in contemporary era. Therefore, it is necessary to suggest the church to take intentional measures and find strategies to help all ministers with training, retraining, and set normal schedules for regular in-service training for pastors and other church ministers.

Conclusion

I would like to make a note that the aim of this analysis was not to devalue the level of education that church ministers already have; neither does the book attempt to ignore the efforts that church authorities have been doing. The analysis in this chapter aimed at pointing out the existing inadequacy of education to ministers in relation to social change. It points out that, despite some efforts that the church has done or is doing, still, something more needs reconsidering. The analysis and discussion shows how cognitive change in people closely links to social change. The change in one's mind-set usually affects his or her ways of life.

Another noticeable feature is that, many members of society are constantly acquiring higher educational status than those of their pastors. In spite of their low education, pastors are leaders of both, those who have less or equal and those who have higher level of education. However, almost every informant acknowledges that the two main roles that a pastor plays are not as easy as one can imagine. They call for the need to up-grade the level of education.

During interviews and in analyses and discussions of data, it shows that there is a big gap between the highly learned and the low learned. Sometimes the educational gaps, in many ways represent a hindrance for pastors to perform their tasks. Furthermore, the educational gap that has existed for many years between pastors and the community seemed to discourage some pastors especially if they encounter constant pressures from the community. For many years now the church has been reluctant to educate its church ministers so that they can respond to the changes. Then

44. Informant H.

I ask myself, what is missing that requires some intentional steps ahead, and why? The Constitution that prescribes the roles does not provide clear and liberal principles that direct pastors to upgrade their education or the church itself to constantly reconsider the educational levels of employees. This process can help both, pastors and society to respond constructively toward the changing realities in life and ministry.

Before moving to another discussion, let us cite one observation regarding the significance of observing the times in which we pastor work and live as recorded in the Bible. The Bible records that their leaders " . . . had understanding of the times, to know what Israel ought to do . . . " (1 Chronicles 12:32). According to this description, the Israelites' leaders read the times, the changes and figured out how to go about with the people and their situations. Moreover, the record in the above quotation calls the contemporary churches and their ministers to take that lesson. They, too, must look for the best ways as to reach the mobile, religious, complex, and diverse groups as far as the changing society is concerned. Yet, there is another important question to me, especially in this book. If such faith leaders who carried out their tasks more than two thousand years ago observed the times, society, and contexts without distorting the mission and life of their religion; how can the contemporary pastors and all other church ministers understand their society, live, and minister in their contemporary situations? I will try to discuss this question in the last two chapters (6 and 7) in which I present some discussions on the contemporary stage of the Church and the implications and responses regarding the changing reality.

6

IN THE NAME OF SOCIAL CHANGE

THE CHANGING PHASE OF THE CHURCH AND ITS IMPLICATION TO THE ROLE OF THE AFRICAN PASTOR

INTRODUCTION

IN CHAPTERS FOUR AND five, I have presented the analyses and discussions of the context in which the ELCT/SD pastor works. As I stated before, a major emphasis has been on some practical features of social change and their effects on both, the role of the pastor, as well as on the mission and life of the Church. The main source of information is from both, the lived experiences of church ministers (pastors and evangelists) and the lay Christians (church elders and others). In chapter three, the discussion points out that a pastor belongs to the Church. It is the church that calls, trains, ordains and appoints pastors for parish and other social roles. Furthermore, the church itself analyzes the responsibilities into which a pastor has to be committed. Therefore, a pastor works as an agent of the church.

The argument from my informants about the changing face of the Church due to growing social changes is the reason for developing this chapter. The informants show that the changes that have been happening are altering the expressions of the Church and bring some tensions to ministers when they implement their pastoral roles. One of the main questions intended for this chapter is this: how does the change in society also change an image of the Church? First, the movements of people from one place to another have been decreasing members in one area while increasing in other areas into which they immigrated. Second, the many renewal movements within the Lutheran denomination changed the religious expressions of the Church. Third, the changing morality of society also changed the appearance of the Church. Fourth, the economic and educational improvement helped Christian people change their lifestyles and become critical toward their leaders. All those stand as examples of how the Church was changing its image and attitude due to the changing society. The present image of the Church reflects the reality of society.

It means that society with its change rhythms can also help one figure out what kind of the Church a pastor serves. Equally, society can also help church ministers determine the nature of the roles they ought to perform according to the nature of society to which they are allocated. The pastors in this book encounter difficulty and pressures because the reality of society and the prescriptions of the church authorities are not in harmony. The authorities and the contemporary society differ in interests. Most of the time, the aims and needs that pastors want seem to collide with, or divert from the interests of the reality in society. As a result, in most cases the efforts of pastors to implement the prescribed roles are less effective because as the pastor wants to fulfill the requirements of his or her church authority, society wants that same pastor to direct the tasks toward responding to its problems. This is a point where the pastor encountered tensions. The tension is between the church authorities and the changing reality and interests of society.

According to the theory of Charles Taylor, those forces are due to the contemporary spheres in which society is living. When society expects its pastors to think about the problem of economy, pastors seem to be silent. Escobar states that in this sphere (the globalized world) communication is a necessary characteristic feature of the contemporary world because of social change. When society feels and demands pastors to live in a "globalized world"[1] where there is fast, effective and better communication and transportation, the pastor is not yet fully practicing the demands of this economic sphere. Again, when society demands and practices the democratic freedom, the pastor wants society to be fully submissive to church authorities. Pastors serve the status quo more than living according to the changing society. Society wants church ministers to realize that the traditional authorities belong to a different space and time. Now society is calling for the church to revisit and reform the stipulated doctrines and rules. Moreover,

---

1. Schreiter, *The New Catholicity*, x, xi, 130.

prescribed rules and order of the church require be revisited because they seem to be unchanging, neither are they flexible to address the problems of a changing society. This is among the reasons for the informants to claim that the Church and the whole society now are in another different phase (sphere) and time.[2] They use the terms like new era, age, time, and the postmodern. Others informant are completely reluctant about the dilemma. The assignment to find its clear meaning and descriptions remain to researchers.

As I have highlighted elsewhere above, the task in this chapter is to explore the location of the present Church and the roles of the pastor in it. I present my discussion by reflecting on the experiences and evaluations of informants concerning the social changes already taken place (see chapter 4 and 5, cf. chapter 2). I also reflect how those changes in turn signify different images: first, the phase of the Church; second, the image of pastoral roles; and third, a call for pastors to be aware about and have positive attitudes toward social change. In this chapter, also we look at the status of contemporary phase of the church, reinterpretation of theological or church doctrines and today's proper practices in pastoral ministry. However, the third issue will be mainly the task of chapter seven where I present the discussion on some challenges and problems that seem to need further attention.

In locating the Church, the chapter highlights some propositions on the alteration of phases of the church, postmodernism, multiculturalism, and other responses that are required for the pastoral ministry in the respective era regarding changes in society. I reflect and review those ideas from various scholars such as Samuel Escobar, John R. Gibbins and Bo Reimer, Robert Schreiter, Sturla Stålsett, Paul F. Knitter, and Samuel Escobar who try to bring forward the reflection about the stages of the contemporary Church and how such phases bring implications on the role of the pastor. The chapter also presents some important suggestions from the American Lutheran bishops about the roles of the pastor as they relate with the present phase of the Church. Essentially important, also in this chapter, I try to contribute by adding the role of the pastor in the economic sphere of society as I pursue my reflection from the theory of social imaginary that I use in this book. I find it important because the theory describes most of the realities that one can observe and apply in Tanzanian society today. The lived experiences of the informants, the analysis and the overview in chapter two testify that the Tanzanian society is facing poverty. The whole society, whether religiously or secularly, is daily struggling to improve its economy. Therefore, it is within a bond of economic sphere.

2. Cf. Taylor, *Modern Social Imaginaries,* 69, 83–89, 97–99, 101–107, 109, 115, 127, 138, 143, 149–154.

THE CHANGING PHASE OF THE CHURCH

We can start with this question: in which era is society and Church living and working? In responding to this question in this section, the discussion concentrates in looking at some characteristics of the era in which both society and the Church with its ministers in particular are living and working. The aim of this sub section is to find the position and locate the Church in its stage regarding social change with its whirls and beats. I call the first subpart, a postmodern era. This serves as one of the age locations in which the Church exists to date. Thereafter, I discuss the phases of the Church, and finally the implications as responses to the role of the pastor.

The Church in the Postmodern Era

Samuel Escobar states that now Christianity is in the postmodern era. On the one hand, this era contains also a post-Christian world. He states that: "The way in which Christianity is displaced from its role of honor and influence in society where it was an official religion in the past has generated what we call a post-Christian world. On the other hand, the renewed interest in all kinds of religion, including those that existed before Christian missionaries appeared can better be described as a sign of postmodernity."[3] Before moving to other sub-features of postmodernity, let us have a look on the meaning and characteristics of postmodernity. The term postmodernity is hereby contracted to its noun, postmodernism.

Gibbins and Reimer state that postmodern era illustrates the pluralism of values and de-alignment that also accompanies the re-alignments in varied lines of contexts and levels of the lives of society. Those pluralizations and alignments alter the performance and expectation of all institutions. As society enters and practices these pluralizations and realignments it produces fluidity and complexities both in religious and in other areas of life; politics is among them. The main cause of all those value pluralizations and de-alignment are economic and social changes.[4] Consequently, the fluidity and complexity bring out some problems in all dealings of management. They write:

> A long-term process of value pluralisation and de-alignment, accompanied by realignments along more local and transnational, group and individual lines–reflecting wider and deeper economic and social change-has produced fluidity and complexity

---

3. Escobar, *A Time for Mission*, 68, cf. Clough, *Ethics in Crisis*, 16, 119, 122–125.
4. Gibbins and Reimer, "Postmodernism," 301.

in politics, as well as problems in the management of self and society, economy and government. Postmodernist value change has altered the way governments, institutions, and politicians are evaluated, and has challenged old ideas and expectations about government.[5]

The above observation from Gibbins and Reimer points out the position of economy and society and their effects on other institutions. It shows that postmodernist value change not only brings and calls for the exercise of carrying out re-evaluations, but also challenges all old ideas and expectations about leadership and organization structures.

After reflecting on the notions that open the idea of postmodernist value change, it is important to explain the aim of this subsection in this book. Gibbins and Reimer reflect the intention for expanding the idea of postmodernity. Therefore, I adopt their opinions because they reflect my goals regarding the objectives and survey outcomes done empirically as presented in this book. Though in a very long phrase, two aims stand valuable for this respect:

> The first is to show that postmodern theory helps us to understand and perhaps explain contemporary value change in [Africa] and its impact on beliefs [and practices] about the role and legitimacy of [pastors and Church] government [regarding present situation in society]. The second is to demonstrate that the concept of postmodernism can be operationalized and put to empirical use. We hypothesize the emergence of new 'structures of feeling' and new formations of values which are united by little else than a common concern of individuals and groups for the right to be and to express themselves. Those who accept this reality and seek to open spaces for the exercise of their diversity, difference, and identity, are postmodernists. Postmodernists are characterized by a high level of cultural capital, and they are directed toward leisure, life-style, and image. *Expressivism* is the core notion of postmodernism, measured by such indicators as the high priority given to individual development and restlessness. Our hypothesis implies that, rather than moving in patterns structured around traditional socio-economic groupings, people move in a multitude of both individual- and group-based directions. This may be discerned in work as well as in leisure, and at all levels-from local to global. New patterns of value orientations affect the behavior of people, and as these

5. Ibid.

affect both beliefs about government and government behavior, traditional allegiances and interests are being transcended.[6]

It seems that, for Gibbins and Reimer, once there is a feature of the emergence of new structures of feeling, the new formation of patterns and values, and people can express themselves, then it must be realized that a postmodern age has come. As a result, all levels of behaviors in people and governments change. Value changes affect the attitude and performance of institutions. Consequently, this is what happens in the Church as well as it does in the life of ministers.

The Theory of Postmodernism

Gibbins and Reimer further describe the orientations of postmodernist age. They argue that as it relates and differs from postmaterialism, postmodernism deals with the following:

I. It seeks to explain shifts in political inputs and outputs through the examination of value change.
II. It detects the emergence of new values, and endeavours to relate these to the development of new selves seeking realization, which are brought into being through generational socialization.
III. It identifies new young cohorts as educated, activist, and prone to belong to new movements.
IV. It pinpoints new issues and axes of conflict.
V. The four orientations above are similar to that of postmaterialists.
VI. It seeks self-expression.
VII. It seeks fulfilment on a developmental scale as against hedonist enjoyment.
VIII. It is concerned with the immediate, the present, and has no agreed narrative for the future.
IX. It relishes the simulated, the image, and the representation.
X. It sees the self as being constantly constructed, deconstructed, and reconstructed throughout their lifetime.
XI. It shows how the value orientation is pluralist and heterogeneous.

---

6. Ibid. 301- 302.

xii. It stresses technology and the media with a growing awareness of existential and social insecurity and risk.

xiii. It stresses exposure to everyday culture, the mass media, and travel.

xiv. Ultimately, postmodernism attacks the canons of modernism.[7]

Unlike postmaterialism, postmodernism can be materialist; unlike postmodernism, postmaterialism can be modernist. However, "The two orientations cannot be collapsed into one, for postmodernist and postmaterialist theory are competitors to explain political change in the . . . world."[8]

A Changing Political World

Gibbins and Reimer continue to state that people live in a changing political world. It implies that the changes that take place in politics do alter other institutions and aspects of life. However, change in political arenas is in most cases undermined by cultural changes. Other changes that undermine the political world include technological, organizational, and social change. Gibbins and Reimer describe:

> In brief, postmodernists claim that many of the practices and preconditions of politics in the modern world are being undermined by technological, organizational, social, and above all cultural changes. Which create discontinuities, incongruity, dissonance, fragmentation, and dissensus. Some key changes include the transfer to a post-industrial information and consumer society; the disorganization of capitalism, socialism, and bureaucracy; transnationalism and globalization processes; the reorganization of employment . . . ; arrival of new classes or segments within classes; heightened conflict between the public and private worlds; and the emergence of postmodern culture. The latter involves the emergence of . . . the reorganization of leisure, the life world, and habitus; the commodification and mass production of a plurality of images, cultures, and lifestyles. These developments entail the creation of new expressive selves reflection and reformulation. We use the concept of . . . and new attitudes, both local and universalized, stressing immediate gratification . . . The self and society, citizen and state, have thus changed-sometimes dramatically. The rate of change demands reflection and reformulation. We use the concept of postmodernism to account for these changes and try to show

7. Ibid., 302–303.
8. Ibid., 303.

how postmodern value change affects political behavior and beliefs in government [and religion]."⁹

The paragraphs in the quotation above highlight the situation happening in political world and the demands needed to meet the dramatic changes. Moreover, Gibbins and Reimer depict that the changes emerging in political world happen even in other aspects of social life. The changes enquire for an awareness of the needs that changes call for and the reformulation in order to match with reality at hand. Therefore, the overall "Attention is given to the everyday; to popular rather than to elite culture; to alternative rather than to dominant ideologies; to divergent life-styles rather than to the dominant social order; and to the emerging power of the mass media in constructing and maintaining them . . . ."¹⁰

Identities of Postmodernism: Conditions, Definitions and implications¹¹

Gibbins and Reimer ask this question: "What conditions should a postmodern value orientation try to meet?"¹² They argue that there has been no survey research conducted regarding this kind of value orientation. Then they show some important conditions that must be met in order to grasp a postmodern value orientation:

I. The value orientation must be conceptually and theoretically coherent.
II. It must be grounded in arguable historically, economic, social, and political context.
III. It must be definable with appropriate indicators.
IV. Hypotheses must be framed about change which may be tested and supported by empirical evidence.¹³

The above conditions are necessary for one to take hold of postmodern value orientation.

After presenting the conditions, now I turn to highlighting the historical meaning of postmodernism. With its volatile history, there are at least six kinds of accounts or usage identified:

9. Ibid., 303–304.
10. Ibid., 305.
11. I borrow this concept from Gibbins and Reimer, 305.
12. Ibid.
13. Ibid., 306.

I. Postmodernism may refer to aesthetic and architectural movements or cultures.

II. It may refer to cultural *avant garde* or elite movement whose cry was 'anything goes.'

III. It may also refer to popular phenomena in which consumer life-style and mass consumption dominate taste and fashion, and in which groups stress differences and distinction in their attempt to accumulate cultural capital.

IV. Postmodernism may also refer to a general cultural orientation with special recognition of the new self and groups rooted in the economic and political context of late modernity, with significant expressions in political culture as well as life-style.

V. Postmodernism may refer to a *Zeitgeist* or the spirit of the age that described to start around 1875 and prevailing until some unspecified future time.

VI. Postmodernism may also refer to a general cultural orientation, which emerges from the wider contextual arguments.[14]

In summary, Gibbins and Remeir state:

> The process of transformation from modernity to postmodernity, is postmodernization . . . Old class allegiances have fragmented; social de-alignments and realignments have emerged. In economic terms, modernity was characterized by two rational forms of production and distribution: capitalism and communism. . . . Thus the broad postmodernist picture is of modern economies becoming unwieldy, unworkable, unpredictable, and disorganized . . . The key dynamic of postmodernity is not economic or social but cultural. . . . According to some observers, the new state will take the form of a revived civil society, with government as umpire rather than provider. . . .[15]

It means that once society has transformed, then all structures in life become altered. The key dynamic process of postmodernism is cultural. What are those process features? The next section discusses about cultural ages that demonstrate the development.

---

14. Ibid.
15. Ibid., 306–310; cf. 311–315, 320, 328–330.

Three Cultural Ages as Process Features of Development into Postmodern Era

Again, similar to the statements above, Escobar notices that the postmodern era has created a new culture that people around the world share. Then he describes that society has undergone through three cultural ages: first, there is a *'premodern'* culture; second, *'modernity'*; third, *'postmodernity'*.[16] For Escobar the contemporary church is in the third era. The present characteristics of the society that pastors experience are some of the marks of the postmodern era. Even so, in the third era both religious and secular societies are in a constant process of change. In this third era, many people are getting educated; there is great interaction among people; there are varied ways of relating, of moving around and of communicating worldwide; and most of the postmodern Christians are spreading all over the world.[17]

Globalization, a Feature of Postmodernity

Several times during the processing of research for this book, especially when I wanted some clarifications from the respondents about the contemporary life of society, church ministry, and about the roles of the pastor; informants responded by stating that the social and cultural context and the times in which they live and work is challenging and changing rapidly. Then they point out that the Church, society and the pastors are now in the global time outlook. They are aware that: *Our Christians and society are in a global point in time.*[18] Their perceptions resemble to the ideas of Schreiter.[19] Schreiter states that the contemporary Church is living in the globalized society. This is a globalized world, where there is a compression of time and space. Schreiter remarks to all theologians that when doing theology in this contemporary world:

> We must be at once aware of how our world has been changing and what skills and practices are needed to understand, communicate, and act within it. . . . we must not merely change the *narratives* of our histories, but transform our sense of what it means to live, to be, in other times and different spaces, both human and historical. Living in a globalized world, where time and

---

16. Ibid. Emphasis original.
17. Escobar, *A Time for Mission*, 69.
18. Informant B.
19. Schreiter, *The New Cotholicity*, 76, 133.

space have been compressed, . . . a truly intercultural way of doing theology between the global and the local is required of us.[20]

Schreiter is raising some essential issues for the contemporary theologians: first, all contemporary theologians need to be aware that the Church is now in a different world, a world that has a global outlook in terms of communication, understanding the meaning of life, time, and in terms of spaces.

Second, the Church exists in the globalized and changing world. For Schreiter, change is one of the characteristics of this world. Third, theologians ought to find the essential skills, policies, and necessary practices needed to understand, to communicate and to act in this world. Fourth, society is living in the age of intercultural lifestyle, "the age of freedom and liberalisation of communication."[21]

Sturla J. Stålsett is one of the proponents of the above arguments. In his article *Religion and Globalisation* he states that religion is within the midst of globalization. Religion has no exemption. He writes:

> As world history has entered the era of globalisation it has become ever clearer that religion is not something that primarily belongs to the past. Contrary to what was held by many social scientists and students of religion some decades ago, global processes of modernization have not led to fading of religion from the public arena. Instead, as the world has become more interlinked we have seen a resurgence of religion in many regions and many spheres of society. Hence, to get the complex process of global transformation in our time, it is vital to study the role of religion in these processes.[22]

Stålsett's observations show that the transformations taking place worldwide in society have transferred both, the religions as well as their ministers into a new era – the era of globalization. The whole world history is currently living in a new world. This era is characterized by interlinks, resurgence of religion, and spheres of society.

Yet, Stålsett and his colleagues bring more insights about the situation of religion in the globalized age. The same as of society, the world history puts religion in the globalized age. In this globalized state of religion, there are great "contemporary developments that affect us all."[23] While defining

20. Schreiter, *The New Catholicity*, 133, cf. 76, 129, 130; Jagodzinski & Dobbelaere, "Secularization and Church," 77–115; Gibbins & Reimer, "Postmodernism," 301–330.

21. Escobar, *A time for Mission*, 12–14; Fihavango, "Leadership and the Family," 184, 186, 189–191.

22. Stålsett, "Religion and Globalisation," 9–10.

23. Ibid., 10.

the concept "globalisation," Stålsett shows that in this era there are great transformations and transfers that:

> involve all regions and societies around the globe although in different forms and to different degrees, creating a stronger *interdependency* between these regions and societies. These processes of transformation are due firstly to the unprecedented acceleration of the speed, range, and cost reduction of communication through the digital revolution in information technology. Second, they are both caused and thoroughly marked by the (re-)organization of world economy according to neoliberal principles.[24]

In the quotation above, Stålsett depicts some important features of a globalized age, the process as well as the causes for the transformations. Likewise, he shows that "The (post) globalised age is the age of the global empire. . . . The process of globalization is notable in at least three fields: economy, politics and culture."[25] This situation leads religion to find itself encountering undefined globalizing dimensions and contradictions, ambiguities, 'transfers and transformations,' and 'integration and resistance.'[26] For Stålsett, "Globalisation means the transfers, flows, communication not just of commodities or money. There is also an important process of globalisation of concepts and ideas, not least ethical and religious concepts and ideas. . . . Globalisation calls for a hermeneutic of transcultural and inter-religious encounters."[27] As a consequent, being in this globalized age, it may be difficult to understand the Christian religion. So, what should pastors and other theologians do in order to sustain the Christian faith while coping with social change as in this age? Hence, in very long statement, Stålset proposes that:

> In order thus to contribute to a better understanding of religion in a globalised age we are convinced that a contextually rooted and case-oriented approach is necessary. . . . The particular focus of these analyses is Christianity's potential for critical mobilization against and resistance to globalizing forces, as well as its capacity as a resource for integration into these global processes, in the tension between its local rootedness (contextuality, particularlism) and its transnational, global outreach and scope (universalism, holism). The task before us is thus empirical-analytical, in that it requires analyses of different sides of the

24. Ibid (Emphasis in italics original).
25. Ibid., 12.
26. Ibid., 12, 13, 14 (Emphasis original).
27. Ibid., 14.

> interaction between religion and globalisation through particular case-studies. But it is also propositional-normative, in that it sets forth, on the basis of these studies, possible (re)interpretations of Christian faith and religious worldviews in the face of globalisation, while at the same time assessing globalisation processes in light of these religious traditions. . . . Globalisation does not only represent a tremendous increase in global communication and transportation, but also in many cases travels in new and unexpected directions.[28]

The proposed approaches for living and working with the globalized age need taking into high considerations. Pastors and other Church ministers have an obligation to undertake constant researches and assessments of contemporary society and Christianity in order not to be carried away or stressed by the tensions and forces of globalization that it brings into contexts; but rather, they should incorporate them constructively to bring out fruitful outcomes.

Similar to the ideas of the scholars above, the data from the informants makes an emphasis on the existence of fast change. They acknowledge that the postmodern era has some characteristics that call for change even in some outlooks and work operations of churches. As I defined above, the following are among characteristics of the postmodern society that informants mentioned frequently.

Generation Gap

They feel that most contemporary members of society belong in the postcolonial and postmodern age. It is no longer a period of modernity although there are those who belong to both generations. For example, one informant witnessed: *We are in a new and changed generation. There is a big generation gap from that of the early church. In addition, we lead society that belongs to old and new generations.*[29] With such arguments, they describe that sometimes there are conflicts between the old and the young generations due to varied interests, attitudes and ways of doing things. The youth is among other groups that struggle for the changes to match with the context in which they are living. Each group wants its needs and interests be realized first. The informants stated that there have been times when the situation made a difficult task to lead such a society. Usually each group wants recognition and its problem be solve in the first place. Some informants complain that

28. Ibid., 14, 15. Cf. 16, and 37.
29. Informant B.

the youth are not listening to their old ministers. In a lamenting voice, an old informant once argued that some youth claim that old pastors are outdated; as he laments, *later on they started calling us as the old people who are outdated and conservative elders.*[30] Such situations make most pastors (especially the old ones) work under great fear of the youth and other pressures.

Science and Technology

As I pointed it out in the analysis and discussion of the findings, society under study has been aware of all changes including the use of science and technology. As noted elsewhere above, Fihavango points out that we live "in the twenty-first century, a century of science and technology, a century of communication . . . At a time when the world experiences a situation in which, as far as communication is concerned there are no longer boundaries. With the World Wide Web information flow all directions around the world."[31] Using a modern science and technology is among major characteristics of the contemporary religious and secular societies. People report daily that this is a time of improved skills and knowledge. For example, in the interview with evangelists, they testified that: *society is advancing a lot today. It is living in a time of science and technology. Many people are doing things in a modern and attractive ways.*[32]

As I stated before, this aspect of skills and knowledge makes communications easier and fast. Right from the previous chapters we hear that African theologians and pastors admit that the Church, pastors, and society are now in the twenty-first century, a century of science and technology and a century of communication. Due to this science and technology, the church is encountering constant forces for transformation and interactive society. This advancement makes both religious society as well as the secular societies of altering some old ways of life sometimes without considering the traditionally prescribed boundaries. The development in communication networks enhances this practice of rapid change. The parochial arena does no longer have a wide room for existence to date. That is why, most scholars argue that "Today, and tomorrow will never be like yesterday."[33] That is why even the morals and other practical matters keep changing.[34]

30. Informant D.
31. Fihavango, "Leadership and the Family," 184.
32. Informant E.
33. Fihavango, "Leadreship and the Family," 184.
34. Fihavango, "Leadreship and the Family," 184, 185, 190; Mugambi, "Rites of Passages and Human Sexuality," 228; Escobar, *A Time for Mission,* 69.

A Culture of Choices and Evaluation of Leaders

The contemporary society has entered into a culture of multiple options and choices. The term culture here means ways of life whereby people develop certain behaviors that they feel are attractive and suitable for their living. Additionally, in this sub-section, I use the concept 'A culture of Choice and Evaluation of Leaders' as it originates from Jackson W. Carroll in his book *God's Potters*. Carroll states that when people get tired or need to meet certain requirements, they develop a culture of choice. Parallel to that, parishioners develop behavior of evaluating their church leaders.[35] This implies that, the present generation is serious of leadership aptitudes.

During the conversation for this study, the informants have been stating that today people have wide freedom to choose what they want, something that was hardly possible in some centuries ago. They also make evaluations of the pastor's spirituality and work performance. Some church ministers (pastors and evangelists) complain that people can even dare to say that their pastor or evangelist has little or high spirituality. This is especially if that pastor has high or poor attendance in gatherings of renewal movements. They can even go to preach to their leader about conversion. I also came across the statements emphasizing on evaluating the contemporary church and social leaders. Society is now trying to evaluate even the ability, credibility and reliability of their leader. If it discovers that the leader is not operating toward responding to the needs at hand, society may force the leader to learn the situation and hence pressurize to work accordingly.[36]

Considering all these three examples of the characteristics above, Christians and the whole society has entered into a different time. Several features of freedom of expressions, decision-making, economic and technological advancements, and others characterize current society. Carroll continues to state that freedom of choice, of belief, and educational development in society in which pastors live and work, creates difficulties for them to reach people with the gospel. In this era, people (whether children or adults) argue that they feel more free to attend worship services. Carroll states blatantly, "Given these broader changes, it should not be surprising that religion has also been affected [because] . . . religious involvement is a choice, a voluntary activity in which they are free to engage or not."[37] The influence of parents has become minimal. The same is true for the influence

---

35. Carroll, *God's Potters*, 48.
36. Fihavango, "Leadreship and the Family," 190, 191.
37. Carroll, *God's Potters*, 49, 52.

of pastors. For Carroll, each generation views, chooses and evaluates what it feels will respond to its needs and interests.[38]

Taylor is also aware of all those characteristics of the postmodern era. That is why in his theory he writes that: "The move to horizontal, direct-access world . . . had to bring with it a different sense of our situation in time and space. It brings different understandings of history and modes of narration."[39] After discussing the location or era of society, now I turn to the discussion on the phase of the Church due to the changing society.

The Third Phase of Church in Continuous Change[40]

In this sub-section, I use the term 'phase' synonymously and interchangeably to mean 'stage or period' by reflecting the ideas of Samwel Escobar,[41] and those of Taylor himself, and Knitter. To this discussion, the names they give to the Church reflect the stages or era in which it positions itself. Escobar argues that the Church is in the Third Millennium.[42] Charles Taylor in his theory of *social imaginary*, prefers the terms 'sphere' or 'space' or 'forms' of social life instead of the term phase when he describes the context in which the contemporary society and its leaders are living and working.[43] Taylor is much less interested in the names phase, stage, or period even though all may relate to the styles or systems of life in the names he gives in his theory.

In the previous discussion about the characteristics of social change (chapter four and five) I stated that demographic change, migration of people with their beliefs, morality, and education are among the factors that bring some effects on Christianity, in society itself and on the role of the pastor. On the one hand, the church authority presses the pastor to be committed to the prescribed tasks than prioritizing society. On the other hand, society also wants the pastor to realize and work according to the realities in society. This is where the pastor encounters tensions. The interests and needs of the church authority and that of the changing society seem to differ in a wide range. Consequently, the implementations of tasks from church authorities face great difficulties. What are the reasons for these problems?

---

38. Ibid., 48–49, 54.
39. Taylor, *Modern Social Imaginaries*, 175, 168.
40. In this section I use the terms Church and Christianity interchangeably to mean the Church universal.
41. Ibid., Escobar, *A Time for Mission*, 13.
42. Ibid., 14.
43. Taylor, *Modern Social Imaginaries*, 69, 83, 86, 152.

In one of the sections above, I have provided some reasons. I pointed out that society, the church, and the ministers themselves are in a new and different era, an era characterized by freedom from submission, freedom of choice, an era of science and technology. It is an era having varied demands, needs, and interests not available in other eras. That is why as society changes its ways of life both, in religious outlooks as well as in secular directions, the changes affect the image of the Church. Consequently, the Church also enters into another phase. While in the new phase, by no means even the structure of the Church will obviously change. The Church may have an obligation to adapt and carry on integrating them in the mission, vision, and approaches.

Since society as a whole is in the postmodern era, so is the third phase of the Church. If that is the case, then the roles of the pastor also become affected. Therefore, as I stated above the Church has been changing stage by stage due to changing society. The main aim of this section is to show the present location or phase of the Church. After that, I will reflect the roles that a pastor ought to undertake in the time of social change, when the church is in the third stage. I find it helpful to use some hypotheses as presented by Paul F. Knitter and Samuel Escobar in my interpretation and the discussion on the face and stages of the Church.

In his book *No Other Name*, Knitter is trying to show how Christians in this third phase are experiencing many Christian expressions and challenges from the mushrooming of religions with their denominations. Knitter confirms that the contemporary society is in a state of change and religious pluralism. Among major issues he addresses in his preliminary pages is that, "Religious pluralism [is] a newly experienced reality."[44] He starts by stating how one person confronts many religions and denominations at present. Then he goes on to describing how the problem has existed for generations, though its increase has been in the younger generation because most of them have shown an interest of knowing at least the background of world religions. Furthermore, he depicts that the plurality might persist for ever because "Not only are ideas migrating, but so are persons. . . . The religious life of humankind from now on, . . . will be lived in a context of religious pluralism. . . . Because we are coming so close to each other, 'we are learning each other's languages, both 'literally and figuratively.'"[45]

Knitter describes also that through missionaries, Christianity had been facing several problems, challenges and opportunities of pluralism from other religions (Islam, Hinduism, Buddhism and other traditions).

---

44. Knitter, *No Other Name?*, 2.
45. Ibid., 3.

Since many centuries, Christian missionaries have attempted to convert as many people as possible. The process or developments follow those of analysts of politics, economics, intellectual, social and cultural awareness.[46] He argues that, on the one hand, there are philosophers and other experts of theology (himself included) who state that: "The world religions are confronting each other . . . and they are experiencing a new sense of identity and purpose because they . . . are moving toward a pervasive unity through . . . relationships with each other. They are . . . within all reality toward a new form of unity . . . "[47] For Knitter and his colleagues, on the one hand, the world religions are holding new senses of identity and purposes. They are in confrontation while approaching a new form of unity. There unity emerges from the relationships they make. They hold individual identities and purposes while eager to unite. These are ambivalences. In such a situation, then, Christianity faces these tensions.

Furthermore, sociologists and psychologists argue that individual people and society are within two horizons of identity and morality: "conventional" and "postconventional." The conventional personal identity relates to the behaviors of children. A person obeys and takes on rules or values in order to gain reward and acceptance from their parents or elderly. The values and identities belong to those parents. Nevertheless, the postconventional self-identity urges persons to grow up and accept values and roles freely, intelligently and critically.[48]

Today people are trying to opt and move into the latter (post-conventional) because it provides more space for them to decide and act toward what they feel will serve their needs and interests. Consequently, due to change in population, movement of people, integration, religious pluralism, and change in their morality, mind-sets, and other factors that I discussed in the previous chapters; Christianity finds itself encountering both threats but also some opportunities from other religions, denominations, and from other external influences. The threats may lead to a loss of Christian tradition and identity of the Church.[49] Since all comprise the social order and influence, the concept social change appears in between. In other words, social change affects the identity of the church. This happens when members of one faith community mix their faith and practices with other faith communities. The same happens when they mix with external influences. Thus, what is the contemporary *Kairos* of Church?

46. Ibid., 4–6.
47. Ibid., 9, cf., 7–8.
48. Ibid., 10.
49. Ibid., 10–18.

Knitter introduces "A New *Kairos* for Christianity." For Knitter, *Kairos* "is a point in history when, because of the particular constellation of events and personalities, genuinely new possibilities and advances are latent."[50] He argues that Christianity has been changing from one phase or stage to another. What are those stages? He starts by the above introduction. Then he describes how Christianity has been changing and affected due to the changing context:

> To propose a new understanding of the gospel and of Christian tradition is not a novelty. Throughout its long life, Christianity has always been profoundly dependent on the ever changing context of history. It is not simply that Christianity affects the world; the world really affects Christianity as well. The church relates to and seeks to transform the world not merely by applying the well-defined deposit of truth to changing historical contexts; nor does the church simply utilize the concepts of a new situation or culture in order to give expression to an already possessed truth - as if the truth were already clear and nearly needed a new medium. . . . The church learns from the world. Christianity and Christian truth are, therefore, evolving with the evolving world. As the church tries to speak to the world, it grows and changes with it.[51]

The above argument depicts that the face of Christianity has ever been changing as the world changes. Those changes are due to evolvements of the world. Again, while Christianity has been attempting to change the world into its goal by mission; the world also in turn is trying to change the Church so that it suits the world's interests and needs. Knitter continues with an example from Church history:

> Knitter goes further to describing that, the history of the Church shows how true this is. When the early community moved from its first cultural context, that of Judaism, into the Greco-Roman world, it underwent a far-reaching transformation. It was a transformation not only in the liturgical, sacramental life of the church and in the structures of the organization and legislation, but also in its doctrine – that is, in the understanding of the revelation that had given birth to it.[52]

According to Knitter, the face of the Church started to change since the first society started to move. The movement of Judaism into the Greco-Roman

50. Ibid., 18, 19–20.
51. Ibid., 19.
52. Ibid., 19.

world affected everything that Christianity possessed, inclined, and adhered. The social movements affected liturgies, sacramental practices, rituals, organizational and legislations structures with their policies, and doctrines. One may presume that, the cultic impressions of moving seem a non-stop practice. Consequently, as the movement takes place, there happens the change and reshaping of congregations with their roles and practices. The social movement strongly influences while changing even the religious traditions. In supporting this argument, Ellingson states that:

> Religious traditions, like many other cultural objects, are not static but are constantly in flux. Most explanations of religious change start from the premise that rituals, theologies, or congregational cultures, like other forms of culture, are relatively stable and do not change until social structures or cultures outside the religious organization change. This is the fundamental premise . . . on culture, action, and change: ideologies and cultural repertoires do not change until the social world becomes unstable, and when this happens individuals and groups are compelled to rework their cultural repertoires or create new ideologies because the "unsettled times" or social crises have rendered the old meanings and practices obsolete. . . . While external social forces influence religious change, they do not necessarily catalyze change as directly as the literature. Traditions change in part because large social forces outside the tradition impinge on our ways of thinking and acting outside the doors of the church. . . . Congregations must decide collectively that the new context is relevant and thus requires some response.[53]

This quotation as well gives a picture of how social movements are very affective to church theories and practices. External social forces have powerful influences over religion with its traditions. It means that, society can change everything depending on its needs, demands and interests. The same happens if society gets into crises or into unsettled times, its impacts affects the Church and all religious practices. The opposite also may be, the stable society, is the stable the church (religion).

In relation to this research, Knitter affirms the arguments of the informants that movements have now become normal actions of society. Furthermore, and here I agree with him, church ministers would not feel much tension because as society moves with its beliefs, so it may transform almost all its outlook regarding its contemporary needs and interests. Rather, as Knitter comments, pastors and all other church ministers must take time to

---

53. Ellingson, *The Mega Church and The Mainline*, 187–188.

investigate and learn the reasons of all problems that are different from what they expect. He also raises the issue of doctrines. However, I will take that into the next chapter where I highlight some challenges.

Furthermore, Knitter agrees with the missiologist Walbert Buhlmann and Karl Rahner. He acknowledges Buhlmann who titled one of his books *The Coming of the Third Church*. As he admits to the arguments of Buhlmann, Knitter claims, " . . . the church must prepare itself for radical transformation as the bulk of its population and influence moves outside its traditional . . . boundaries into the cultures and religions of the Third World."[54] He provides a summary of the way in which the church has been changing stage by stage.

> The first stage was the church in its Judaic form, as found in the earliest period of the New Testament; the second stage was the church transformed into Greco-Roman, European (or Western) culture – a stage that, for the most part, has characterized Christianity for most of its history. The third stage, or world church, will be the church as it incarnates and reassesses itself within new cultures and enters into dialogue with [other] religions.[55]

Knitter's point seems to be that changes are also due to the cultural integration of people and their attitudes as they move and interact with each other. For Knitter, the church is constantly incarnating and reassessing itself as it enters into every new culture.[56] The expression culture here reflects to the new context and new ways of life regarding the respective society. Furthermore, the Church (that is, Christianity as a whole) is now in a daily dialogue with other religions. So, the contemporary pastors as agents of the church are currently living and serving in the third stage. Whilst living and working in this phase, religious dialogue with their fellow religious leaders is one of their tasks.

The missiologist Samuel Escobar agrees with Knitter. Escobar argues that from the beginning of the twentieth century to the early twenty-first century the situation of the Christian church has been in a rapid "sequence of phases, . . . In our times, . . . we seem to stand at the threshold of a new age of Christianity."[57] The Third Church will comprise members from almost all nations with their varied ways of life. This Third Church will demand changes that go with the present time and technology. It will also claim

---

54. Knitter, *No Other Name?*, 20.
55. Ibid., 20, 223; Escobar, *A Time for Mission*, 12–14.
56. Knitter, *No other Name?*
57. Escobar, *A Time for Mission*, 13.

the need for "a change of mind and attitudes . . . "[58] He emphasizes that together with the culture of Christianity, almost all things " . . . are in a constant process of change . . . " due to time, needs and interests.[59] Thus, he suggests that the ministers of the Christian faith utilize any available opportunities when doing their work "to interpret the current social and cultural reality of Africa in the twenty-first century . . . "[60] within which people are living.

Since pastors and other church ministers seem to deal with practical matters, Bevans emphasizes that this can be possible if "that context is understood in terms of social change."[61] Again, what should the ministry of the Church look like? Before I discuss the roles of the pastor in the third phase, I will discuss how the pastor is in the midst of a multicultural society and how this pastor ought to understand a diverse population. Thereafter I will discuss the need to rethink the role of the pastor in both a multicultural Church and a changing society.

THE PASTOR AND CHURCH IN A MULTICULTURAL SOCIETY: UNDERSTANDING FULLY THE CONTEMPORARY DIVERSE POPULATION

Why does understanding the contemporary society become important? Again, how can the church and pastors understand it? In Chapter 4, we noted that among the first and biggest social changes in the contemporary society of Tanzania are the movements of people that lead into population changes and into the general multicultural life of society. In the conversations with informants, we discovered that people are very free, mobile, constantly integrating, intermarrying, and changing their moral behaviors. As a result, the pastor as head minister of the parish is encountering a dynamic community. This affects him or her especially when performing the tasks as defined in the church documents. Furthermore, the greatest problem is how to understand fully that diverse, multicultural, free, mobile, integrative and an ever-changing society. Ignorance of this leads into ineffective ministry.

On the one hand, pastors are among the first to describe how society in which they are living and working is in a rapid growth of multiculturalism. On the other hand, they acknowledge that they have not yet clearly

---

58. Ibid., 19, cf., 14, 17-19, 68-81.
59. Ibid., 69.
60. Ibid., 179.
61. Ibid., Bevans, *Models of Contextual Theology*, 71, cf., 76.

understood it society owing to its volatile dynamic statuses. In one of my interview sessions, one pastor strongly accounted how the challenge appears to be of crucial stance:

> *The first problem and challenge I have been facing myself is how to understand this society. The present society has not yet completely revealed itself. Since it has a mixed and varied cultures; it is not an easy task to understand its ways of life, before one start leading it. This is because there is a character of each society [into which you may be sent by the church to minister] to have its own demands depending on its own context and needs. It means that each parish has its own demands. The challenge here is that the pastor is therefore a person who will be in a daily learning of the contexts. He or she is transferred into other contexts after a few years of ministry. Therefore, as society changes rapidly, so should the pastor change rapidly his or her ways of doing things in order to catch and manage it. This is how we try to live and work without messing up the Christian faith.*[62]

Another informant supports that the contemporary society is so complex that there are: "*big problems and challenges on how to understand this society.*"[63] In view of that, most informants complained that the life of the contemporary society in the ELCT/SD is such that difficult for pastors and other church ministers to define and serve freely and effectively.

As the type of the contemporary society is complex, varied, undefined, demanding and forceful, most of them are carrying out their responsibilities by just being keen to the given tasks so that they do not "mess up" the Christian faith. Over again, the quotation above points out that sometimes there are attempts to change into steps of social change, without success. By being attentive only to the given responsibilities, pastors encounter many tensions. On the other hand, by harmonizing with society they seem not committed to their church authorities that appointed and ordained them. Therefore, most time they find themselves in dilemma.

Through this research, I learnt that the challenge encountering the church with its underlying authorities is primarily to understand society in which the Church is placed-the phase or spheres, to the words of Taylor, with its behaviors. The pastor is challenged to fully understand the diverse population in which pastoral ministry has to be done, and in which the personal and family life of the minister has to subsist.

---

62. Informant C.
63. Informant E.

I agree with and adopt the definitions and comments of the theologian David C. Cook and Anthony Giddens on the concept *Multiculturalism*. Cook states that our contemporary pastors are undertaking their pastoral ministries in a complex multicultural society. The challenge is on how to perform those enforced roles to this complex multicultural society. Cook strongly comments: "Ministries in the past, present, and future millenniums . . . are facing the challenges of reaching diverse populations with the gospel. To be effective in doing so, we must be a multicultural ministry to be relevant to those who surround us—they are the prize to 'win'. But to win this [society], we must choose wisely on how to go about it."[64] Cook describes that believers in the past ages and the ages to come have had to change ideas, traditions and tactics to carry out the Great Commission of Jesus Christ (Matthew 28:19). The church has been constantly changing throughout the ages to reach new generations. This task first, began right at the birth of the Christian Church as one finds it in Acts 2. From that very point, pastoral roles and ministries have been facing a great challenge of being *multicultural* so that they match with the social and cultural changes in changed contexts.

To make his propositions more clear, Cook tries to highlight some definitions of the word *multicultural*. He asks, "So what is multiculturalism?" Some Christians and church leaders ignore this notion probably because they do not want to familiarize themselves with the contemporary social changes. Cook states that some church ministers seem to reject the multicultural life of society and do not want their tasks to reflect the changes that are constantly coming up. Still, the realities in the present society and even in Scriptures portray that there is a cry for a multicultural ministry, a ministry that observes the complexities and changes in the contemporary society. Cook maintains that, every church and every pastor ought to "be aware of the challenges one might face. Out of this challenge, our [pastoral] ministries will become relevant and healthy multicultural ministries that carry out the Great Commission."[65]

Then Cook describes the meaning of *multicultural* as follows: first, he points out that many Evangelicals associate "multiculturalism" with a compromise of faith and values for those who practice sinful lifestyles with regard to sex and religion. Cook thinks that probably we do not really listen fully nor do we try to understand society because "We have allowed our ministries to become politicized. This does not mean that you are not entitled to a political opinion, or that you should not be politically involved.

---

64. Cook, "Multicultural Ministries," (Online).
65. Ibid.

What I am trying to point out is that when it comes to ministering to the hearts, we cannot be so hasty and spiritualize all of our political stands to the point that they affect the ministry."[66] For Cook, the actual definition of the word multicultural is a relational rather than a political word. He quotes from the Webster's Dictionary that states that it is "relating to, or including several cultures."[67]

Becoming similarly to the descriptions above, Anthony Giddens in his book *Europe in the Global Age* provides the origin and intended meaning of the term *Multiculturalism*. Giddens states that "The 'home' of multiculturalism is Canada, both in terms of policy practice and intellectually, since some of the leading scholars in the field are from that country."[68] He goes on to defining its meaning. For Giddens, "'Multiculturalism', to repeat, is not a description of a society in which there are diverse cultural groups. It is best to reserve the term 'cultural pluralism' for that. Multiculturalism is a policy or a set of policies. It refers to policy programs that recognize the authenticity of different ways of life within a social community, and seek to promote fruitful and positive transactions between them – but within an overall, and singular, system of citizenship rights and obligations."[69] In his descriptions, Giddens provides great precautions on defining the term. He argues that we should define it according to the Canadian understanding. The definition should reflect the meaning from which the term originates.[70]

After stating the correct (as he deems to argue so) meaning of multiculturalism as I use it in this book, Giddens gives three conditions that facilitate the successful adoption of multiculturalism. As he quotes from Kymlicka, he points, I summarize by paraphrasing them:

- It is difficult to gain public support if the main beneficiaries are illegal immigrants. In most countries such migrants are seen as flouting the rule of law and 'jumping the queue.' It means that in order for the context to be multicultural, it should have legal immigrants.

- A second influence is what kind of cultures figure in multiculturalism. Public support is very hard to get if the cultures in question are perceived as illiberal – a situation that primarily today concerns Muslims. Such a situation generates of multiculturalism morally risky.

---

66. Ibid.
67. Ibid.
68. Giddens, *Europe in the Global Age*, 123, cf., 122 (Emphasis original).
69. Ibid., 124.
70. Ibid., 122–125.

- The third factor is the perceived economic impact of immigrants. If those who would benefit from multicultural policies are seen as taking more from the welfare state than they contribute to it, public support again tends to lapse. For example, in Canada, immigrants largely seem as net contributors – reflecting the reality that they have been chosen for their skills or education levels.[71]

Hence, Giddens illustrates that with those conditions, until 2007 "Multiculturalism has so far barely been tried in Europe. The main exception is the UK, which in spite of many difficulties, has proved so far to be the most successful country in coping with cultural pluralism and turning it to positive effect."[72] The above factors are among other conditions that every pastor of the twenty first century should understand when doing pastoral ministry in the contemporary changing society. A pastor must realize a kind of a society he or she serves.

It means, together with other ministers, pastors perform their roles in times and contexts where most people have diffused their cultures. The emphasis is made here that, when pastors need to move out and reach society, they ought not to reach people with their full cultural standards, traditions, and with strict set of responsibilities. This helps avoid racism when performing the pastoral office and ministry in the context. Pastors are supposed to observe the realities of society and hence cope with the religions and inhumane traditions that exist throughout the world.[73] Pastors should tolerate and manage the differences they encounter.

Why is it important for the pastoral ministry to be multicultural involving the changing society? The reason stands on relating to the community. Pastoral ministry has to be multicultural in order to relate to the community we are trying to reach. It was clearly stated by informants that the church at large must constantly seek to learn the social changes. It needs to learn the tasks of reformulating the roles so that they include the position of society, enforcing the roles, performing, and evaluating the church ministry. During conversations in the research process, I realized that there is more or less a one-way and top-down flow of communication. I learnt that society is inadequately involved when the church sets its roles. Probably, society can help if the church finds some most effective communication means relevant and adaptable to diverse groups in the community. This would also help to meet the needs, interests as well as the intellectual development in people.

---

71. Ibid., 125.
72. Ibid., 126.
73. Cook, "Multicultural Ministries," (Online).

This may probably help to minimize or avoid unnecessary challenges that pastors encounter due to social change.

In addition, I suggest that all pastors, theologians, and the church consider, internalize and put into actions some remarks from Cook. He recommends that: "We must be wise and realize the times we are living . . . in and not let them pass by without this generation."[74] I also agree with Cook that both pastors and all other church ministers should not be completely submerge in certain stipulated roles of the church. Rather, they have to seek some contemporary and significant alternatives that can be useful in these times, as they perform their tasks in their areas. As it was in the time of Chroniclers, the outstanding challenge to the contemporary church (ELCT) with its pastors and all other leaders is to observe the times, the context and society with its ever-changing realities in the life. This can be one of the strategies to become effective and less attacked by social changes.

Referring again to the concept of a multicultural minister; multicultural ministry aims at reaching the community and listen to its voices and the suggestions it makes. This is possible if pastors have undertaken intensive training in their profession so that they may be able to use all their skills to understand society and work with it effectively but with efficiency. I would therefore suggest that the church rethinks the intensive training tasks at the right time that the intended Church mission and goals may be accomplished in this multicultural context.

In the following section, I discuss the roles of a pastor in the third phase. I use one framework from the Evangelical Lutheran Church in America (ELCA) to serve as a model for the African pastors in general, and for the ELCT in particular. I try to respond to the question 'What does the 'changing face and phase of the Church' imply to the role of the pastor in the contemporary society?'

RETHINKING THE PASTOR'S ROLE: AN AMERICAN RESPONSE AS A MODEL FOR ELCT AND AFRICAN PASTORS

In the previous discussion above, I have presented the three phases of the Church as a result of social change. It is easy to note that the whole process of transformation to the third phase has brought both, great impacts and effects in the Church and on the role of the pastor. One of the impacts is the

---

74. Cook, "Multicultural Ministries," (Online). See also Schreiter, *The New Catholicity*, 93–97, 118–120, 133;
Giddens, *Europe in the Global Age*, viii – ix, 122–139.

complex life of society and the tensions to church ministers. In the analyses and discussions, I found that social change is the major factor for the constant transformation in the expression of the Church. We have seen also how the contemporary church ministry ought to be multicultural due to the nature of the contemporary society.

Up to this stage, the church documents referred to in chapter three, in most cases appear to be static, strict, sealed and protected from responding to the fast social changes with their effects on the role of the pastor and on the whole mission and life of the Church. The church documents with their roles serve to maintain the status quo, while people with their Christian faith and affiliation have moved into a different and new age, phase (spheres), and context. This serves as a sign to the church, to pastors, as well as to all church ministers to think anew about the present situation of the Church and the stipulated roles for pastoral offices.

The third stage of the Church is calling for the church authorities and the pastors to consider the changes that constantly take place in society. As the expression or phase of the Church changes, the role of the pastor increases, widens and or reduces. By locating the Church into the third phase, Paul F. Knitter, Samuel Escobar, and Charles Taylor place the life of the pastor into that same phase. What implications does the present phase make to the role of the pastor? How should pastors do all those role in contemporary Church, in a society: characterized by a postmodern ethic, in a globalized age, of rapid intimate and communication growth, an educated community, a community that fights for democratic rule, a community of criticisms, of commercial stance, and a multicultural community?

In this discussion, I consider the responses of the bishops from the American context to be the best paradigm in evaluating, securing, implementing, and illustrating the roles of an African pastor in the changing society. The model presents ten faces of pastoral roles as the book *The Many Faces of Pastoral Ministry* presents them. The bishops of the Evangelical Lutheran Church in America (ELCA) have perceived, analyzed, demonstrated, and illustrated those roles. The book was edited by Herbert W. Chilstrom and Lowell G. Almen in 1990. By that time, Chilstrom was also a bishop while Almen was secretary to the ELCA.

The book shows that there are ten roles and nine bishops who reflected and described the roles that every pastor was required to perform. The general secretary of that ELCA added the tenth role. Why did those bishops and the general secretary need to embark on that task? The book describes that, first, there were great changes in society, pressures and growing challenges upon pastors in the American society that bishops and the secretary of the ELCA had to reflect on some basic areas of the roles of the pastor in that context. Those roles have a stipulation and reflection according to the ELCA constitution. Second, according to the ELCA Constitution among the tasks of the bishops are both, the teaching responsibilities and that of pastoral care to all people, starting with the members of various administrative structures or organs (for example, synod), the Christian society, ordained ministers, and its associates in ministry. Another task was that of leadership.[75]

However, in his preface to this book, bishop Chilstrom describes that it was the first time those bishops agreed to contribute with some lived experiences according to the ELCA Constitution and from pastors' lived experiences. They did this task through reflecting and writing down materials on the contemporary responsibilities that every pastor had to perform. The nine bishops and the secretary of the church describe that the context in which the Church and the pastors were living and working was quite different from the previous. There were constant, rapid and countless changes in people and in communities at large. As a result pastors experienced numerous and daily effects due to the demands, pressures, and challenges from the community. Those situations were bringing several burdens that caused splinters and differences between bishops and pastors, and between pastors and their congregations.[76]

I now turn to my reflections on those ten roles that the ELCA pastors have been performing. On the one hand, the aim is to provide some basic information that can be useful in the process of studying the spheres and stages of the Church as Charles Taylor and Paul F. Knitter analyze and emphasizes them. On the other hand, the aim is to reflect their relation and applicability for pastoral ministry in the African context. The roles are very similar to the ones that the ELCT pastors carry out at present. Furthermore, at the end of the ten roles I add one role of the pastor regarding the economic activities of society according to the findings. I am also aware that the reflections I draw from the American context in this book date back to the 1990s. However, in my view, the materials are still important and relevant because most of the roles can apply to the present church authority and the pastor of the ELCT, as well as to African pastors as a whole. Conclusively, I suggest that the reflections that those bishops made can serve as a model for the ELCT and to all Christian pastors in the African context to rethink on their attitude and position about social change and the contemporary role of their pastors.

---

75. Chilstrom and Almen, *The Many Faces of Pastoral Ministry*, 7–8.
76. Ibid., 11–10, cf., 23.

The Pastor as Spiritual Guide

The bishop who reflected on this role pointed out that in a time of growing social transformations, demands, skepticisms, pressures, and numerous other challenges from the community; among the first qualities of a Christian religious leader for the church of the 1990s was to know his or her own sheep, and in turn that sheep to know their shepherd. Why was this guiding principle so special that it is in the forefront of all other roles? As insisted above, the bishop describes that it is a Biblical fact as we quote: "John 10: 14, I am the good shepherd; I know my own and my own know me."[77] He emphasizes that every pastor soon from the time of seminary training grasped and realized this task has correctly. The bishop held constant visitations in parishes as well as during other schedules for pastoral ministry and meetings. In his visitations and meetings, he reminded and emphasized on this role right from the day of ordination.

Making more emphasis on this role, the second quality of a pastor in the era starting 1990s is to practice what they preach. He emphasizes:

> The task of being a pastor to a congregation is an overwhelming responsibility. You as a pastor are entrusted with the care of God's precious people. This keeps you and other pastors (shepherds, in the biblical image) on your knees searching for God's wisdom and guidance. No requirement of the pastor's office causes such deep concern as the responsibility to guide the baptized in their spiritual growth. Sometimes, it seems, the challenges grow and the burdens increase. . . . Sadly, we are living in a period of time when Americans have become skeptical of those who claim to be authentic spiritual guides. We have much damage to undo in order to lift high Christ's cross and proclaim the gospel of salvation to a desperate world. . . . 'Skepticism toward institutional religion is growing deeper among baby boomers.' . . . one of the Ten Commandments for the church of the 1990s is to 'scrupulously practice what is preached.'[78]

The above quotation highlights how difficult it is the era for the pastors to be faithful spiritual guides amid the demanding and a doubting attitude of society toward religious beliefs and in almost all other individual and social practices.

Fortunately, that bishop was aware that pastors are like any other human beings. Therefore, as he gives the third quality that the pastors have to

---

77. Ibid., 9.
78. Ibid., 10, 11.

know that they possess both qualities—abilities as well as some defects. He writes: "Jesus—the only perfect person—will not come to be their pastor. They [society] will have to accept as pastor a woman or a man who has many abilities but who also has some defects. God only gives us pastors who are saints and sinners at the same time."[79] Therefore, he urges them to show to people that they as well live and work by the grace of God through faith in the Lord Jesus Christ.

Finally, the fourth quality that every pastor should abide to is on being a model in terms of moral conduct and devotional life. With this model, bishops seemed to be very harsh toward their pastors, especially if a pastor was caught with dirty stories that ruin the expectations of parishioners. He wrote:

> Occasionally, we encounter some pastors who overreact and knock themselves out to prove their humanity.... We then hear complaints from pastors of a double standard in the church... While some members of congregations may tell dirty stories, drinking excessively, and recount intimate details about their sexual activities, this is never acceptable for the clergy. Every bishop has had to encounter pastors who do not understand this and who find their ministers in ruin because of such misbehavior. ... we recall Paul's words to Timothy (1 Tim. 4: 12). A good pastor must be an authentic man or woman in Christ.... We pastors are the spiritual mothers and fathers of Christ's people.[80]

Thus, the above description shows that the pastor has to work effectively according to the Christian faith and within the framework of church constitution. Pastors have to make sure that they are authentic by any means; otherwise, their bishops will convict them.

The Pastor as Bible Scholar

According to the ELCT constitution, the second role of every pastor is to teach and undertake evangelism. However, most of the pastors argue that despite their attempts to use the Bible in teaching it has become a hard task for them to perform that role. One of their reasons was the lack of education. Despite the shortcomings, the task of being a competent scholar of the Bible rests upon the pastor. The role seems to be more essential especially in the third stage of the church as far as the contemporary spheres of society are concerned.

79. Ibid., 11.
80. Ibid., 12–15.

One of the emphases put in this role bases on being knowledgeable on the centre. An emphasis is that every contemporary pastor has to know the kind of a church that he or she serves. Each church has its own characteristic that ministers ought to know, learn, listen and follow. Following the Lutheran Church, the bishop argues that despite the fast changes that are taking place in society: "You may be many things, friend, but if you are not a student and a teacher of the Scriptures, you are not a pastor."[81] Every pastor should keep learning the Bible. That bishop continues to state that this prerequisite is essential because the pastoral ministry primarily centers on the Word of God, that is, in both the Old and New Testaments. It is from the same Scriptures that rules, norms and doctrines people make and give some appraisals and judgments. For example, a pastor uses the Scriptures to teach the Christian confessions, the sacraments, in pastoral care, and when teaching several other church doctrines. Hence, there are strong emphases that a pastor has to be competent in learning and teaching Scriptures. This bishop concludes that:

> I contend that a pastor is a particular kind of scholar and teacher of the Scriptures. There are and must be academically trained and oriented, professional Bible scholars and teachers whose task is to 'objectively' study and reflect on the Scriptures, using all tools of responsible research. As pastors we do our work taking into account all that we can learn from the best of those faithful teachers; but our approach is shaped by our call.[82]

Accordingly, there are important things that need to consideration in order for a pastor to become qualified as a Bible scholar. First, there is a need to undergo some regular academic training and orientations. Second, there is a need to practice the knowledge that is, teaching the Biblical Scriptures by using all necessary tools and reliable researches. Third, to be students of Scriptures, that is, to be daily involved in learning; fourth is the need for a pastor to have a call into pastoral ministry; and fifth, faith in Biblical Scriptures as a Word of God.[83]

Most pastors in the research sample argue that they are teaching the Bible by using their old knowledge and a little experience they get in the course of their ministry. The old knowledge and little experience they have are some of the things that make them become incompetent ministers. Consequently, they sometimes feel inferior before the community in which they live and serve. Consequently, their lack of competence makes them

---

81. Ibid., 17, cf., 19.
82. Ibid., 19.
83. Ibid., 20–26.

The Pastor as Parish Theologian

become less students and teacher of Scriptures. In that case, they sense as less Bible Scholars in their changing and curious society.

Connected to the Bible scholarship is the task of making theological issues well understood in and outside the premises of the Church. This model points out that in the "New Age" the pastor deals with theological questions such as, death and life after death, judgment, sin, grace, ecumenism and Social Gospel, sexuality, salvation, love, and the question of revelation.[84] In this role, "the pastoral task is not only relational, therapeutic, and functional. It also concerns the truth as we know and believe it."[85] Considering it to be a crucial task in church ministry, every pastor has to be aware of serious theological and sociological issues especially when preaching, teaching and making dialogue and theological debates with other people in society; because in any formal occasions the people expect serious theological reflection and preparation.

The reflection made on this role suggests that, in order for a pastor to qualify for this task the following steps need attention: first, a pastor must read as many theological books as possible. Yet, a pastor has to be up-to-date also by reading for example newspapers, biographies of important theologians, and other materials. Why? This "helps you understand contemporary life. . . . Theology informs the self-understanding of the church at every turn. . . . It helps people make connections between life and faith. . . . Theology provides the critique of all the church does."[86] Second, a pastor should understand him or herself as an individual who is at the same time saint and sinner. A pastor should understand how to describe the way God addresses humanity, that is, on how He relates to human beings. Moreover, as a parish theologian, a pastor uses theological reflections to "understand the relationship of individuals in the society."[87]

Third, a pastor has to be careful in using the Word of God as his or her authority in theological work. The pastor's appeal to the Bible needs high carefulness because "Today there is no consensus about biblical authority for the contemporary social issues. In much Christian social teaching, the quotations from the Bible are almost a matter of convenience or

84. Ibid., 27.
85. Ibid., 28, cf., 29, 32, 34.
86. Ibid., 29.
87. Ibid., 30.

ornamentation."[88] Fourth, pastors should keep reminding themselves that the criterion for their theological work is grace alone. As pastors preach and teach, as they lead in evangelism and stewardship, as they organize and administer, and as they undertake the care and counseling for souls, pastors have to realize that the criterion is whether they are helping people see that centre (grace of God) in their lives, and in the life of the parishes.[89] Finally, fifth, pastors have to realize the principle of priesthood of all believers, and that "we are not to do theology *for* our people but *with* them. We are to help them become theologians. This means we help people make the connections . . . to celebrate the grace of God when they experience it and believe it."[90]

The above reflections end up by a comment that the contemporary theologian is called to tend the gospel and to serve '*with*' the people in the place where contemporary people are looking both for the satisfaction of their needs and for the ultimate answers to questions of life and death. Together with those people the pastor has to discover ever anew God's grace and the meaning of the church as the sign of God's sovereign rule in their midst.[91] In my opinion, by reflecting from the theory of Charles Taylor, it seems that now a pastor becomes more of a facilitator than an instructional boss for society to reflect on various theological issues and how they can reach consensus with a common opinion.[92]

Bevans argues that in this new age where contextual theology is essential, the role of being a parish theologian is only for the professional, that is, a qualified theologian. A qualified theologian helps people to discover anew the grace of God and carry the image of God through the church in their contexts. The pastor acts as a midwife to the people during the process. He observes:

> WHO DOES THEOLOGY? . . . classical theology understood the form of theology to be discursive and academic, it understood the theologian to be a scholar, an academic, a highly trained specialist with a wide knowledge of Christian tradition and the history of doctrine and with a number of linguistic and hermeneutical skills. . . . But . . . ordinary people . . . are not the real theologians. . . . The role of the trained theologian (the minister, the theology teacher) is that of articulating more clearly what the people are expressing more generally or vaguely,

---

88. Ibid., 32.
89. Ibid., 32.
90. Ibid., 33.
91. Ibid., 34.
92. Taylor, *Modern Social Imaginaries*, 83–141, 143–154.

deepening their ideas by providing them with the wealth of the Christian tradition, and challenging them to broaden their horizons by presenting them with the whole of Christian theological expression. . . . The role of the theologian is to function as a midwife to the people as they give birth to a theology . . . and, . . . to conceive theology in terms of a constant dialogue between the people . . . .[93]

In supporting the above argument, I agree with Bevans that, today people want to make theology the living, the theology that responds to the realities in their life. Therefore, I suggest the reflection above and Bevans' arguments be adopted into the ELCT so as to help pastors who are the parish theologians become competent scholars through academic training. This may help them serve the gospel *with* the community.

The Pastor as Liturgical Leader

Another reflection strongly emphasizes, "Although lay members properly have significant roles in worship, liturgical leadership is the primary and central task for which the ordained ministry was instituted."[94] In liturgical leadership, the pastor conducts a service in a way that is more spiritual. It is where the Word of God confronts the congregation (Isaiah 12: 6; Hosea 11: 9). It is a gathering place where worshippers in their faith receive the grace, promises and other blessings offered by God. By means of the liturgy, Christians experience the presence and manifestation of the mystery of Christ.[95]

The pastors as well as some other church ministers such as evangelists perform the liturgical role. I pointed out that this is the first task as the pastor performs the sacramental ministry. In the analysis and discussions sometimes pastors have to perform this role under a tense situation due to increase in the number of worship services and the pressures of the community regarding time and type of the conservative liturgy processes. The ELCT pastors used the Lutheran liturgy book or the *Mwimbieni Bwana* and the *Tumwabudu Mungu Wetu*[96] book in almost every worship services. Informants argue that their present liturgy is in crisis due to the: length in content, rigidity, and conservative processes. Most Christians insist their pastors and the church at large adjust it so that it is flexible, inclusive, and as short as possible. Moreover, church ministers state that they face similar

93. Bevans, *Models of Contextual Theology*, 17–18.
94. Strohl, "Ministry in the Middle Ages," 37.
95. Ibid., 36–37.
96. KKKT, *Mwimbieni Bwana*, 267–530; *Tumwabudu Mungu Wetu*, 329–707.

complaints when it comes to sermon delivery. Some lay informants argue that several times choirs complain to have little time to sing during worship services, whilst they spent a lot of time in preparing songs during the week. It means that the church liturgy and sermons occupy a larger space than other activities during worship services. Thus, people feel less involved in church worship services.

Referring to the above opening descriptions for this liturgical role: "The term *liturgy* . . . does not really mean a sacrifice but a public service."[97] In liturgy, the congregation shares their valuable gifts for the corporate worship of God, such as musicians and other participants. Once pastors recognize themselves as spiritual leaders of society; they sometimes work cooperatively with society in planning and leading the worship services. However, a pastor does not leave some issues to management by consensus. These are matters not subject to majority votes, such as the proper conduct of worship.

I certainly agree at least with some emphases made by the bishop in this reflection. Somehow, the bishop seems flexible to allow pastors to make some adjustments in the given liturgy of the church. The bishop argues that pastors need to be very careful with some old traditional practices and make some alterations as they conduct the liturgy. They should always preserve some Lutheran traditions but also make some sensible changes in order to make worship services accommodative, joyous and attractive to the community.[98] Pastors need a reminder to seek and accept constructive criticisms from people in order to avoid distracting and misleading ways of acting and speaking, especially as they make theological statements in the public.[99] This precaution is an essential to pastors that are quite sure of what they know and tell other people.

The Pastor as Parish Administrator

The pastor is also an administrator of the church. In reflecting this role, the concerned bishop opens the discussion by stating that once you notice that the congregation begins to express a desire for some changes in pastoral leadership; then know that one of the reasons is a failure of the pastor's administrative task. Why can society rise up and desire those changes? In responding to such a question, the bishop argues that the role of administration is a gift. This bishop writes: "Living in a society where administrative

97. Strohl, "Ministry in the Middle Ages," 37.
98. Ibid., 39–42.
99. Ibid., 43.

skills are essential to much of life, the gift of administration is ironically undervalued, even denigrated, by ordained ministry."[100] This shows that to live and administer the present society a pastor requires some special knowledge and skills. That is why once society discovers that the pastor does not have that gift; it may attempt to take over his or her role.

In this role, we learn that, further descriptions about this task can are studied from Jesus himself. Jesus is an ultimate model for the contemporary pastoral administration. Jesus studied the context in which he worked, whereby he tried to identify and analyze the problem. He worked with visions, shared visions, and taught others the tasks he was performing, trained other people, developed some alternative, delegated, encouraged, strengthened and also was a model. It seems that almost every plan that Jesus made was done.[101] The pastor has to make some follow-ups; accounting and records keeping are also among many responsibilities of the present pastor. In trying to conclude, this bishop emphasizes that the goal of administration is to build up the community for ministry and mission. Therefore pastors are advised to consider this role essential just as Jesus did, otherwise it might be very difficult to win the contemporary society.

The Pastor as Parish Educator

In chapter five, the analysis and discussion has shown that pastors work within the learned and the learning society. They are community educators. At this level, I just highlight some few issues that another bishop reflects. I already discussed it in detail in chapter five when I dealt with the role of the pastor as a community educator. Nevertheless, I will reflect it again in chapter seven where I discuss it as one of the responses. In this ministry, a pastor deals with matters of providing religious education in a parish to people whom he or she leads and to society. Christian teaching in Sunday schools, in confirmation classes and other schools are among the classes that he or she conducts.[102] In general, a pastor works as an executive director of the education system and as mentor for a religious community. The bishop who presented this reflection accounts that it is an obvious fact that the present congregations bring some educational challenges to a pastor. Therefore, he advises pastors to use some resources that might help to promote new ways to approach those educational challenges of the congregation. One of the

---

100. Ibid., 45.
101. Ibid., 46–50.
102. Jansen, "The Pastor as Parish Educator," 57–58.

opportunities that pastors may exploit is by incorporating other people in this task of educating society.[103]

The Pastor as Evangelist

Herbert W. Chilstrom observes that: "[A]s a synodical bishop for more than 10 years, I have come to a fundamental conviction about evangelism in the parish setting: A pastor must be convinced that nothing else is of importance compared to the call to share the Good News about Jesus Christ. Most any program or technique will work if there is this basic commitment; no program or technique will work if it is missing."[104] Chilstrom demonstrates that evangelism is among the major tasks of any pastor. Evangelism deals with the sharing of the Word of God so that people by their own will make decisions to join the Christian faith. It deals with invitation for people to join the Church.

Chilstrom continues to state that evangelism is an "enterprise of telling people first and foremost what is fundamental to the gospel."[105] Due to its significance and wide dimensions, he suggests to incorporate others members of the church in this task. Second, the commitments on the task and to Christian faith are essential features for the success of evangelism especially in the time of rapid change in people.[106] Third, pastors ought to learn some evangelism techniques from other non-theological fields that seem compatible with the doctrinal emphasis.[107] Chilstrom insists that there is no important programme in the church and to pastoral ministry than evangelism. For him, evangelism is the backbone of all pastoral roles. Other programs exist and operate after the sharing of the Gospel to society. Evangelism first, preaching in the church later. Other roles exist because evangelism exists.

The Pastor as Ecumenical Leader

Since there have been a growth of religious groups, under this task a pastor works as an agent of ecumenical unity between members of his or her Christian Church and those from other Churches. Despite some doctrinal differences that have existed in the American Church, a pastor deals with

---

103. Ibid., 59–63.
104. Chilstrom, "The Pastor as Evangelist," 65.
105. Ibid., 67.
106. Ibid., 69.
107. Ibid., 56–69.

the common elements in Christian faith such as the faith in Christ, Church confessions, trinity, and the use of the Bible as the central reference for the Christian faith.[108] In this place, the bishop emphasizes that a pastor ought to carry out this role while aiming at promoting Christian unity, in spite of some other doctrinal differences and competitions for Church members.[109]

In the interview, I noted that there are religious collaborations between Christians. In this role, the pastor engages much on uniting his or her church with others. This task relates to being a link between two sides. He or she stands neutral, a collaborator. Moreover, regarding the existing pluralism, in case religious conflicts rise, the pastor is there to work as a mediator than an opponent. Now he or she enters another role regarding the need for peace.

The Pastor as Peacemaker

Another Church leader contends that injustice, wars, cultural or ethnic conflicts, religious conflicts, catastrophes and many other tensions occupy the planet in which the society lives. Therefore, due to those problems, a pastor works as a peacemaker.[110] The pastor has to offer alternative perceptions of reality so that the ones in conflict may change their minds into positive perception toward each other and understand each other. The pastor has to help these people understand that they have to hold no destructive powers over others. By using the Bible and other tools, the pastor calls people to unity and hence creates alternative structures of global security and nonviolent means of winning freedom from various social problems.[111]

Why this task is to a pastor? The following are some of the reasons for a pastor to be responsible for peace making. First, pastors are stewards of the life of this planet. Second, in Christ pastors reject the planned immorality that leads to bloodshed. Third, in Christ pastors have to emphasize loving enemies. Pastors are responsible to destroy enemies by reconciliation, not annihilation. Fourth, pastors have a task of calling people to understand that we live beyond the distinctions of race, class, ethnicity, and nation and that all people are called to be among the forerunners of a new global community. Fifth, pastors have to help people realize that security does not

---

108. Chilstrom, "The Pastor as Ecumenical Leader," 72–84.
109. Ibid., 83, cf., chapter 4.
110. Ibid., 85.
111. Ibid., 86–87.

consist in the abundance of fire weapons. In general, pastors are committed to goals of justice; freedom and peace.[112]

There has been a vivid saying that, no peace no preaching; no peace no happiness, and many other slogans. Once peace has gone out, there happens chaos situation. The presence of a pastor in the church and in secular communities assures people on the presence of peace. The pastor makes reconciliation by using his or her available resources, for example, the Bible.

The Pastor as Historian

The Secretary of the ELCA, Lowel G. Almen, presents this tenth role. Almen describes that the pastor is a recorder of many faith issues within the congregations of his or her service. The pastor collects or orders someone to collect and preserve postscripts of the parish in an orderly way. He or she arranges and keeps the photographs, constitutions, letters, contracts, diaries, booklets and parish records, for example to write Church history. These are essential tasks for future references. For Almen, without this task the parish may lose its history.[113]

However, in my research, this role of a pastor as an historian is not clear. The reflection from the American context serves as an essential contribution for the ELCT pastors and bishops to commence their role in their context. I suggest the ELCT to consider this contribution from the secretary of the ELCA as important for the Church to be faithful and lenient in preserving its history. There is a saying in Tanzania that goes: *Mali bila daftari hupotea bila habari* (literary: wealth without proper records is lost without information). This means that if you do not keep records of what has happened, you will end up with no clear information of your presence. The same loss affects the parish. We have the future because the past and the present exist.

The descriptions of Americans about the roles performed by their pastor teach other bishops and other head office bearers of the ELCT that they have to learn how to make follow-ups in the parishes and obtain real information. Heads of the Church keep surveying and analyzing the prescribed roles and help pastors work effectively while updating those roles.

After reflecting the roles that American pastors carry out in their pastoral ministry, it is better now to look at another essential task that a pastor performs. Despite all those roles that I have reflected above, we ought to add another role from the informants - the role that relates to the first sphere

---

112. Ibid., 87–95.
113. Almen, "The Pastor as Historian," 97–101.

of the contemporary society–the economic sphere. He or she becomes an advisor of economy in society.

Taylor's Theory and the Pastor as Economic Advisor

Why do I add this role to the above roles that American bishops reflected on? It is because first, this role is missing in both the constitution of the ELCT church and in the reflections of the ELCA bishops. Moreover, there is the fact of poverty and poor standard of life in my society. That is why my society is struggling daily to raise up its economy. Second, according to Charles Taylor's theory that I use in this book; economy is one of the most important spheres of society in the Western Europe as well as in Africa. Taylor accounts that economy obviously links with the self-understanding of a polite civilization. It is certain that, as he observes, most informants with whom I conversed argue that now the church and pastors need to position themselves in a commercial society.[114] He continues to highlight that currently "humans are engaged in an exchange of services. The fundamental model seems to be what we have come to call an economy."[115] In this case, I find it important that a pastor also becomes fully committed to the role as an advisor of society about its economy.

Some places in chapters 2 and 4 above show the importance of economic sector and the way in which it takes place in Tanzanian society bearing in mind that poverty exists in the context. Economy has become more dominant in almost the whole life of society. Some informants stated that an increase of problems in the economic production in Tanzanian society leads some people into becoming mobile in search for better economic status and life at large. Other people become powerful in their political standpoints. On the one hand, good economic status can lead one to be financially independent. On the other hand, poor economy leads one become dependent upon others.

Better economy helps people promote both their ordinary and religious life. Due to improvement in their economy, people can improve their communication means, their shelter and other contributions in the whole society.[116] Likewise, in this twenty-first century, economy seems to define even the status of the pastor in society. For Taylor, economy defines how people link together or separate one another. Economic improvement

---

114. Taylor, *Modern Social Imaginaries*, 69.
115. Ibid., 71.
116. Ibid., 72–75.

gives people a freedom of movement, freedom of speech, and freedom of self-rule.[117]

Other researchers have come up with some evidences that economy attaches to education in Tanzanian society. For example, in 1990's it was obvious that due to social change the government and other non-governmental organizations carried out research to look for strategies to respond to the economic crisis. The crisis caused the decline in education quality, severe shortage of staff, buildings, equipment, and other resources. These problems affected the life of teacher and their families. Consequently, other human resources in the education sector failed to tolerate the situation; hence, they had to quit their jobs by force. It reads, "The economic crisis . . . had a severe impact on the educational sector, . . . The effects have been far-reaching. As Tungaraza (1990) has noted, the period has been one of declining education quality . . . in severe shortages of staff, buildings, equipment . . . The meagre salaries which teachers receive have forced them to either quit their jobs, ..."[118] As many other Non-Governmental Organizations have been building and running their private schools, the fees increased. However, the economic crisis in people leaves them unable to send their children to schools with high fees. The government has been asking all Non-Governmental Organizations to join their hands to reform all essential policies and in order reduce the problem. This problem is dominant in most African countries.[119] Certainly, religious leaders have been playing this important role in helping society improve its life.

Hence, within this sphere of society, the pastor as a leader, he or she is also expected to give some advice on people's better economy. Similarly, Istvan Czachesz highlights that religion is an agent of economy. This tells society that their religious leader is an agent of economy. Thus, Czechesz concludes with an emphasis that this role is essential, and so he briefly observes, "a religious agent is also an economic agent."[120]

CONCLUSION

From the first, we have noticed that almost each role points to a pastor, and the pastor points to society. Moreover, the American reflections I discussed above admit that due to some fast transformations in society pastors enter into many and tough roles. The loads of pastoral responsibilities burden the

117. Ibid., 76, 82.
118. Gibbon, *Social Change and Economic Reform in Africa*, 195, 203.
119. Ibid., 185–243.
120. Czachesz, "Theory-Forming in Biblical Studies," 57.

pastor. There are two main observations that ought to putting clear regarding the emphases made by the ELCA leaders (the bishop sand the General Secretary) on those roles. On the one hand, I appreciate them for taking trouble to analyze and discuss some contemporary roles for their subordinates. It shows how serious they are in their work. I therefore suggest that church leaders in the ELCT as well as in the African context as a whole adopt this kind of spirit.

On the other hand, the above observations on the roles are individualistic because they hardly show how a pastor has to have a two-way traffic relationship with community. Despite the many and good directives for their pastors to follow in their responsibilities, a few reflections emphasize on ministering *with* people. One can expect that most or all of them could show their views on working *with* community in most parish programs. Another observation that I want to make from the reflections is that pastors have to learn from other people. There is very little emphasis on gaining knowledge and experience from the community. The reflections do not show the pastor to be a student of the community. Therefore, I suggest that the reflections define and urge pastors and other church ministers learn from society instead of just throwing instructions toward their followers. I suppose that there are countless potential contributions in society that may help the church accomplish its mission.

I suggest that authorities of the ELCT, and the church in Africa as a whole, assume this endeavor to define and constantly redefine the roles of their pastors and provide them with such useful materials as the American reflections did. My informants show that even if they acknowledge to have undergone some pastoral training and have some church documents such as the constitution and the confessions, the training does not cover all essential roles according to their individual areas. Further, throughout the research most informants complained that church documents were so old that they did not address most sensitive and contemporary issues pertaining social change and the pastoral ministry.

The discussion in this chapter shows that as society changes, so the face of the Church changes. Furthermore, as the Church changes its era and phase, so it affects the role of the pastor; hence those changes with many demands cause severe tensions to the pastor. Then, what should we do in order to help pastors respond constructively to changing society? I deal with this question in the forthcoming chapter. The focus is on the Tanzanian responses toward social change. Additionally, other experiences from literature and or interviews will be useful to substantiate the suggestions and in proposing better alternatives.

7
RESPONSES TOWARD SOCIAL CHANGE

INTRODUCTION

Due to space and time, it is high time now for me to enter into discussion of some general implications and responses to the issues I raised in the previous chapters. The task of this chapter is to highlight some further steps that need to be done in order for both the church and its pastors to think about and take a step forward toward responding to the changing realities of society. I find it important to develop more ideas in the process of finding some alternatives for the church authority and church ministers to think more about social change and ways to respond to it constructively and effectively. Otherwise, the present situation might exacerbate the existing tensions to pastors such that the pastoral ministry in the Church might enter into a situation of unrest. What should we do then in order to meet the challenges? Some responses ought to highlight.

UNDERSTANDING AND ANALYZING THE CONTEMPORARY CONTEXT OF PASTORAL MINISTRY

Emmanuel Y. Lartey opens this discussion on responses to social change by stating that pastors execute their tasks for church ministry in a context of "an intercultural community, . . . a dynamic recognition of interaction, mutual influence, and interconnectedness."[1] For Lartey, it is important

---

1. Lartey, *Pastoral Theology*, front cover.

for a pastor to be conscious of the context of the contemporary society in which he or she serves because the "Societal and cultural factors influence the shape and form of all caring activities."[2] Lartey emphasizes that pastors and all other church ministers have to understand fully the complexity and context of society they are serving. It is a mixed up and dynamic, interactive, influential and interconnected. This complexity of society influences both, the shape and the form of all pastoral roles. Those effects bring burdens over the pastor. Lartey states openly that pastoral ministry is performed in a multicultural world in which there are many different social forces. He asserts that: "We live in a multicultural world and are influenced and informed by many different social forces."[3] He declares that currently, pastors are within the twenty first century, a century that is full of criticism, inquiries, relies and calls more for context awareness and practice oriented ministers. It is "a world currently characterized . . . by postmodernism and postcolonial criticism."[4] Once these characteristics are well known and analyzed appropriately, it makes easy for pastors to interact and serve the society comfortably, effectively and efficiently.

Lartey describes further that, the above characteristics of the society urges the church to re-evaluate itself before it understands society. Then, he argues that, the life and action of the Church relates to two directions. The first, it relates to its own self-understanding and comprehension of its faith. The second direction is to relate to the changing reality of society. Then he states that it is from those two directions that the church and pastors receive forces. Therefore, he urges pastors to be conscious: of those changing realities of the society, on interrelationships and differences of faiths; and on their practices as they carry out their tasks. Additionally, pastoral theologians have to be conscious as they live within their communities and as they interact with society. He considers this essential, especially for theologians. It is essential because:

> The church's life and action is related not only to its own self-understanding and comprehension of its faith, but also to the changing society in which it [the church] functions, practical theology is triadic, concerned with the interrelationships of faith, practice and social reality, and is aware that the lines of force flow in both directions. This dynamism between faith, practice and social reality . . . moves [pastors and churches] continually . . . to . . . begin doing theology by attempting to

2. Ibid., 2.
3. Ibid., 6. More descriptions can be obtained in 42–43, 84, 126–127.
4. Ibid., 42.

become as conscious of the real situation that surrounds us as we possibly can.[5]

I agree with Lartey that currently the major challenge that the contemporary church and pastors face is changing society itself. As this book depicts (see chapter 6), Lartey also shows that the church and most ministers are not yet conscious enough about the rapid dynamism of faith, of practices, and of social reality. For him such ministers seem not to bother about the changes in society. It means that they do not care whether their pastoral service responds to the contemporary problems of the people or not. After giving the two directions of forces then Lartey suggests what theology should carry out its mission according to that changing reality.

He adds another important challenge that certainly pastoral theologians in the twenty – first century ought to be conscious, to understand and analyze the context in which they do the pastoral ministry. Good awareness will come after they have done a context analysis. Pastoral theologians have to undertake a "Context analysis" before and as they continue with their tasks. He writes:

> It is of utmost importance that pastoral theologians pay attention to the contexts in which they work and interpret the experiences of those they work with, as well as their own, in context. Context analysis includes an examination of social, cultural, economic, political and religious factors at work in given geographic locations. . . . a thoroughgoing contextual analysis is necessarily dynamic and historical, exploring changes through time.[6]

He insists in paying attention to people whom pastors preach the gospel. There must be an exploration of change and an intensive inspection of all factors that affect ministry and personal life. Pastors should perform the context analysis constantly and thoroughly.

Lartey is not alone with such responses; Carroll supports them in his chapters two to five. He discusses the need to understand and respond to contextual changes.[7] For Magesa, understanding and analyzing the context goes hand in hand with bearing differences. He challenges the leaders of the Church for their failure to bear the differences. He laments that: "The real problem is that the leaders of the church cannot bear differences and alternative ways of doing things in the church. For them, differences mean

---

5. Ibid., 84.
6. *Pastoral Theology*, 42–43; cf., Bergmann, *God in Context*, 1–18, 67–84.
7. Carroll, *God's Potters*, 31–158.

opposition, and if you do not comply with what they want, you become a rebel and a heretic."[8]

It implies that, the church is doing its theology based on its established norms. As a result, pastors and other church ministers are encountering many pressures and situations of unrest in their roles due to lack of context analysis and failure to bear the difference that social change exposes to them. It seems also that the church formulates its principles for pastoral ministry in hidden from social reality. During implementations, much ambivalence emerges – whether in sacramental roles, in teaching and evangelism, during disciplining and leadership or in the whole task of pastoral care and counseling. Almost every task has encountered great challenges. I suggest that the ELCT adapts the above approaches in order for pastors to work joyously and effectively in this time of social change. Thus, I pick a few implications as suggestions for responding to the main challenges.

DISCOVERING NEW APPROACHES FOR MATCHING WITH SOCIAL CHANGES

The church documents that I discussed in chapter three gave a list of the tasks that every pastor and other theologians who had to carry out theological tasks had to abide with. The documents do not provide any reflections on how the tasks can be implemented. As a result, pastors encounter numerous ambivalences. For example, since society has undergone several changes, the roles appear to be outdated. Due to their responsibility into the given tasks, church ministers find themselves getting more into tensions than happiness in ministry. The social changes that are taking place claim new ways of doing theology. Members of society at times require the incorporation of their demands, needs, interests and expressions in church principles and practices.

The following informant describes that educational change that takes place in people forces the church ministers to be creative and innovative in terms of the methods to be used in doing pastoral ministry in the time of social change. There is call to find new and attractive methods for preaching, teaching and in other roles inside and outside church circles. The informant comments:

> *The educational change of society calls for the church ministers to create or find new styles or approaches when preaching, teaching or doing their functions in the church and outside it. People*

---

8. Magesa, *Anatomy of Inculturation*, 49.

> like changes in styles from one week or one lesson to another. The same is for the preachers. People need changes of preachers, not always him or her. Therefore, pastors need to study and know their contexts and people. Pastors should ask themselves some questions such as, why do these people live the way they live? What and why do they like certain things and not the other? What demands do they have upon me as their leader?[9]

Apart from the methods, this informant claims that there must be an exchange of preachers and teachers in the church. One preacher should not perform those services frequently. Society wants fresh styles every week. Moreover, pastors need to be inquisitive by asking themselves several questions. Among most important questions are about inquiring to know the constant needs of people and learn the special demands they put upon their leaders.

As for this response, my discussion with some lay-Christians, they made some claims that the contemporary society in and outside the Church needs new type of leaders: *Christians and society today need competent, flexible and visionary leaders, leaders with a global outlook.*[10] Anybody may agree with this informant in the fact that, obviously, the roles as well as a serious Church ministry cannot be effective if pastors and all other church ministers are not competent in terms of education, leadership knowledge, and skills. From the demand of the survey, I suggest that this is among genuine issues the Church ought to consider from the very early stages of recruitment, training and in-service training, and allocation processes as regards the existing strong social changes. That is why the challenge about up-grading church ministers is included in their responses. The following four issues serve as major steps on how pastors and the church might respond to social change.

LISTENING FROM BELOW: LISTENING TO THE COMMUNITY[11]

When I refer to the conversations with interviewees, pastors and most of church ministers seem not fully combining church documents with the realities of contemporary society. It appears that in most cases the church itself and some ministers perform their tasks in an individualistic way. They do not to listen to society. Most needs, knowledge and experiences, and

9. Informant F.
10. Informant F.
11. I use the term 'listening' to mean understanding and matching with the contemporary reality.

interests of the contemporary society get little room in church documents at an action level. Social change somehow put aside. As a result, ministers keep complaining of society with its many affective and forceful changes. It is now high time to listen from below, to listen to the community, to recognize the reality, and thereafter share together what they have, both theoretically and practically.[12]

I do not use the concept "listening" to mean that church ministers do not listen to their people, neither do I denote that everything from the social change is totally fine. Rather, I use it to highlight that listening to society is still inadequate because almost every guideline and function depend on a norm (prescription) from the administrative structures, the church only. There is very little space for the majority to contribute in the making of those principles and tasks. The involvement of society can properly address the problems according to social change. The ways in which the processes are undertaken seem to bring numerous dilemmas.[13] There is a lack of consensus between the church and society below it. Then, what needs change: the church documents (with their analyzed tasks), the agent (pastor), or society according to the contemporary situation? Why and how? To me, I would suggest the church documents need constant reformulations to suit the reality, that is, social change.

RETHINKING CHURCH DOCTRINES

The first question concerns marriage. Most pastors complain that at times of social change the question of marriage and its administration raises numerous challenges. In this section, I discuss two interrelated issues: the first is the need to rethink the current marriage doctrine and the second is on the administration of marriage–wedding liturgy. One informant observed:

> *Marriage has become a difficulty enterprise. This is because there are different religious traditions and customs that may need emphases from each partner's faith tradition. For, example, there are varied denominational teachings. Now, how will you administer a marriage where partners belong to different religious traditions? May be for Christians at least it can be easier because our Lutheran denomination allows the so called 'a cooperation in administration of intermarriage', but what if they belong to different religions, for example, a Christian and a Muslim?*[14]

12. Taylor, *Modern Social Imaginaries*, 88–89; Lartey, *Pastoral Theology*, 42, 124.
13. Kijanga, *Ujamaa and the Role of Church*, 70.
14. Informant A.

As discussed it in chapter four; it appears that intermarriages are typical practices in the postmodern society. As a result, almost the whole procedures, its liturgy and the doctrine of marriage are among serious problems attributable to social changes. The research shows that there is a need for the church to rethink again about the teachings on marriage, especially, by using new information from the contemporary situation of society. This will probably help in order to produce a better guideline for both, pastors and society itself to refer in the time of social change. Again, the problems that suppress society inform of the need for all churches to rethink the liturgical administration of intermarriages following religious pluralism. Otherwise, it is becoming very difficult to administer marriages to date.

For this reason, the cry from pastors for the church to revisit the marriage doctrines and to rethink its liturgy for a shared wedding administration comes out due to the pressures of social changes in terms of freedom of movement (mobility), integration, interaction, freedom of marriage that resulted in intermarriages, and religious pluralism. There is a need to rethink and reframe all traditions according to changes in society.[15]

UP-GRADING PASTORS' EDUCATION: A CHALLENGE FROM A HIGHLY EDUCATED SOCIETY

There is a great challenge due to pastor's lack of education that matched with contemporary society. As noted in the previous discussions, most informants complain that although church ministers try to do good work, yet the majority of them are not well educated. Since education is one of essential tools for the pastoral ministry, both the church and its ministers are challenged to rethink on how to up-grade their levels of education. One of testimonies from an urban parish pastor expressed the complaint: *Most of the pastors in our diocese are complaining about the role of the diocese to educating her ministers in both theology and secular education. The less educated pastors face a challenge to up-grade their levels of education; otherwise, they will miss churches to work in future.*[16] Accordingly, the complaint is first directed to the church authorities being the superior and the one that enacts and activates the educational principles for ministers. The minister stands at the second stage. This pastor also points out that the problem seems so big and serious since there are many pastors who need the upgrading of their education. They are waiting for their employers to upgrade them.

---

15. Ellingson, *The Mega Church and the Mainline*, 78–106, 187–192.
16. Informant B.

Evangelists in substations of parishes supported the above testimony when they gave some descriptions of how educational changes are gradually taking place and how society is feeling when those ministers performed their tasks. They stated:

> *According to the present situation and the signs that society is revealing; in the future the church will have less or no un-educated Christians to the level of secondary education. This means that also the church ministers will be only those with the same level of education, otherwise Christians will not accept some pastors and evangelists as their leaders. It is a good time for ministers and the church at large to be aware of this and go or send people for further and professional education.*[17]

The above description highlights the need to up-grade the level of education so that in future pastors and other ministers may not miss the opportunity to work with the Church. This informant shows the possibility for the Church in future to be only for those with higher education. The reason for that prophecy is that most people might be having higher education, or that society might decide to need a minister with higher education.

The problem and complaint seem to be serious especially when I conversed with other co-workers, that is, evangelists. During my interview with them, I was interested to know how those evangelists perform their tasks in the context in which most pastors complain that they have inadequate education and encounter numerous pressures. Moreover, I was also interested to know the approaches used to respond to those challenges. After a long discussion on the issue of education, this was their response:

> *We believe that we are called by God to serve even this educated society. We just do what we can and leave what we do not know. Sometimes people are cooperative, while in other times they are not. They challenge us by using their high knowledge especially when they ask tough questions. Truly, low education, being uneducated, or having less education on the work you are doing is a big problem and a great obstacle, especially in terms of leadership and in preaching or teaching. Contemporary Christians and society urge and want an educated and modest leader. We just tolerate, otherwise we would not continue.*[18]

The quotation above reveals how ministers work amid social pressures. They tolerate many forces. However, most of them show to be ready if the

17. Informant E.
18. Informant E.

church is willing to up-grade their education. Working under the shade of tolerance is good but on the other hand, it might bring problems in future. Education goes with age and time. It is better to up-grade while still young.

On the one hand, I agree the way this challenge precedes. I presuppose that one of the most important responsibilities of any employer is to educate employees. On the other hand, since knowledge is primarily of individual benefit, I suggest that individual ministers themselves have some responsibilities toward developing their educational levels. I came about the descriptions that some young ministers are attempting some secondary examinations as part of upgrading their level of education. In a summary way they described that, the majority of those who are trying to up-grade their level of education are the youth: "*Many young pastors and evangelists are joining secondary schools and universities to increase their knowledge. It is very difficult today if you are not or little educated. Since pastors carry multiple roles, it is important that we have to change habitually and cognitively. This is how society is behaving.*"[19] When I asked how education was to be improved and about the type and level of education that seem to be needed for church ministers' work, my respondents suggested the following:

> *It should be the education that responds to people's needs, context and type of people. The education must make them aware and helpful in the people's social, political, economic, physical, intellectual and spiritual life. Such type of knowledge can be attained if pastors get both secular and theological education. . . . So, the problems are in both sides: in the church that sends them for theological training before helping them with secular education, the training institutions themselves may have poor or inadequate curriculum that could equip ministers with required knowledge and skills necessary for their ministry; and to ministers themselves who do not up-grade their levels of education. Churches do mainly drain the pastors' knowledge without updating it. Due to change of time, generations and varied problems in society, pastors should be re-equipped with additional knowledge, skills and experiences. Social science studies and other related disciplines are needed to all pastors.*[20]

In a brief way, another informant added similar descriptions: *A church minister requires having both theological and secular education. He or she needs an education that matches with the present changes in society, and that goes*

---

19. Informant B.
20. Informant H.

with science and technology.[21] These descriptions focus mainly on two areas. First, there is need for extensive and intensive training in both theological and secular courses to all pastors and other theologians. According to my informants, courses that cover both theological and secular ones seem to be of great importance. Secular courses such as social science and natural science studies appear to be essential to date. Then I probed with another question: why is this essential? Among the reasons they gave are the following: to be constructive from the preparation of sermons, during the preaching, and teaching in the Church and in schools; and another importance stands on the need to widen the horizons. The third reason is for obtaining some knowledge that might be helpful if a minister has to prepare and present some papers in conferences.

> *He or she can be asked to deliver a speech or lecture about a certain issue to educate them. If this pastor is not well educated, he or she can be tempted to refuse that appointment. Sometimes even the theological education that he or she may have may not be enough according to time and context in which he or she is in service. For example, some pastors and evangelists may not involve themselves fully in teaching Christian education in secondary schools due to their low education.*[22]

For this informant, training of pastors and other new theologians for pastoral or other theological responsibilities in the Church should match with the contemporary changes in society. Another example of the changes from society is that of science and technology. This also forces church ministers to think about their levels of their education in order to match with science and technology. Additionally, the suggestions above emphasizes the need for a regular training to church ministers in order to equip them with new and additional knowledge, skills, and other tools for meeting some new issues in their societies.

My informants state that they are surprised with the church for being idle to up-grade its church ministers with education. Their surprise is because society is active but the church is very slow as if it is comfortable with this situation. They state:

> *It will be a surprise if Christians and society are actively widening their intellect . . . but the church and its ministers are idle. Currently most of our leaders (pastors and evangelists) have no secondary education. In addition, most of the evangelists have not*

21. Informant A.
22. Informant F.

> being trained with theological education. This thing is outdated. Our church is supposed to change so that it may not be denied by society. One of the most important qualities of a contemporary pastor is good education and its proper application.[23]

Second, there was a suggestion that the curriculum be revisited so that the courses catch and much with the social change. Most of the interviewees asked for trainers to include other courses relating to new issues such as homosexual marriages and religious pluralism:

> The past and present theological training seems to be insufficient into this society. There are additional issues that need incorporation in the whole process of pastoral training. The issues of new forms of marriages, homosexual marriage, liturgies as I said . . . they exist also in Tanzania, religious pluralism and their impact on the church. Colleges should teach such issues so that theologians are enlightened before they are ordained.[24]

Another informant who worked in one of the training institution responded on the above claims. This informant first did not completely agree with the above argument, however, he admits some arguments:

> We make researches to see whether the curriculum reflects contemporary situations of society. We study the challenges that pastors get from their contexts. From such researches, we renovate, introduce or change some programs. It once happened that one of the graduates from this college shared to us a type of knowledge he could have gained. That former student said that people whom he was serving had some other different problems that need new strategies and methods of solutions. Unfortunately, he did not have them because such courses were not in our curriculum. This meant that the training did not meet his existing situations. As Christians become learned, so their pastor ought to be.[25]

With the arguments above, it shows that sometimes the plans of curriculums are prior to the research of the reality. Once we do a research, it becomes easy for the curriculum to include most current and practical experiences. It shows that if the review of curriculums will be constant, the training will match with the existing reality. Mwombeki reminds the ELCT on the important practice that now need resuming. He states:

23. Informant F.
24. Informant B.
25. Informant H.

Today *we have entered into a different generation.* Whereas pastors remain with their *'ordinary* [and old]*'* education, other people have learned and become competent persons in different sectors. Doctors, Engineers, Professors, Lawyers, Politicians and many more academicians have increased to date.... [Currently,] a pastor can no longer claim any competence in other professions, except this pastor has undertaken training in those fields. . . . Secular courses have to be established in seminaries to *impart them with the reasonable and needed skills for leadership.*[26]

Contrary, some pastors seem to leave church ministry. The informant communicates:

Those who up-grade themselves under their expenses when they come back, the church does not use them well. However, the situation is changing slowly to a better use of well-learned ministers, although they are very few. The church is also challenged to retain the learned from running out of it. However, why do the highly educated pastors run away from church ministry? If one asks them, they show to be willing to serve the church; but why is it so? The challenge remains on the top church leadership.[27]

The issue of how to handle and use both those who up-grade their education and all other church ministers, seem to click and remain a puzzle in the thoughts of my informants. Despite the significance of the problem for the betterment of the church, I will not discuss it in detail in this book due to lack of space and time. Moreover, this is not among the primary objectives of this book. Therefore, with those arguments about how to handle church ministers, the church remains challenged.

At last, I find the following comment about education to match with the ministers and society to be very essential. From the conversations, they suggested that: the church, other leaders in society, training agents, and all agents of social change that they realize and consider for implementations:

It is good for a pastor and the church at large to match the level of education of . . . with that of society. This is important because society discovers many things and terminologies that this pastor ought to be aware at least some of important ones. This is the same for our evangelists and other theologians. So, the church should take intentional initiatives to educate and constantly upgrade . . . ministers so that they may carry their roles effectively

---

26. Mwombeki, *Uongozi wa Usharika,* 9, cf. 10, 11, 12; Knutsen, "Left–Right Materialist Value," 160–161, 171, 173, 189–190. Translation and emphasis mine.

27. Informant B.

and confidently. Theological education, social sciences and other courses relating to leadership and managerial skills are one of the most important and needed knowledge in this generation.[28]

Third, I suggest to the church, pastors and any other church ministers consider education as a resource and tool for their pastoral ministry. They need to struggle for it as hard as possible, and with all their efforts. I noted in chapter five where I discussed the intellectual changes in people that, education is one of the major factors to help pastors avoid or minimize a large part of tensions and pressures they encounter. Education is a resource in a sense that it helps one to have unlimited alternatives in the course of performing the tasks especially in this time of fast social change. In one of my discussions with my informants, my focus group describes that in generally, education liberates. *The contemporary society is academically equipping itself with how it can liberate through education.*[29]

We learned that most pastors as well as other ministers such as evangelists have a low level of education. The level they have is of little help in this time of fast social change. This problem leads them feel inferior, less confident, and become attacked by a feeling of withdrawing from the ministry. The biggest surprise to me is when informants state that their employer (the church) is somehow comfortable with the situation. For them (pastors) their employer is very slow in dealing with this problem. Even if the church knows the problem well, yet, it is more reluctant. Long service pastors and lecturers in the training organizations confirm on how most employees have been less considered in relation to education: "*For a very long period of time the Church has been led by less educated [ministers]. Now the church is challenged to up-grade their level of education. It should not remain enjoying the services this person does without considering his or her side.*"[30]

Although there may have existed some genuine reasons; still, the number of those who are less upgraded is growing. Special strategies have to be undertaken. Therefore, because of the pressing social change, the church can better devote much effort to deal with the problem of less education in church ministers. Pastors need a reasonable education because, apart from it being helpful in their ordinary life; education helps in finding some more approaches for preaching, teaching and for new techniques for mission and evangelism in the time of rapid changes in society. Education helps in finding techniques to address the problems of morality and church ethics. Also education helps a person get some essential tools and skills for

28. Informant F.
29. Informant G.
30. Informant H.

administrative tasks and, skills for care and counseling tasks. Finally, yet importantly, education helps in effective communication.

Again, there are some emphases that education helps one become an independent thinker. One informant from a training institution emphasized on independent thinking by stating that: *education can help the pastor be an independent thinker. He or she can take measures if a problem arises than crying for unnecessary transfers or parishioners driving pastors away from parishes frequently.*[31] Through the discussions I held with this informant, I learnt that if all church ministers in the ELCT/SD and Africa will get chances to up-grade their education, they become independent in decision making. Fine enough, they will become effective ministers in their parishes.

Before looking at the tasks to be in another inquiry, I find it necessary to propose another crosscutting alternative for responses toward social change. Though it may look similar to some of the above-proposed approaches, however, there are slight but important differences that one may realize. There are some general suggestions on how the process of responding to the changing reality in society. That is, the process of reframing the tradition.

REFRAMING THE TRADITION: OFFICIAL ACCOMMODATION OF OTHER SPIRITUAL EXPERIENCES

As we notice from the survey, there are vivid complaints and unofficial practices in the Lutheran denomination. Without official authorization, the Christian society is adopting other religious practices from wherever attracts it into their denomination. The reasons for their adoption of those practices are already open in the previous discussions. May be we can have the following questions again to guide us in this subsection: Why do congregations accommodate other spiritual experiences into their denomination? How can one manage this behavior? Furthermore, how will pastors honor and preserve their (Lutheran) tradition? Cannot the mother tradition be violated and hence lose the identity of the mother denomination? To respond appropriately to those questions, I use the model as proposed by Stephen Ellingson. I derive the subheading above "Reframing the Tradition"[32] from his work. However, before I enter into the whole process of how pastors can use this model in response to social change; let us visit other important

---

31. Informant H.
32. Ellingson, *The Mega Church and the Mainline,* 78.

questions on "the trouble with tradition."[33] What is the problem with the Lutheran church to the extent the congregations may need to reframe their tradition? How can the process be done successfully and comfortably?

"The Trouble with Tradition": Why Accommodate Other Spiritual Experiences?

Ellingson states that congregations enter into trouble with traditions because of varied reasons. We need to understand the ways through which the trouble arises and exists. Ellingson's observation can help us reach that goal.

Personal Religious and Cultural Flavors

People want to experience what they feel flavoring their spiritual and cultural interests. They want the language that they can feel. During his research, Ellingson came across the following feelings: " . . . I hear more members talking in the language of American evangelicalism than traditional Lutheranism, and worship does not follow the structure and practices set out in *The Lutheran Book of Worship*."[34] In the analysis and discussion of data in chapters four and five, show this kind of spirit. Most Christians demanded freedom from strict and conservative principles. Congregations want freedom of spiritual exercise. Congregations of this inspiration will always be against any set and strict tradition.

Encouraging the Born-again Experiences

Another cause that makes pastors and their congregations troubled with tradition is the fact that pastors and congregations want to sustain the born-again. One of his respondents replied to Ellingson: "I don't want to dismiss the born-again experience as illegitimate. . . . we want to encourage the person to explore what that experience means and to go deeper."[35] Most pastors in congregations that over-emphasize on born-again spiritual experiences have been under church discipline or excommunicated from the church. There is an example of how the church has lost many Christians due to the problem of restricting Christians from being free to express their born-again experiences within the Lutheran premises: "We Lutherans have

33. Ibid., 20.
34. Ibid., 21.
35. Ibid., 21.

driven thousands of people away from Lutheranism and into evangelical and fundamentalist churches because we have rejected the born-again experience and language out of hand."[36] Instead, the church authorities have to find constructive ways to maintain the born-again persons: "we have to figure out how to maintain the culture of the church in light of these people who are coming in who say, 'What does being Lutheran matter?' . . . People are literally coming to us with no church background. That's going to change the culture of this place almost whether we like it or not. As those kinds of people come to church, the church has got to shift."[37] It means, change in Lutheranism is inevitable.

Pastors and all other church leaders have to repackage the content of the Lutheran doctrines continually in order to accommodate all people who join the church in this postmodern era. If this problem remains unresolved, most people will leave Lutheranism.[38] There is a need to consider and work on the challenges facing Lutheran tradition today so that in turn we may reduce or solve the problems we encounter from these congregations. There is a cry resulting from the problem in leaders. It is very unfortunate: "Most of our leaders don't have a clue how to grow a church."[39] They need help with further training.

Restructuring of Religious Traditions: Indicators for Unofficial Reframing

During his exploration in the American context to the publication year 2007, Stephen Ellingson exposed himself to "The Restructuring of American Religious Traditions."[40] There were great and high rhythms of religious and cultural change in "The Mega Church and the Mainline." He noticed thus: "The Mega Church and the Mainline" were "Remaking Religious Traditions in the Twenty-first Century", to use the main and subtitle of his book as an outcome of his survey.[41]

Very early in his participant observation, Ellingson noticed that many of the congregations he visited were restructuring their religious traditions. He witnessed how the worship services were administered with some alterations or in the liturgy, in preaching styles and emphases, as well as in

36. Ibid., 21.
37. Ibid., 21.
38. Ibid., 21.
39. Ibid., 22
40. Ibid., 1. Cf., 2–19.
41. Ibid., see title of the book, i, iii.

honoring their ceremonies. He noticed that different from the principles prescribed in the "Lutheran Book of Worship,"[42] congregations had additional practices. For example, unusually, in one of the ordination services, he witnessed the congregations under motivations of their pastors dancing with their hands in motions. Ellingson shares that, after a newly preaching style and emphasis that seemed to depict exceptional emotional expressions as observed from the congregation, "The bishop then led the official ELCA ordination service. We ended the service with a lively South African hymn, for which the newly ordained pastor taught us the words and hand motions and the senior pastor taught us a sort of line dance that involved a lot of foot stomping. Within minutes, the entire congregation was dancing and singing along with the incessant beat of the African drums."[43] It seems that according to his experience the change from either standing – still to stomping their feet gave him a new lesson. Mind you, Christians did this in the presence of the bishop and other significant church leaders. I presuppose they joined the new religious experience.

Then, Ellingson points out how the tradition included the social – justice that marked the liberalism, ecumenical and global additions. Witnessing the way the congregation enjoyed the worship service in one of the ordination and installation occasions; he mentions the significance of opening up the tradition in order to include other ritualistic practices in the worship services,

> Ordinations and installations of pastors are extraordinary rituals in the life of a congregation. They are moments when the foundational beliefs, distinctive theological worldviews, and the most important elements of a community's religious culture are displayed. [Since] rituals are the vehicles through which we tell ourselves stories about ourselves, then these rituals should tell us a story about the nature and salience of the historic religious tradition that should govern the congregations. At . . . the congregation's Lutheran theological and liturgical commitments [are] rehearsed but the tradition [is] opened up to include the social – justice concerns more central to liberal Protestantism as well as the ecumenical and global additions to the music and liturgy of the service.[44]

As the quotation reveals the need that contemporary congregations enquire, pastors ought to realize and adopt some rituals that help people strengthen

---

42. Ibid., 2.
43. Ibid., 3.
44. Ibid., 3.

their faith than reorienting them into rigid and conservative traditions. Ellingson displays how other congregations are integrating the ecumenical and global experiences to the music and liturgy but without 'making Christianity palatable.'[45]

The congregations were questioning the old and conservative practices that honor only the prescribed tradition than the experiences of the contemporary religious needs and flavors. Consequently, unofficially, parallel to their questioning, they constantly took their initiatives to start remaking the tradition. To me, it implies that, there are times if they are tired or are in fond of something, the congregations may found a religious ritual and start practicing it without official authorization. They accommodate what they feel helpful to them even before official inauguration by the authorities. From the quotation above, one can note that, the integration and practice of South African hymn, the dancing and singing with the incessant beat of the African drums had no inauguration. Everything started like a surprise. Even though that was a Lutheran worship that used to honor the traditional worship practices, Ellingson argues that in that day:

> The Lutheran tradition was dismissed as irrelevant and humorously outdated, and Lutheran theological ideas and liturgical practices were absent from the installation ritual. Instead, we heard the kind of music used at growing evangelical churches around the country; we heard about the centrality of the Bible for authentic Christian faith and saw how it was used instrumentally to solve problems; we heard about the important mission to convert people to Christianity . . . ; and finally we heard that foundational evangelical story about individuals' personal relationship with Jesus.[46]

When I reflect the history of *Ujamaa* in Tanzania, and relate it to the history of the American Protestantism, there are some elements of similarities. I noted in the preliminary chapters that, soon after independence in 1961 slight social changes started to emerge. But immediately after the introduction and strong emphases of Arusha Declaration and the *Ujamaa* Vilagization, rapid changes started to gain another momentum. Let me highlight some reasons as to why congregations and individuals are no longer abiding seriously to the religious traditions to date. I draw the reasons from Ellingson to interpret the situation happening in the African Christian Churches, especially, the ELCT in particular.

45. Ibid., 3.
46. Ibid., 4.

Ellingson states that the history about the religious change, especially the American Protestantism and Lutheranism, has been familiar since 1960s. Almost the same as the history of the Church in Tanzania, "In general, the restructuring literature suggests that since the mid–1960s congregations and individuals are less likely to consider a particular religious tradition important, meaningful, or binding than in previous decades."[47] When the congregations are restructuring, what are the indicators of growth or decline toward the commitment to the given traditions, moreover, what are the effects in the historic denominational traditions? The following are some of the features showing the effects of restructuring of religious traditions on the Church as a whole. By summary, I paraphrase:

'First, the common practice of dropping out of organized religion or switching from one church body to another suggests that commitment to a given denominational tradition has weakened. The old, former tradition is probably not very important, as individuals must abandon much of the unique history, theology, culture, and worship practices of their former denomination.

Second, the rise of religious consumerism encourages individuals not only to switch from one church body to another but to pick and choose among doctrines, practices, beliefs, or values from different traditions and put them together to form a religion (or a sect) that meets individuals' interests. This religious eclecticism may undermine the authority and integrity of a given tradition because it pulls individuals out of the community that preserves and practices the tradition. Usually, the search for spiritual experiences and the creation of "multilayered spirituality", takes place outside religious communities that can provide support and some degree of control over the creative process.

Third, restructuring implies not only the denominational decline, but also that the tradition is rediscovered and reworked. Some scholars argue that aliveness of the denominational identities and traditions stand in the activeness of the individuals and congregations who actively seek to rediscover and hold on to the distinctive ritual practices and identity narratives or to develop new traditions from a burgeoning religious marketplace.

Fourth, the proliferation of nondenominational congregations and the growing importance of church growth consultants may be weakening the historic traditions of mainline Protestantism.'[48] Thus, once a pastor or anyone notices those features, he or she realizes that the existing tradition

---

47. Ibid., 6.
48. Ibid., 6–7.

is in trouble. Then, intentional measures to restore or improve the situation must be in place.

Strategies for Reframing the Tradition

Why reframe the tradition? In the above discussion, we have realized that congregations want to accommodate some religious rituals that flavor them. It is noted: "Tradition is intrinsically problematic." 'Tradition has two faces, or two temporal dimensions.' "One face looks to the past and views religious tradition as a set of religious beliefs, doctrines, values, worship practices (e.g., rituals, liturgies, hymns), and educational and decision – making practices that are passed on down historically and stored in a denomination's or congregation's collective memory."[49] "The second face of tradition looks to the present and refers to the current religious activities and vehicles of expression in use by a given religious group."[50] This deals with "the adaptations on the core made by successive generation."[51]

Due to these characteristics of a tradition, in this postmodern age, once they are tired with the tastes of their own, "people and congregations freely borrow one another's traditions."[52] Thus, to make the tradition their own, pastors must be willing to reframe it with the congregations and individuals. If one ignores and destroys this process, the postmodern Christian society dares to reframe or remake it unofficially. At this stage then there emerges some conflicts between the leaders and society. When pastors would want society to listen to them, 'the society (congregations, Christians) remains in either reconstituting the lived tradition or struggling to over the legitimacy of borrowing from other traditions and deciding which traditions are the legitimate ones from which to borrow.'[53] Therefore, the best way is to reframe or remake it officially with them.

Thus, Ellingson provides the reasons and the process undertaken regarding the task of remaking religious traditions. He articulates that:

> in reframing, the intent is to dislodge old meanings or create new ones, and in particular, the strategy suggests that reframing advocates will take a critical and even confrontational stance against traditional religious language and symbols. At the same time it is a strategy by which religious leaders can help people

49. Ibid., 23.
50. Ibid., 23.
51. Ibid., 23.
52. Ibid., 24.
53. Ibid., 27., cf., 84.

find a new language (or provide one for them) with which they can make sense of their religious experiences. Given the larger shift in [African] Protestantism away from doctrine and toward experience, and the lack of familiarity or even salience that religious doctrine has for many Christians (including Lutherans), reframing becomes a way to develop a new language for articulating the religious truths contained in doctrine without using the religious jargon."[54]

Ellingson shows that when Christians reframe the religious traditions, they can even use confrontational approaches. This approach is also used by religious leaders themselves when they attempt to make their religious senses. Among significant reasons for using the reframing process is to stand as a way that helps in developing a new language in finding truths in doctrines in a straight and simple terminology. Hence, this reveals how postmodern society wants clear and understandable languages in religious expressions.

In this paragraph, let me share five strategies that can be used in reframing or remaking a tradition to cope with the reality—the social change as envisioned and expressed by Stephen Ellingson in his research.

I. *Translation*—whereby the congregational leaders translate core theological concepts from the Lutheran tradition (or from one of several other traditions such as the pietistic or revival tradition of other Protestantism, or the ancient church) into a language that is more contemporary and understandable.

II. *Reemphasis*—whereby church leaders shift the theological, symbolic, or ritualistic emphasis away from certain elements of the tradition in favor of other elements.

III. *Contextualization*—is the attempt to adapt the tradition to fit more closely the demographic and sociocultural context of the local religious setting. For instance, the congregation tries to incorporate religious practices, symbols, or ideas from the non-Lutheran traditions of new or prospective members or from the ethnic populations the church is serving or trying to serve. Contextualization serves to reframe a tradition by shifting the emphasis away from certain elements of the tradition, such as the intellectual and none motive style of worship and stressing other elements, such as the pietistic or emotional strand of Lutheran worship by adding music or the call - and - response style of preaching. It is similar but technically different from reemphasis. Reemphasis simply means that the congregation ignores

---

54. Ibid., 82., see also 23–27.

some elements of the tradition and highlights, uses, talks about other elements more. Contextualization means that the congregation intentionally tries to alter the tradition to fit the religious interests, needs, or expectations of a particular population, such as African Americans.

IV. *Retraditioning*—the congregations create new religious practices, especially rituals, by incorporating parts of other religious traditions into the life of a congregation. Retraditioning is "a way of creating new cultural formations that provide alternative visions of spiritual and ethical life." Retraditioning tends to be used periodically at a few congregations as the means to expand the ritualistic repertoire of the congregations and sometimes to shed new light on certain features of the Lutheran tradition without remaking or replacing the tradition with a totally new or different tradition.

V. *Reconnecting*—congregation leaders turn to this strategy to help members connect with lost, forgotten, or unknown elements of the tradition. This strategy is mostly used when church leaders want to push for departure that is more radical from the Lutheran tradition. It is used to remind members of the deficiencies of the tradition or to signal continuities with the tradition. This strategy mostly takes the form of appeals or reminder about the churches' connection to Lutheranism as leaders try to defend or gain support for proposed changes[55]

We should neither perceive this proposition negatively that it denies or ignores the significance of tradition in the church, nor should any reader of this book draw and implicate negative notions from this proposition. The selection, interpretation and discussion of this strategy aims at sensitizing pastors and other church ministers of the many alternatives to be employed in trying to match our pastoral roles with the changing realities of society. As author of this book, I am aware that,

> A tradition helps members of a church answer the question "What's going on here?" by providing theological rationale for religious activity, a cosmology that orients individuals in the world, and ritualized activities (in the form of the Lutheran liturgy and hymnology) that guide and teach individuals how to worship God and instruct them about what to expect intellectually and emotionally from worship. Reframing, then, becomes a way of altering the taken-for-granted primary framework of the tradition of a religious group.[56]

---

55. Ibid., 82–83, cf., 79, 78, 103.
56. Ibid., 82. Emphasis original.

The model of reframing the tradition is here adopted in a sense that "I do not have eyes in my back, but there are eyes in my back." The saying calls pastors and any other ministers both in the religious circles as well as in the secular ones to live, work, and serve with precautions that "I know something, but at the same time I do not know something. And as well, I like this thing or practice, but also they like that thing or practice." Thus, together with other proposed as alternatives for responding to social change; reframing calls all people, knowledge and skills to sit down together and make or look for the commonalities for walking together or for influencing each other. I agree with Ellingson that, "As suggested in the previous section[s], how members perceive change is an important part of determining its success or failure. In particular, members' perceptions about the tradition–its importance and the degree to which its core is buffered–and about the process of change are critical for building consensus."[57]

LOOKING AHEAD: PROPOSITIONS FOR FURTHER RESEARCH

It is no easy task, nor is there a clear end of exploration, especially, when one tries to make a research about the interaction of people and the way they organize and perform their functions. This book of social change and its effects on the role of the pastor highlights the need for more and detailed research on how society is transforming its ways of life. The second challenge that this book tries to bring up is the need to research more on the way those transformed realities of life in society match with the programs of the church. This holds true right from the formulation of principles and guidelines for pastoral ministry to its daily operation in the local settings.

The third challenge is the need for the church and its agents to read the signs of the times in which they live and serve, to read the threats and opportunities, and find knowledge and skills useful to respond adequately to social change, and help enhance the mission and life of the Church. The need for more focus on education of pastor's education is central. This goes hand in hand with the good use of the resources available – constructive use of highly learned ministers as well as proper use of any other resources around us.

Time, space and other factors have limited me from exploring all parts of the African context, and the ELCT in particular, and present it in this very small book. Furthermore, it is hardly possible for me to present everything about the characteristics of social change and their effects on personal and

---

57. Ibid., 165.

pastoral ministry. In addition to the above challenges (see chapter 4 to 7), this book proposes looking at the relationship between social change and: communication, globalization, urbanization, culture, and Church identity in the postmodern times. Other issues relate to religion and postmodernity, and the Church and mass media, to mention but a few, and to explore the way each phenomenon affects the role and life of the pastor in the contemporary world (spheres of society). In this book, I have highlighted some issues on how a pastor is living and working in the globalized and multicultural world – the postmodern era. Since the tensions that church ministers get cause them become unrest, there is a high and great need to make an extensive study on the scope and impacts resulting from those effects. How safe are the pastors and other ministers owing to the problems they encounter from social change? Unrest situations that pastors encounter due to social change and other features of life may lead pastors enter into stress, burnout, loneliness, and many more psychological and sociological problems. How and who reassures the pastor amid pastoral and life crises? These are among crucial themes for further in-depth research.

Finally, along with other theologians, I would like to recall Robert J. Schreiter to elaborate my suggestions on the way in which both, the Church and pastors should encounter the problems and challenges regarding their life and pastoral ministry in the twenty - first century. Schreiter's ideas point out to the significance of being aware of the contemporary context and situations when performing pastoral roles. He suggests starting with 'globalization'. He argues that globalization brings many changes that in turn those changes bring many effects on the ministry and life of the Church and on the role of the theologian. He states:

> *Communication technologies compressed time and space* in a process known as *globalization*. Globalization has created a certain homogenization of the world in its wake, . . . religious protest movements, nativist reassertions of sovereignty, and fundamentalisms of a variety of stripes. . . . What has globalization meant for local theologies, as social relationships are realigned, cultural production is at once homogenized and fractured, and *peoples migrate and mix* at an unprecedented rate, creating a cultural melange in the *urban centers* of the world? . . . *the changed world* and . . . *some of the issues* . . . *are reshaping theology today*. Theology stands today between the global and the local. The Global is not the same as the old universal or perennial theologies. . . . To live and act in such a changed world will require new theories of interpretation. . . . a theology that must live constantly in a *multicultural context*. . . . Now communication-including

issues of *culture, identity, and social change*-becomes the third and necessary addition to the theological concept of catholicity.[58]

A serious challenge that African Churches with their pastors perhaps ought to consider is this of "taking the age seriously."[59] Designated even more specific as to the reflections made from the data collected, I suggest that the ELCT interprets and reformulates its existing church definitions and guidelines concerning pastoral roles and helps pastors become reliable resources to Christians concerning the changing society. To be a Christian in the changing society is indeed a challenge. To be a pastor today in the context where social change affects most of the roles of the pastor is even more of a challenge.[60]

---

58. Schreiter, *The New Catholicity*, ix, x, xi; cf. Beyer, *Religion and Globalization*, 15, 33, 226–227 (Italics mine).

59. Carroll, *God's Potters*, 32; cf. Beyer, *Religion and Globalization*, 15, 132, 226–227.

60. Cf., Bevans, *Models of Contextual Theology*, 86.

BIBLIOGRAPHY

Almen, Lowell G. "The Pastor as Historian." In *Called and Ordained: Lutheran Perspectives on the Office of the Ministry,* edited by Todd Nichol and Marc Kolden, 97–101. Minneapolis: Augsburg Fortress Press, 1990.
Bahendwa, L. Festo. "Uchungaji Leo." *Jarida la Kichungaji,* 4: 3 (1997) 94–102.
———. "Kusimamia Neno na Sakramenti." Seminar Presentation, 2004.
Ballard, Paul and John Pritchard. *Practical Theology in Action: Christian Thinking in the Service of Church and Society,* Second Edition. London: SPCK, 2006.
Bergmann, Sigurd. *God in Context: A Survey of Contextual Theology.* Aldershot: ASHGATE, 2003.
Bevans, Stephen B. *Models of Contextual Theology.* Maryknoll, New York: Orbis Books, 2002.
Beyer, Peter. *Religion and Globalization.* London: SAGE Publications, 1994.
Browning, Robert L. and Reed, Roy A. *Forgiveness, Reconciliation, and Moral Courage.* Grand Rapids, Michigan: William B. Eerdmans Publishing Company, 2004.
Bryman, Alan 2004. *Social Research Methods.* Second Edition. New York: Oxford University Press, 2004.
Carroll, Jackson W. *God's Potters: Pastoral Leadership and the Shaping of Congregations.* Grand Rapids, Michigan: William B. Eerdmans, 2006.
Chalfant, Paul H. and Emil Labeff. *Understanding People and Social Life: Introduction to Sociology.* New York: West Publishing, 1988.
Chilstrom, Herbert W. "The Pastor as Evangelist," in "The Doctrine of Ministry in Martin Luther and the Lutheran Confessions," 65–83. In *Called and Ordained: Lutheran Perspectives on the Office of the Ministry,* Todd Nichol and Marc Kolden (eds), 49–95. Minneapolis: Augsburg Fortress Press, 1990.
Chryssochoou, Xenia. *Cultural Diversity: Its Social Psychology.* Carlton: Blackwell, 2004.
Clegg, Stewart R. and Rhodes Carl (eds.). *Management Ethics: Contemporary Contexts.* London: Routledge, 2006.
Clinebell, Howard. *Basic Types of Pastoral Care and Counseling: Resources for the Ministry of Healing and Growth.* Revised and Enlarged Edition. Nashville: Abingdon Press, 1984.
Clough, David. *Ethics in Crisis: Interpreting Barth's Ethics.* England: Ashgate, 2005.
Cook, David C. "Multicultural Ministries." Online: *http://www.davidccook.org/MRPastors/sam_journal/index.*

Cook, J. Keith. *The First Parish: A Pastor's Survival Manual*. Philadelphia: The Westminster Press, 1983.

Czachesz, Istvan. "Theory-Forming in Biblical Studies: Contributions to an Interdisplinary Dialogue." In *Complexity: Interdisciplinary Communications*, edited by Willy Østreng, 55–58. CAS: Oslo, 2006/2007.

Detachment and the Writing of History: Essays and Letters of Carl L. Becker, edited by Phil. L. Snyder, Ithaca, New York: Cornell University Press, 1958.

Dobbelaere, Karel and Wolfgang Jagodzinski. "Religious Cognitions and Beliefs." In *The Impact of Values*, edited by Jan W. van Deth and Elinor Scarbrough, 197–217. New York: Oxford University Press, 1995.

Drønen, Tomas Sundnes. "Communication, Conversion and Conservation: The Dii Meet the Norwegian Missionaries Northern Cameroon 1934-60." Ph.D. Dissertation. Stavanger, 2007.

Eide, Oyvind M. et al. *Restoring Life in Christ: Pastoral Care and Domestic Violence, African Experiences*. Arusha: Makumira Publications, 2009.

Ellingson, Stephen. *The Mega Church and the Mainline: Remaking Religious Tradition in the Twent –First Century*. Chicago and London: The University of Chicago Press, 2007.

Escobar, Samwel. *A Time for Mission: The Challenge for Global Christianity*. England: Inter-Varsity Press, 2003.

Evans, David M. *The Pastor in a Teaching Church*. Valley Forge: Judson Press, 1983.

Fihavango, George M.D. "Leadership and Family in the New Testament." In *Marriage and Family in African Christianity*, edited by Andrew A. Kyomo and Sahaya G. Selvan, 178–192. Nairobi: Acton Publishers, 2004.

———. *Tupate Wapi Mtu Kama Huyu?: Uongozi Karne ya 21 na Dai la Uadilifu na Uwajibikaji*. Moshi: Moshi Lutheran Printing Press, 2009.

———. *Jesus and Leadership: Analysis of Rank, Status, Power and Authority as Reflected in the Synoptic Gospels From a Perspective of the Evangelical Lutheran Church in Tanzania (ELCT)*. Arusha: Makumira Publication Sixteen, 2007.

Furnham, Adrian. *The Psychology of Behaviour at Work: The Individual in the Organization*. Hove and New York: Psychology Press, 2006.

Forde, Gerhard O. "The Ordained Ministry." In *Called and Ordained: Lutheran Perspectives on the Office of the Ministry*, edited byTodd Nichol and Marc Kolden, 117- 136. Minneapolis: Augsburg Fortress Press, 1990.

Gerkin, Charles V. *An Introduction to Pastoral Care*. Nashville: Abingdon Press, 1997.

Gibbins, John R. and Bo Reimer, "Postmodernism." In *The Impact of Values: Beliefs in Government*, edited by Jan W. Van Deth and Elinor Scarbrough, 301–331. New York: Oxford University Press, 1995.

Gibbon, Peter (ed.). *Social Change and Economic Reform in Africa*. Uppsala: Nordiska Afrikainstitutet, 1993.

Giddens, Anthony. *Europe in the Global Age*. Cambridge: Polity, 2007.

Holland, Jeremy and John Campbell (eds.). *Methods in Development Research: Combining Qualitative and Quantitative Approaches*. Wales Swansea: ITDG Publishing, 2005.

Jansen, E. Harold. "The Pastor as Parish Educator," in "The Doctrine of Ministry in Martin Luther and the Lutheran Confessions," 57–66. In *Called and Ordained: Lutheran Perspectives on the Office of the Ministry*, Todd Nichol and Marc Kolden (eds), 49-66. Minneapolis: Augsburg Fortress Press, 1990.

Jagodzinski, Wolfgang and Karel Dobbelaere. "Secularization and Church Religiosity." In *The Impact of Values,* edited by Jan W. van Deth and Elinor Scarbrough, 76–119. New York: Oxford University Press, 1995.

"Julius Kambarage Nyerere," in *Britannica Concise Encyclopedia.* Online: http://www.answers.com/topic/julius-nyerere

Kijanga, Peter A.S. *Ujamaa and the Role of Church in Tanzania.* Arusha: ELCT, 1978.

KKKT. *Katiba.* Moshi: Lutheran Printing Press, 1989.

KKKT. *Mwimbieni Bwana.* Nairobi: Acme Press, 2000.

KKKT, *Tumwabudu Mungu wetu.* Arusha: KKKT, 2012.

KKKT. *Kalenda.* Moshi: Moshi Lutheran Printing Press, 2007.

KKKT-DKu. *Katiba.* Njombe: DKu, 1980.

KKKT-DKu, "Ibada ya Ubarikio wa Wachungaji." Liturgy for the Ordination of Pastors, 2007 (Unpublished)

Knight, C. Gregory. *Ecology and Change: Rural Modernization in an African Community.* New York: Academic, 1974.

Knitter, Paul F. *No Other Name? A critical Survey of Christian Attitudes Toward the World Religions.* Maryknoll, New York: Orbis Book, 2005.

Knutsen, Obbjørn. "Left-Right Materialist Value Orientations." In *The Impact of Values: Beliefs in Government,* edited by Jan W. Van Deth and Elinor Scarbrough, 160–196. New York: Oxford University Press, 1995.

Kolb, Robert. "The Doctrine of Ministry in Martin Luther and the Lutheran Confessions." In *Called and Ordained: Lutheran Perspectives on the Office of the Ministry,* edited by Todd Nichol and Marc Kolden, 49–66. Minneapolis: Augsburg Fortress Press, 1990.

Kyomo, Andrew A. "Pastoral Care and Counseling to Families." In *Marriage and Family in African Christianity,* edited by Andrew A. Kyomo and Sahaya G. Selvan, 193–216. Nairobi: Acton Publishers, 2004.

Lartey, Emmanuel Y. *Pastoral Theology in an Intercultural World.* Werrington: Epworth, 2006.

Lutahoire, Sebastian K. *The Human Life Cycle Among the Bantu: With Reference to the People of the West Lake Region, Tanzania.* Arusha: ELCT, 1974.

Lwehabura, Jonathan Mutayoba Kakulu and Ndyetabura, Jeanne Karamaga. "Implementation of the Tanzanian National Policy on HIV/AIDS in relation to the defence sector." In *The Enemy Within: Southern African Militaries' Quarter-Century Battle with HIV and AIDS,* edited by Martin Rupiya, 125–155. Pretoria: Institute for Security Studies, 2006.

Maendeleo Dialogue: Democracy in Tanzania. "48 Years of Our Fight against Poverty, Ignorance and Disease: Have We attained Our Goal? Issue VI, January 2010. Online at http://www.kas.de/wf/doc/kas_19111-1522-2-30.pdf?110125174938

Magesa, Laurent. *Anatomy of Inculturation: Transforming the Church in Africa.* Maryknoll, New York: Orbis Books, 2004.

Mtaita, Leonard A. *The Wandering Shepherds and the Good Shepherd: Contextualization as the Way of Doing Mission with the Maasai in the ELCT - Pare Diocese.* Makumira Publication Eleven, Erlanger Verlag fur Mission und Okumene, 1998.

Mugambi, J. N. K. "Rites of Passages and Human Sexuality in Tropical Africa Today." In *Marriage and Family in African Christianity,* edited by Andrew A. Kyomo and Sahaya G. Selvan, 178–192. Nairobi: Acton Publishers, 2004.

Munga, Aneth Nyagawa. *Uamsho: A Theological Study of the Proclamation of the Revival Movement within the Evangelical Lutheran Church in Tanzania.* Sweden: Lund University Press. 1998.

Mwendamseke, A. N. S. *Mass Media and Female Images: Reality and Possible Reforms.* Iringa University College Publications, August, 2003.

Mwombeki, Fidon R. *Uongozi wa Usharika.* Arusha: Scripture Mission, 2004.

Niwagila, Wilson B. *From the Catacomb to a Self-governing Church: A Case Study of the African Initiative and the Participation of the Foreign Missions in the Mission History of the North-Western Diocese of the Evangelical Lutheran Church in Tanzania 1890-1965,* edited Edition. Ammersbek bei Hamburg: Verlag an der Lottbek, 1991.

Njinga, Meshack Edward. "*The Shift from Ujamaa to Globalization as a Challenge to the Evangelical Lutheran Church in Tanzania: A Theological Reflection on Relationship Between Religion and Globalization.*" Master Thesis. University of Oslo, Oslo, Norway, Spring, 2003.

Norwegian National Committee for Research Ethics in the Social Sciences and the Humanities (NESH). *Guidelines for Research Ethics in the Social Sciences, Law, and the Humanities,* Oslo: De nasjonale forskningsetiske kommiteer, 2006.

Ntloedibe-Kuswani, Gomang Seratwa. "The Religious Life of an African: A God-given Praeparatio Evangelica?" In *Talitha Cum!: Theologies of African Women,* edited by Nyambura J. Njoroge and Musa W. Dube. Piertermaritzburg: Cluster Publications, 2001.

Nyerere, Julius K. *Ujamaa Essays on Socialism.* Dar es Salaam: Oxford University Press, 1974.

Parker, Yvonne. *Mke Aliyechaguliwa na Mungu: Mke wa Mchungaji.* Nairobi: Baptist Publications House, 1990.

Peterson, Eugene H. "Titus: Starting Out in Crete." In *The Unnecessary Pastor: Rediscovering the Call,* 183-204. Edited by Peter Santucci. Grand Rapids, Michigan: William B. Eerdmans, 2000.

Pope John Paul II. "Address of His Holiness John Paul II to Priest and Religious of Tanzania." St. Peter's Church, Dar es Salaam, Sunday, 2 September, 1990. Online: ttp://www.vatican.va/holy_father/john_paul_ii/speeches/1990/september/documents/hf_jp-ii_spe_19900902_clero-tanzania_en.html.

Pragman, James H. "Ministry in Lutheran Orthodoxy and Pietism," In *Called and Ordained: Lutheran Perspectives on the Office of the Ministry,* edited by Todd Nichol and Marc Kolden, 67-76. Minneapolis: Augsburg Fortress Press, 1990.

Schreiter, Robert J. *The New Catholicity: Theology between the Global and the Local.* Maryknoll, New York: Orbis Books, 1997.

Slee, Nicole. *Women's Faith Development: Patterns and Process.* England: Ashgate, 2004.

Snyder, Katherine A. *The Iraqw of Tanzania: Negotiating Rural Development.* Cambridge: Westview Press, 2005.

Strohl, Jane E. "Ministry in the Middle Ages and the Reformation." In *Called and Ordained: Lutheran Perspectives on the Office of the Ministry,* edited by Todd Nichol and Marc Kolden, 35-48. Minneapolis: Augsburg Fortress Press, 1990.

Stålsett, Sturla J. "Religion and Globalisation," in *Religion in a Globalised Age: Transfers & Transformations, Integration & Resistance,* edited by Sturla Stålsett, 9-18. Oslo: Novus Press, 2008.

Swalo, Solomon Y. "Mtumishi wa Bwana Karne ya Ishirini na Moja (Mwanzo 2: 15): Mkutano wa Kujengana Kiroho." Paper Presentation, Makumira University College), 25-26 May 2006 (Unpublished).
Taylor, Charles. *Modern Social Imaginaries*. Durham: Duke University Press, 2004.
Taylor, H. *Tend My Sheep*, Applied Theology 2, ISPCK Study Guide 19. Delhi: ISPCK, 1989.
Tracy, David. *Plurality and Ambiguity: Hermeneutics, Religion, Hope*. Chicago: University of Chicago Press, 1994.
Tumbo-Masabo, Zubeida and Liljestrøm, Rita (eds.). *Chelewa, Chelewa: The Dilema of Teenage Girls*. Uppsala: Nordiska Afrikainstitutet, 1994.
Westerlund, David. *Ujamaa na Dini: A Study of Some Aspects of Society and Religion in Tanzania, 1961-1977*. Motala: Borgstroms, 1980.
Wright, Walter C. *Relational Leadership: A Biblical Model for Leadership Service*. Carlisle: Paternoster, 2000.

www.ingramcontent.com/pod-product-compliance
Lightning Source LLC
Chambersburg PA
CBHW062015220426
43662CB00010B/1337